TRAIN YOUR BRAIN FOR A
FAST-TRACK CAREER

DR JACQUELINE RENAUD

TRAIN YOUR BRAIN FOR A *FAST-TRACK CAREER*

foulsham
LONDON · NEW YORK · TORONTO · SYDNEY

foulsham

The Publishing House, Bennetts Close,
Cippenham, Berkshire SL1 5AP, England.

ISBN 0-572-02290-5

Typeset in Great Britain by Typesetting Solutions, Slough, Berks.
Printed in Great Britain by St. Edmundsbury Press, Bury St. Edmunds, Suffolk.

CONTENTS

INTRODUCTION

Virtually every week scientific journals publish the work of experts from all over the world, bringing more and more fascinating news about the way in which the brain functions. Increasingly, a lot of these discoveries will be put into practice for the benefit of people who have suffered cerebral lesions.

Normally, much of what we are able to do – talk and understand speech, move our limbs to walk, write, play a musical instrument and so on – depends on very precise zones inside the brain. When one of these zones is destroyed, for example by a cerebral haemorrhage or the removal of a cerebral tumour, the activity that relies on that zone can no longer be operated.

Increasingly thanks to re-education techniques which are continually being improved, the patient does in numerous cases recover this function. How has this been done? By working on another area of the brain and teaching it to do what it was not doing before – namely, the work of the defective part. This clearly illustrates that when it is asked – and worked on – the brain can provide a lot more than it does in its normal daily routine.

We are all a bit like the farmer who owns a top-class racehorse and uses it to pull a cart! But that's not to say that we should adopt more grandiose ideas and tell ourselves we are going to become superhuman; in any event, that is not a particularly desirable goal. Knowing what we have available, our aim must be to use this marvellous tool to do what we have to do really well, without tiring ourselves too much. And sometimes without even thinking about it!

This can start with a sensible life style – that is to say, fitness exercises, a good diet, regular sleep and so on. We know things like these are better for us. But sometimes they can be a nuisance! Well, as a matter of fact, we can do them automatically, without thinking about them. And, since the most painful part is getting going, and the brain can do that all on its own, we can even gain pleasure from our aerobic sessions, healthy food and good fresh water to drink.

This search for an easy way to becoming more effective applies just as much and just as readily to our mental performance. We can acquire an 'elephant's memory' as easily as playing a good tennis shot, strumming a guitar or learning how to whistle – and at any age.

Finding those 'tricks' – the way of fixing a screw without a screwdriver or selling shoes that are out of fashion, that is to say being creative – is not always possible immediately, but can be learned. Yes, perhaps the idea does come into our conscious mind spontaneously. But it is the well exercised brain which does the unconscious work that makes the idea pop up.

Our internal discussion

For practically all of us, life today seems a lot more difficult than it used to be – for our parents, for example. It is useless dwelling on this conclusion, albeit perfectly justified, but it is necessary to face up to the fact. Quite simply, we have to fight against bad-temper, petty aggression, constant fatigue and increasingly nagging worries just in order to live.

We can no longer be content with simply living, working (hopefully with pleasure, if this is possible!) and making the most of our leisure. We keep on saying all the time: I MUST do this. I MUST do that. I MUST go there ... We live under permanent pressure, because we know that if we ease up for one moment we will be overwhelmed.

This reminds me of a book about teaching which is regularly quoted among educationalists, in which a little girl asks her teacher the following question during play-time: "Do I have to play?" Taking this to its logical conclusion, one has to ask whether lovers who eventually find themselves alone say: "I MUST have pleasure!"

So to succeed – to succeed simply in living – we do everything with maximum effort; we even end up breathing, dare I say it, by sheer strength and sometimes not very well. And we clearly talk in this way to our children: "You MUST do your homework"; "you MUST learn your lessons"; "you MUST go to school". As though they did not enjoy class! With all those fascinating facts that their teachers will tell them, and all those questions which are certainly entertaining when they are asked in popular television quiz shows!

Learning is a game that children and adolescents should enjoy quite naturally and it is very often the adults who put the idea into their heads that it is a DUTY and that they must FORCE themselves to do it. Moreover, one learns a lot better without knowing one is learning: today's children of three or four are clearly more 'awake', in the sense that they know a lot more, than those of the same age thirty or even twenty years ago. They are in a much better position to make new discoveries because they have more contact with other people, they travel, they have more varied games, and this is a precious training for life – obviously without them knowing they are learning!

By repeating: "I MUST do . . .", we sometimes end up quite despairing. When it comes to insignificant tasks that we could, in fact, do without even thinking about them, we then say to ourselves: "I can't manage that; I'll never manage that; I couldn't possibly . . ." This is desperation in the true sense of the word. We have lost all hope because we believe we can no longer have confidence.

So how, in today's world, can we avoid falling victim to such depression, at least from time to time? It is a problem which could be a serious handicap to a person's career prospects: for it's true that those who 'lose their grip' are overtaken and have little chance of regaining their place. And it's also true that when we start to tell ourselves that we can't do something, we really believe it. And we believe it because we have put it to the test. We force ourselves right up to the point of exhaustion. But we all know it is not by saying "I won't make it" that we throw away our chances. Equally, it is not by continually saying "I will make it", since it is precisely by repeating "I MUST make it" that we reach a point of exhaustion and depression. It is essential that we find another way.

There is another little phrase which is noteworthy because when we say it to ourselves, we believe it and that pushes us even further down the wrong path (that of failure, unhappiness and even illness). "It is stronger than me" is an expression of false indulgence when said in relation to our own behaviour. We know that we mustn't drink more than a certain amount of alcohol; we know that we should exercise our body (a quarter of an hour of aerobics once a day is not exactly purgatory!); yes, we know, we know, but we don't do anything about it, repeating to ourselves "I can't; it's stronger than me". This is false indulgence because the truth would rid us of the feeling of guilt; and when we say "It's stronger than me", we double up our guilt with a feeling of impotence and at the same time increase our own lack of confidence.

Such internal discussion is commonplace and normal given the conditions under which we live. It is only necessary to recognise it, to be conscious of it when it happens. At that point, we can start changing something; not to refrain from thinking like that, but to act in such a way that we no longer have occasion to think like that.

The key is to have confidence in ourselves, not as a result of any moral decision, but simply because we know that, from the sole fact that we are human beings, we possess an extraordinary machine, a super-computer, which only asks to work for us – if we know how to use it.

In reality, lots of things happen on their own

Already, before any special training, we benefit from an incalculable number of 'services', which function without us having to think about them for an instant, and with which we only get annoyed on the rare occasions when they fail.

Let's not talk about the obscure toils of the body: we don't need to think about how to breathe, to digest, to put one foot in front of the other to walk, and so on. Imagine what it would be like to learn to play the piano if, suddenly, we had to say to each muscle: "You contract . . . you over there, stretch . . . a little more energy . . . but not you, the one next door . . . !" All your teacher has to say is: "Hold your hands like that and hit the notes, harder or more softly . . . and practise your thumb movement until the notes are all equal . . ." The teacher plays the piece so that you know what has to be achieved and you practise it until the fingers move automatically. But during your practice, in which you are concerned only with the end result, there is behind your efforts an incredible machinery adjusting almost to a thousandth of a second the electric currents that are passing permanently across the brain.

To take this example a little further, because it illustrates a common theme, all pupils have found that on certain days, first thing in the morning, the fingers run up and down the keys like little geniuses, while on other days, without any explanation, they get tied in knots and totally tangled up. Unnoticed, a grain of sand has momentarily upset the mechanism ... Such minor failures remind us that there is a mechanic, somewhere, beyond the orders we give ourselves, who is in fact the one who does the work.

Thus, during a walk in the forest, our foot can inadvertently hit a stump: we wobble for a moment and then regain our balance. On the odd occasion, we fall over: then we look at the obstacle, which is tiny, and can't understand how it happened. A worrier can even end up telling himself: "Something isn't right. I must be ill." The balance mechanism is one of those absolutely automatic functions to which we never give a thought and which neverthe-less keeps us from falling over more than a thousand times a day and equally stops us from knocking over objects we touch at vir-tually every moment during our everyday activities – to say noth-ing of tight-rope artists and other professional balancers ...

Generally speaking, once we have learned something, for example to drive a car, once it is well fixed in our head and we have picked up the habit, we do it without thinking. To be honest, do you think when you stop at a red light or indicate to turn? It is often so well 'oiled' that very busy people can, while driving in a traffic-jam, dictate letters into a hand tape-recorder, or the agenda for the next meeting or a list of what they have to prepare for a forthcoming visit from some important businessmen.

If I were to ask you to jot down your address, would you have a moment's hesitation? The Gulf War, Henry Cooper, Sir Laurence Olivier ... these evoke something, surely, and straight-away. We are so accustomed to this type of phenomenon that we forget to see at what point it can seem magical. It is a lot better than an automatic ticket machine: here we have to press buttons in order to get our ticket, while ideas and memories come to mind immediately, all on their own, without us having to press anything!

Yet this is no more magical than Father Christmas's presents: Mother and Father have saved some money, gone off to buy the gift, looked for some pretty wrapping-paper and then gone to ridiculous lengths to keep it all secret so that their lucky child discovers nothing before the day itself.

For us adults, as well, all the underground services are there. When staying in a comfortable hotel, we know when we ring for breakfast that in a few minutes the bedroom door will open and an appetising tray of food will be placed on our knees. We don't have to bother ourselves with how the order gets to the kitchen, how the coffee-pot and milk-jug are filled or how the chamber-maid collects the tray and brings it to our room, complete with a pleasant smile.

For so many of our activities, we have nothing more to do, spoilt children as we are (without knowing it!). We ring up a friend. The number comes from a touch of our fingertips. We go to do the shopping, each with our own strategy (without thinking any more about it, because we really don't study how to do it!). Some of us have a good look round to compare prices and then head for the best in terms of 'quality at the right price'. Others know that tomorrow night the Smiths are coming to dinner and they need such-and-such; Jean doesn't like carrots, so a soup without them, etc, etc. All that happens automatically; we don't need to think about it.

Or rather we don't need to tell ourselves that we MUST think about it. We think, that's for sure; we never stop thinking. And that's something we should think about for a moment. Don't you agree that it would be a good idea sometimes to stop thinking a little? Of course, that's not really possible – except, perhaps, for those people who have spent years training in the discipline of Yoga or Zen.

For most of us, one thing is clear; the machinery inside our skull is in perpetual motion, like the mechanical movement of the same name. Why then do we have to force ourselves to attempt some training, reasoning or creativity? There we are, repeating: I MUST get up every morning at such-and-such a time . . . I MUST not drink more than one glass of wine at lunch time, I MUST learn twenty French words each day, while in fact, once again, each of these things can happen on its own – or almost. By wanting to do everything by force and consciously wanting to control everything, we are a little like the chief of staff who felt he must check the coat buttons of all his soldiers.

The trick is to rely on the work of our little grey cells

Like Hercule Poirot! They perform well in any case, but we can plan new tasks for them since they are really biologically made to do new things all the time – or almost. So let's organise all these activities and when it is time to act, all we have to do is let the impulses in the brain start to flow! That will relieve us of the continual pressure of feeling obliged to watch over everything and so, automatically, enable us to go much further.

If we put our confidence in 'machines' to make the base of a building, we give ourselves plenty of time to choose what will be the most harmonious and best adapted style for the different floors above. But if we are unsure about the base, we will have the nagging feeling of creating a dangerous balance as the construction continues.

It is the same for musicians. When they have mastered their technique, that is to say when their fingers do what they want without them having to think about it, then they can concentrate entirely on the art of interpretation. But if they try to interpret a Schubert sonata without the basic skills, it is like the labour of Sisyphus (who was forced to haul up the side of a mountain a rock which kept falling back down before he reached the summit). Behaving like this we will be overworked and stretched . . . and the result will always be in doubt.

We must therefore register new mechanisms in the brain which will subsequently work all on their own. It is like learning a foreign language: when we know it, the words come so instantly that we sometimes end up dreaming in that language when we are in the country where it is spoken!

Now you surely know that learning a foreign language is within everyone's capability, whatever the age, if the appropriate new methods are adopted. The moral of this is that with appropriate methods we can learn anything – that is to say, by registering in our brain a very large (incalculable!) number of new mechanisms and automatic patterns which enable us to dispense with having to force ourselves in order to succeed, and to succeed well.

WE MUST START BY WORKING – WORKING ON OUR-SELVES – TO 'EDUCATE' OUR BRAIN

Thanks to modern methods, we can all easily learn a foreign language. Certainly, but all the same we have at least to make the effort to follow these methods. You can arrive – EASILY – at being 'master of yourself and the universe' without having to think about any discipline, but you have to start by doing some exercises.

You can exercise your brain a lot better even than the top-level sportsman exercises his muscles. However, to be at the top level, the sportsman (of any discipline) rightly exercises something other than his muscles: he exercises his brain!! And when it is trained, you can relax and profit from its performances. You will not have to worry about seeing them deteriorate with use. The more the brain is made to work, the better it functions, and this is true for people of all ages.

The brain's work slows down its ageing and, as a result, that of the whole person. Once an automatic system has been well installed – for following health rules as well as for putting creativity to work – you will only have to check often enough that it is working properly. Any period of slackness will soon be sorted out with the help of a few exercise.

So rest assured that you can rely on a brain in good form, which will always find solutions to your difficulties and problems. 'Impossible' is a word that doesn't exist in the brain's language!

Have you never noticed that if you go to sleep with a problem turning over in your head, when you wake up the following morning a solution appears as if by magic? Even when not trained, the brain operates on the quiet, sometimes while we are thinking about other things or, better still, at the moment when we get ready to go to sleep, and finds the solution to the problem. This is because our brain is so made that any problem posed automatically prompts the search for a solution. And if we don't disturb it, the brain will do its work until it has reached that goal.

This skill, which is part of our hereditary stock of knowledge as human beings, can however be greatly increased. We can reach a point where the brain automatically seizes the important pointers, plans its strategy of associations and deduces the relevant decisions. And because at the same time it directs all our thoughts, it releases the energy necessary for the operation in hand.

We talk about 'brain' rather than 'psyche' to remove any ambiguity: it really amounts to the functioning of the cerebral nerve cells, the configuration of impulse circuits inside the brain, which enable us to do all that we do. And these circuits depend on the secretion of chemical products by the brain cells. We have to learn to make them secrete more depending on what we want to achieve, just as we learn to develop certain muscles to practise particular sports.

WE MUST WORK ON OURSELVES IN HARMONY WITH OURSELVES

Given that we have a brain in a working state, we can all improve its performance. But each one of us is what we are by reason of our heredity, as well as of what we have experienced right up to the moment when we read these words.

Some of us are more inclined towards action and others towards reflection; some of us like to lead, others to follow; some of us enjoy inventing, while others find satisfaction in following well-proven traditions, and so on. It is difficult and often disagreeable to try to go against our nature, against our tendencies. That does not imply that inactive people will not be able to take up aerobics, but rather that active ones will manage far more easily. This means that those who are generally inactive will have to apply themselves in a different way.

So we have to start by knowing ourselves as well as possible and, in all honesty, understanding our own habitual thought patterns in the different areas where we envisage taking up training. This doesn't involve high-powered psychology: we can find out enough by 'testing' certain key points, just like the mechanic can do a spot-check of our car before we take it on holiday. He will tell us perhaps: "Be careful of your spark-plugs; they're not new and you could have trouble starting the engine in damp weather." Then it's up to us whether we change our spark-plugs or whether we make sure we always leave our car somewhere in the dry.

As far as the results of the spot-check on our personality are concerned, unfortunately the solution of a part-exchange of a weak link in the system does not exist! But plenty of other solutions are available to us ...

PART ONE

BASIC PRINCIPLES

The pharmaceutical industry always mentions on its products the fact that the item is a medicine and what precautions should be taken depending on different factors – age, state of health, etc – and whether professional medical advice should be sought before taking that particular product.

HOW TO USE THIS BOOK

This book is a training manual, or you might like to think of it as a tool. You will learn to understand it by using it. Keep it to hand to consult it, criticise it and improve on it all through your period of training. But first you should read it from cover to cover, just like any other book. Then go back to those points that interest you or seem unclear to you or with which you do not agree. Where possible, discuss them with family or friends, look for further information and allow yourself to reflect.

Then take up your training.

Are you going to have a go at all the sections simultaneously, perhaps, since there are seven, devoting each day of the week to a different one? Or are you going to launch into one area and work on that until you feel you have 'changed' sufficiently and easily mastered all that is involved in that area?

Both strategies have their advantages and their difficulties. With the first you may risk spreading yourself too much, although you will avoid boredom. Depending on whether you are the 'active' type who likes novelties and change, or the 'meditating' type who prefers working in depth, you can choose which suits you best.

In any event, once you have begun your training, each day must bring you some new task, some new problem and some satisfying results.

Ideally you should look for the best way of noting down (1) your plan of action, (2) your task for the day and (3) your results. As far as each section is concerned, I would suggest a filing system that allows you to prepare your plan of action based on the information from your 'test-standard'.

Choose a method that suits you, but you must find a good method for making notes: notebook or pad, files, coloured felt-pens, etc. Don't laugh at these apparently childish details. They represent the seriousness with which you approach your training and they will act as a daily reminder (subconscious, perhaps, but you must use every device – even your sub-conscious!). And don't use your daughter's old school exercise-book or pinch the pens off your son: buy your own material and keep it in a safe place where no-one else can come and 'borrow' it! A few pages have been left blank at the back of this book so that you can use every opportunity to practise your skills, try a new exercise or make a note of your progress, even when you are in the bus queue!

The method you adopt also includes the amount of time you must devote to your training, which of course will vary. Setting up your training programme and records will take some time; how much will depend on you. And you may need to go back to these at a later date. Once all is set up, your daily commitment can be just a few minutes. It's not much, but it is indispensable (like cleaning your teeth!). So, before you dive in, work out the particular moment of the day, whenever that is, when you will have the peace and quiet to keep this extra 'diary'.

TO BE IN GOOD HEALTH

It is clear that to tackle any form of training, or learning, we must be in good health. Nevertheless, purely intellectual learning, which does not involve us emotionally, puts less strain on the body than training that affects us physically.

On the other hand, people who have undergone psychotherapy will know that a session of three-quarters of an hour with their therapist can tire them out a lot more than a three-hour walk. When we ourselves are the actual substance being modified, that demands a great deal of physical energy. And this energy must be supplied by an organism that will not suffer from the effort involved.

To feel fit we must, like the athlete preparing for a competition or the student for an exam, pursue a health regime. This includes watching our diet, the pattern of our sleep, the consumption of alcohol and tobacco (what we smoke ourselves and what we breathe in from the surrounding atmosphere!) and so on. It also includes regular daily physical movement, if possible aerobics.

Evidently, this regime will require quite a degree of commitment – and this can often be a lot more than you initially envisaged. It's a vicious circle. And all the more so because to get started on your training in whatever field, you will have to have the will to do it.

Let's be pragmatic: if your lifestyle is choking you, if you are suffering from depression, you will not be comfortable with training exercises; but it will be counter productive if you hold a gun to your head to do them. This will produce EXACTLY THE OPPOSITE TO THE GOAL FOR WHICH YOU ARE STRIVING.

So, if you are not feeling on form and do not have enough energy to follow a health regime, ask for medical help. Tonics can help you get going, just enough to start you off on your regime. After that, the mechanism will be set into gear, your stimulants will become unnecessary and your training will make quite satisfactory progress.

Aerobics

The word *aerobics* comes from America. It was imported into Europe some years ago amidst a blaze of publicity. Television, videos and magazines saw to it that everyone who didn't do it was definitely unhealthy, not to say OUT. Unfortunately the gymnastic exercises often suggested were far in excess of what is needed and, more importantly, were in total contradiction to what aerobics is all about: progressive exercise adapted to the individual.

As its name implies, aerobics came about from research into the physiology of the cells of the human body, which work chemically in *aerobe*, that is to say directly using the oxygen carried by the blood, or in *anaerobe*, first burning up their energy reserves. The transition of the metabolism (the succession of chemical actions) from one to the other works automatically according to the demands made by a person's level of activity. To achieve respiration in aerobe (the best for the body), the best method is to control this activity: not too much and not too lazily!

The principle of aerobics

The principle of aerobics is to practise lively but not violent muscular exercises, inducing a controlled cardiac acceleration. You must avoid breathlessness at all costs, since this would indicate a transition to anaerobic functioning – that is to say quite a different metabolic rhythm which is rarely beneficial.

With aerobics, energy in effect comes from the fatty reserves burned by the regular acceleration of oxygenation. This increase in oxygenation, due to cardiac acceleration, must be maintained at the higher level for at least 20 minutes (15 minutes minimum). This means the exercises must not be stopped or slowed down during this time.

I stress this period of 15-20 minutes every day, repeated at least five days a week. Medical evidence has shown that in less than one month of regular exercise, the whole of the body undergoes a real transformation. Psychologically, this regime also induces a sense of well-being which helps bring about or maintain our good humour.

A rhythm adapted for everyone

When we talk of lively muscular exercise, we mean whatever pace is necessary and sufficient to increase our heartbeats in a precise way. For a strapping lad of twenty, who is bursting with health, this could mean fast running or the sustained pounding of a punch-ball. For a frail elderly person it would probably be a series of arm, neck and leg movements from a seated position.

The rate of heartbeats to aim for depends on your age, and the rules only apply to those whose heart is in good condition. Obviously if you are in any doubt over this you must seek your doctor's advice before starting.

The rule is: you must gradually and progressively reach the permitted rate and maintain this for 20 minutes. If you have the time, you can continue for up to half-an-hour; but it is pointless to go beyond this.

The exact rate is calculated as follows: you start by determining a maximum by subtracting your age from 225. So, if you are fifty, the maximum would be:

$225 - 50 = 175$

That is to say, 175 heartbeats per minute.

But in no way is it a question of reaching that point. According to your age and your state of health, you must reach a modest percentage of this maximum rate depending on what you feel capable of doing. For example, if you are fifty and have never done any gymnastics, you should begin by aiming for 50 per cent of the maximum. That means doing exercises which make your heartbeat at around 87 or 88 per minute. If necessary, ask your doctor to show you how to take your own pulse!

At the end of two or three weeks you will notice that, to maintain this rhythm, you have to speed up your exercises. After about two months, you will feel capable of moving up to 60 per cent of the maximum, that is to say 105 beats per minute. In this way, you can increase the rate progressively up to 70 per cent of the maximum.

However, you should never go beyond 75 per cent of the maximum (130 if you are fifty), even with good training.

You should do your aerobic exercises in a well-aired space. The ideal would be a brisk walk or run, and certainly outdoors if you can. Failing this, since you may not have the time to find somewhere suitable, you can practise your exercises in front of an open window: but remember, no stopping and take deep breaths between exercises to maintain the continuity.

If you can, get yourself an exercise bike (with a speedo to check your pace) or even a rowing machine. If you lack space or imagination, do some running 'on the spot'. But a word of warning: start gently and respect your allotted heartbeat rate.

Generally speaking, whether it is a question of aerobics or your overall health regime, don't ask the impossible from yourself. You will do your aerobics for three days; then, on the fourth, you will oversleep and just make the office on time. What a shame! You will make up for it the next day. And if it's not this week, then it'll be the following one.

Have you noticed that you already feel better on those days when you have done your session of exercises? If you don't, wait a few days before starting again. It must give you pleasure, if not at the time (because to begin with you are going to treat it as an obligation) then certainly a little later.

I know of people weighed down with heavy professional responsibilities who need their aerobics like others need a stiff drink! And, in fact, this is a feeling that awaits us all once we have reached a certain point in our training.

So, at the beginning, you will have to steer your way between annoyance at the obligation and the anticipated feeling of pleasure. Push yourself a little, but not too much, and avoid any thoughts of dodging or skimping the exercises. Don't aim for perfection. Perhaps you over-indulge yourself one evening, maybe two ... That's a pity, because it slows down your training. But you equally have to remember that you have your life in front of you!

Common-sense must prevail in everything we do. It tells us that for all training we must make an effort, of course, but this effort should still be pleasurable, if not at the time then just afterwards. If you find it a chore and nothing more, then why make yourself suffer?

TO REALLY WANT TO DO IT

To undertake your personal training, you must really want to do it. You must really want to live better, with others perhaps, but especially with yourself. You must really want not to be obliged to force yourself to do anything, not to feel forced to be ever more productive – while at the same time being sure to do as well, if not better, than before . . . You must really want to see the good side of life.

In a recent interview, a well-known philosopher used the following expression: "When one has the honour of being alive . . ." Have you the desire to feel fully the pride of 'having the honour of being alive'?

You must be sure of having this real desire and not just try the method presented here as one of those little gadgets that one tries for a while and then abandons for another novelty. If you do, you have wasted time and energy in trying it out and you will find you are more tense and bitter than before.

We talk about faith moving mountains. The wanting, the desire to succeed, is a kind of faith, and it unleashes a formidable energy in those who believe.

So you must really work on yourself, reshape yourself in a deliberate way, but equally in a way you want – and this in the space of a few months.

Every day life moulds us in its own way, usually without us taking any notice, until now and then we notice that we have changed. So it is possible to change; it happens all the time and to all of us. However, this training is something we want – sometimes contrary to the direction in which our life is going at the time. And it must change us faster than outside factors which push us the other way. People can find themselves, in both family and professional life, caught up in a kind of monotony that never requires them to use their free will. They can let themselves go. If they are aware of feeling uneasy about this drift, any efforts to strengthen their own will are going to be much harder to make than the temptation not to have it in the first place!

So here is the first test-question, a matter of confidence . . . to stand in front of the mirror and look yourself straight in the eyes (just an image, but perhaps a good thing to do in reality) and ask yourself:

"DO I REALLY WANT TO DO IT?"

If, in all honesty, you reply "yes", then you can continue. If you reply "I don't know", wait a while and try to find that desire. Because you can give yourself the desire for something. Here is how to do it:

- You think about it as much as possible and at every opportunity. You talk about it, in one form or another. (It is not necessary to speak directly about your hesitation over this particular method; that can be boring. But you can discuss the general principle of doing some 'mental exercises'. There are numerous methods for improving your memory, being more self-assured and so on.)

- You daydream: it could be in the cinema, in a waiting-room, on a bus or in a train, before you go to sleep . . . You imagine yourself in various situations where you have developed the very skills it is suggested you have a go at here. For example, you imagine yourself in an office and the boss says: "We must come up with a brilliant idea." You feel the little wheels turning at full speed in your head and you reply: "I propose that . . ."

- You start to think about some projects, which can only be considered if you have acquired a certain skill. For example, you imagine taking up evening classes: but for that you must have a very good memory. Think seriously about this project, check up on the registration details, etc.

AND ONE FINE MORNING YOU WILL WAKE UP WITH THE REAL DESIRE TO DO SOME TRAINING!

THE REINFORCEMENTS

Training is an apprenticeship: here, it amounts to an 'apprenticeship on normal behaviour', but it is an apprenticeship all the same. And as such it obeys all the laws of apprenticeships, of which possibly the most important is the **law of reinforcements.**

All apprenticeships involve a strategy directed towards a goal, in this case the marking or noting of something in the memory. Now this marking is 'reinforced' when, the goal being achieved, there is a 'reward'; or, if after a certain time the goal is not achieved, there is a 'punishment'.

These terms of 'punishment' and 'reward' were first used by psychologists carrying out learning experiments on animals. But, since the biological demonstrations they devised are the same with human beings, these words have been retained, even in human psychology.

In effect, when a goal is reached, the brain automatically secretes a small quantity of internal morphine, which produces a feeling of well-being but also acts directly on the brain cells to mark in them the activities they have just undergone. This is already a 'reward' which the brain spontaneously offers itself. But if one tops it up by giving a little additional satisfaction – for animals the present of a little tit-bit and for human beings some words of praise and appreciation to boost their image – the internal morphine is discharged in greater quantity and the cell marking is stronger.

When the effort towards a goal ends in failure, the brain secretes other substances which have the effect of pushing it and creating an even greater desire to act. And under the effect of these secretions, the action is a pleasure in itself. As soon as there is a feeling of pleasure, the brain is ready to mark in the memory what it is doing. So, biological 'punishment' is not a non-pleasure, but rather a different kind of pleasure which acts as an incitement to pursue the action. It is why animal trainers never hurt their pupils when they fail: they arouse them with a little tap of the whip, for example, to increase that bit more their drive to action. At the same time, we all know that circus animals receive little tit-bits after each performance.

We all know the role the team trainer plays in today's sport: he works at making his players perform ever better. An Olympic champion of fifty years ago would today no longer recognise his or her sport. It's not just the techniques which make people ski faster, hit the tennis-ball harder or jump higher; it's also the trainer who works on his trainees at the highest mental level.

First he is an experienced 'reinforcer': he knows how to show his appreciation and maintain a warm atmosphere of mutual admiration among members of the team. Imagine the scenes when goals are scored in football, where the scorer is immediately overwhelmed by his team-mates who all embrace him at once and lift him off the ground in triumph! The trainer also knows how to spur on his team just at the moment when lapses appear, how to inject renewed strength into his players ...

You must therefore be your own trainer and play the game of reinforcements properly – knowing that the positive reinforcements, that is to say the 'rewards', are always more effective that the negative ones, the 'punishments'. You must think carefully before deciding what your rewards could be: first, and essentially, is your appreciation of yourself. You must not be afraid to say

"Well done! I have succeeded. I really am exceptional" – or at least to think it. Then, if it's possible – and this is the best situation – you must get the approval and preferably admiration of someone close.

Finally you must not forget material rewards (buying something you like or going out to a show you want to see . . .). Such rewards must not be given for just anything, but should mark a really important success. As well as the pleasure biologically reinforcing the marking in the brain cells, the presence of the object you buy or the memory of the show you saw will irresistibly evoke this noting and further reinforce it.

More difficult to handle are the 'punishments': don't forget that these must not cause suffering, but should be in the form of an obligation which should result in satisfaction. First, you must certainly note it in your conversation with yourself: "That's not working, old boy (or girl); I must put matters right. Starting from today, I have decided to push myself to do . . ."

It is not a question of adopting the attitude of forcing yourself with everything in life, but of giving yourself a precise objective – "and I'm not going to mess that up!" This could be rearranging a drawer, catching up with your personal accounts or writing an overdue letter that same day . . .

OTHER PEOPLE

Other people, first those immediately around us, but also everyone with whom we have contact, clients and professional colleagues, shop staff and even strangers with whom we are travelling or just queuing . . . all make up an integral part of our life. We are human beings and our interaction with other human beings is as vital for our brain's chemistry as air or water is for our body.

We are not conscious of it, but a person who stops us in the street to ask the time or the way is like a little echo which rebounds on us. We decide, without even thinking about it, the way in which we reply: "I was afraid of being attacked, stupid I know . . ." or "I wasn't very friendly!" or even "I think I was helpful. I would like to meet someone like me if I was lost in a strange town."

Obviously people closest to us, and especially family and very good friends, foster in us an emotional reaction – often there is an exchange of feelings which can sometimes be overwhelming. Generally speaking, these people reciprocate, more or less directly, their appreciation of us and that in turn releases in us different reactions ...

All this happens spontaneously; but we can make deliberate use of such appreciation, even the echoes that reach us. To do so, we must begin by reflecting quite pragmatically on our social situation, that is to say on the other people in our circle.

- First there is 'SELF'. Then those nearest to us: there are one or two people whose opinion of you, appreciation and occasionally advice are, for you, very important. These can be your husband (or wife), a member of the family, a close friend. This person or, possibly, these two people are not necessarily those you 'love' most. You can have a very loving relationship with someone, but just the certainty of that love means that his or her judgement, perhaps on an off-day, does not bother you too much! On the other hand, if it is a sister-in-law or a former professor whom you continue to see ... you know them well and you set such store by their opinions that their judgement will influence you.

  It is to this person (or these people) that you must know how to talk of your desire to train yourself and with whom you must regularly share your results. Their praise or disappointment will be your best reinforcements.

  Of course, it is not always possible: we don't always enjoy this kind of relationship with someone close to us ... In the absence of being able to tell ALL, at least choose the people with whom you can share some of your successes, even if this just involves dropping something into the general conversation, such as "I manage to do my aerobics at least five times a week" or, when you are sitting down to eat with the family in the evening, bring up the business meeting you had where it was you who provided the solution everyone was looking for. You will sense the praise of others from this kind of remark and that will give you a boost.

  So make a list (at least in your head) of the people with whom you can talk about yourself without pushing the point too much, just enough for them to voice their appreciation of you.

- A little further still from 'SELF', there are all those on whom you will be able to aim your training: those with whom you will have the chance to exercise your will, your creativity, your anti-stress defence mechanism ... They are like pawns in your game, without whom you can't play. You must recognise who the pawns are and know what they can be useful for and how best to use them in your overall strategy.

And these are human pawns! They always carry a little piece of mirror in which you can look at yourself – and appreciate yourself – if you only choose to think about it.

PART TWO

THE AREAS
OF TRAINING

Anyone who takes an honest look at themselves will be obliged to find flaws in plenty of areas! It happens quite naturally that we say to ourselves: "I am going to get better." And for most of us, everything can be improved: the speed of our repartee, our attention, our sociability, etc, etc.

You are being offered training in just seven areas, since experience has shown that together these encompass the art of living well. They are also the areas in which weaknesses tend to show up most.

- **WILL-POWER** is the nerve – not for fighting, since there is no question of a war, even with yourself – but the nerve for action. It is the basis of choice, decision and perseverance. And it's here that we often suffer the most and push ourselves the hardest.

- **MEMORY** is the basis of all our activities: it demands our attention, leads our observations, organises our perception, feeds the association of ideas or images and provides us continually with words, thoughts and gestures at any given moment. Too often we believe that exercising the memory involves repetition, like a production line, which is tedious and, in any case, not very effective against those 'gaps' and other 'failures' which grow more and more numerous with age – sometimes even from our forties onwards! Exercising the memory in fact involves playing with the techniques of observation and association: this is of immediate practical use for things we have to memorise and saves us from those gaps and failures.

- **PROBLEM SOLVING,** or the knack of finding the appropriate strategy, is always necessary and becomes the more so with the ever more sophisticated conditions of life. In the past we could quite simply have dealt with matters like our parents (professional life, family life, the children's education ...). Today the new technology, the impact of society, the increasingly complicated demands made on us, all mean we have to 'manage' and this 'management' can no longer be just a sort of following the old methods established once and for all. Of course we must have basic strategies, but at the same time we have for ever to respond to new factors introduced into every situation. We often call these 'problems' – and everyone has these 'problems': professional, family, personal.

- **SELF-CONTROL** is obviously difficult, given our modern day surroundings of stimulation and even continual aggression. We overcome our desire to throw a punch, we swallow a broadside of insults we want to utter, we make ourselves walk or smile, we continually live under restraint. And sometimes we crack. Natural self-control brings a feeling of self-assurance and allows us to be pleasant but assertive.

- **COPING WITH STRESS** is a more precise and, at the same time, more far-reaching technique: it certainly relies on good self-control, but it also includes the knack of transforming stressful conditions, otherwise known as controlling one's environment. Coping with stress is very often the knack of transforming aggression into beneficial stimulation, finding the knack of putting stress to work to our advantage.

- **BEING CREATIVE OR INVENTIVE** is a more than useful

necessity. It consists not only in knowing how to manage when we don't have what we should have, but it is also the knack of changing tack, diverting from the well-trodden route and other stereotypes imposed by our daily life. By being a sheep – and we are all under plenty of pressure from, among other things, the media and all-powerful publicity machines – we destroy ourselves. It therefore becomes vital that we are always ready to 'invent something'.

- **STAYING YOUNG** is not just a preoccupation of old age. Whatever its faults, our society has at least one quality: its dynamism. In other words it is made for the young, in every aspect. To keep up with it, we must stay young! And here, particularly, it is no use trying to push yourself too hard. Youth displays itself in many ways, but the most common and evident are: curiosity, plans and ambitions, activity, easy contact with other human beings ...

This is the order in which the book provides you with its training method. However, follow it as you want. Now it's your turn!

CHAPTER ONE

WILL POWER

W e are not talking here of will-power as a moral virtue: you do not have to make a value judgement on what is morally 'good', 'better' or 'bad'. The objective is to find how to improve our way of life from a practical point of view; if we use words like 'good', 'better' or 'bad' it is in reference to the success or failure of proposed strategies.

For us success and achievement are facts, both resulting from reaching a goal: they positively confirm an effective and well-followed method. It is true that conduct leading logically to personal efficiency is in full accord with moral rules. We live better in practice when we live morally well . . . But it is neither within our competence nor our role here to formulate morality.

What we tell ourselves

We all talk to ourselves, which has a considerable influence on our way of life and especially on how we experience life. And, most of the time, we have completely the wrong ideas – at will!

- Thus we generally consider having will-power as being capable of making ourselves do what we would prefer not to do –

or, put another way, being stronger than our desires or dislikes. Superficially, this can appear to be true.

Take a child who does his homework rather than going out to play; surely he has got will-power! Especially if he does it without his parents making him, whether immediately or a bit later after being punished for failing to do so. What we don't perhaps know is that he gets real satisfaction out of doing his homework! And not only that of a 'duty accomplished', but also because he gains real pleasure from this task.

Don't laugh: grown-ups have a tendency to make fun of a youngster who *likes school*: "As if one could actually like working!" they say. But at ten or twelve, we are still discovering for ourselves what is fascinating, what is just a game, and we still like to 'win the challenge' of learning a poem or history lesson. Has your child never come bounding up to you and declared joyfully: "That's it, I've done it! I know my lesson!"?

And, finally, between the pleasure of preparing a little meal for her doll and that of homework and lessons, a young girl can really hesitate ... What may perhaps swing it is the fact that tomorrow the homework well done will be recognised with agreeable consequences, while the fun of the doll's meal will stop right there.

The choice of the 'studious' child is perfectly logical: between two pleasures, with an extra plus for one of them. Is this will-power? We'll come back to this point later.

- So, when we are not always able to make ourselves do something, we tell ourselves: "I don't have the will-power". And that's exactly what we say to ourselves when we don't manage to get up a quarter-of-an-hour earlier during the week to do our aerobics. However, we do get up half-an-hour earlier on a Saturday and Sunday to go and play tennis, because that is the only time the court is available! Don't we need some will-power to get up half-an-hour earlier at the weekend?

The truth is that we enjoy tennis, while aerobics hasn't yet provided us with the same pleasure. We would like to make ourselves do things we don't really have the urge to do. We believe we should, because we tell ourselves: "I MUST do my aerobics". But saying "I MUST" is not enough to make us have the urge! In general, it actually works the other way!

So, what we call will-power is not the energy to get up early, but the ability to make ourselves suffer – because to make ourselves suffer is to do something we really don't have the desire to do.

• We also tell ourselves: "In life, particularly nowadays, we achieve nothing without will-power." In saying that, we have all been taught by our own experiences. For most of the things that we succeed at we have achieved 'under pressure, pushing ourselves to the limit'!

Furthermore, when we look at life's 'winners', the 'successes' of all sorts, and hear them talking about themselves, the emphasis is always on their continuous 'struggle', albeit a victorious one. There is no respite; the pressure is always on. And clearly this is the model which makes its mark a little deeper every day.

What they don't tell us (or not enough) is that they gain a lot of pleasure from their efforts; or, to put it another way, what they want to show us as their 'forcing' effort is, for them, just following their natural bent. For Winston Churchill, tenacity was clearly in his nature – which in no way diminishes his achievements. On the contrary, he had to force himself to let go!

WHAT IS WILL-POWER?

The previous examples well illustrate cases of what we call will-power. While it seems that the protagonists – the child, the sportsman, life's winners – are behaving very soundly and positively, it should be remembered that they are doing what they do *from the point of view of their pleasure* and not the other way round.

Let's go back to our definition of will-power. It is certainly in the action that it shows itself and if possible in the effectiveness of the action; but it is definitely not in the fact of going against what one wishes.

Sometimes we are convinced – and wrongly – that efficiency is opposed to pleasure (as if pleasure was about doing NOTHING!), which leads to the equation: 'To act efficiently is to act against one's pleasure, therefore to force oneself.' Nothing could be further from the truth. We can be efficient by forcing ourselves, but at what price! And in any case we are always MORE efficient when we are doing things we want and find pleasurable.

You say that it is efficient to have regular aerobic sessions but that it is also a struggle. NO. It is only a struggle to begin with: you have to force yourself for a few weeks (we will see how ...). But once you start to feel the benefits, it becomes a pleasure, a need that you want to satisfy!

Do you consider that in the first weeks you are using your will-power and after that you won't have to any more? Well, no; it is always the same thing: only, after the first month, it becomes will-power without any effort. That is the aim of this book – and for plenty of other things apart from aerobics.

IN REALITY, will-power is the convergence of several factors which act in sequence and as one in perfect harmony with each other.

1. First comes the **DECISION** to act.

We use the word 'act' for all actions, whether they are demonstrative (gestures, behaviour, etc) or mental (reasoning, forming an opinion, etc). Certainly refusing to do something is an action, even if it is primarily internal, mental. Naturally you must not confuse voluntary refusal with oversight or laziness ...

We can DECIDE to do something because we have CHOSEN to do it or we can be forced into it. In both cases it is a decision, but there is a difference. When we choose, we are following our inclination, what biologists call 'pleasure' (which corresponds to chemical secretions and particular activities in the brain). When we decide under pressure, we are showing our will-power, of course, but paradoxically less strongly than if we choose to act; we are going to make ourselves do it, because we don't have the strength to refuse.

2. Next, there is the **LAUNCHING** of the action.

This comes after, and does not necessarily follow, the decision, if the will-power is lacking (strong enough to decide, but not enough to get going). For example, you can decide to do your aerobics: you are convinced of its benefits, it's true, and you're going to do them; but it is still necessary to launch yourself into them each day, to get yourself going! This launching is the transition from the act of deciding, which happens in the head. This requires some internal energy. But to move to the act of a chosen decision obviously uses up less energy than to act on a decision into which one was forced. It is therefore easier.

3. Following this, it's **TENACITY** which comes into play.

This will have to be maintained right through until the goal is reached. Generally actions take up a certain time, whether all at once or because there is a question of repetition – such as the repetition of the aerobic sessions – or perhaps because the action is complex and requires a whole sequence of operations (for example: inquiry, then choice, then the formalities and finally the actual purchase or sale . . .).

Thus we have to find the strength to carry on through to the end. Obviously we will sustain our effort a lot more easily when the goal is more attractive and also if the different stages are closer to our own inclinations.

4. During this time, we must keep our **SELF-CONFIDENCE** and not be distracted or influenced.

When we tackle a task, whatever it is, when we come to a decision, there is often some kindly soul to hand who insists: "Leave it alone, at least for a day or two; you'll do even better if you come back to it later" or, equally: "I wouldn't do it like that, if I were you; I strongly advise you against taking this risk", etc . . .

The danger is to 'play the miller'. According to the fable, the miller heeds the 'good' advice, which recommends that he puts his son on the back of the donkey, while he walks; then he meets some outraged people who believe, that on the contrary, it is for the boy to walk while he rides on the donkey. A little further on, someone suggests to him: "Why don't you both ride on the donkey?", with the result that the poor beast collapses under the weight . . .

This illustrates a characteristic lack of will-power, through a lack of self-confidence. If the miller had been sure of himself, he would have sent his advisers packing and done what he had decided.

To keep going right to the end, ignoring all contrary advice, however well-intentioned, demands real strength of mind, of will-power!

5. Finally, you must **MAINTAIN YOUR MORALE.**

Don't be discouraged by things that happen, even failures, and, most important of all, maintain your morale despite the critics.

How many budding creators have abandoned their projects, after initial success (proof of will-power . . .), crushed by the weight of criticism? A good number of our greatest writers not only continued to insist when their editors rejected their manuscripts, but also carried on writing despite an initially cool reception. And what did the Beatles do when the first major recording company they approached turned them down?

So will-power is, at the same time, the capacities of decision, launching, tenacity, self-confidence and strength of morale. And all these function so much better when the voluntary act goes the way we want it to, that is to say when we get pleasure from it (in the biological sense of the expression).

PERSONAL ASSESSMENT

Having the will-power 'without any effort' is making all the capacities involved work harmoniously together. But before suggesting that you exercise these various aspects of personality, it is necessary to assess your existing situation, your tendencies, your weaknesses . . . as far as your will-power is concerned.

It would be a waste of time asking you straight off: "Have you got will-power?" Perhaps you would, in all honesty, reply yes, because you know you are capable of forcing yourself. Possibly you do nothing but that! And your aim will not be to acquire will-power, but simply to achieve what is being proposed here: having the will without pain! Perhaps you would answer no, because you do not manage to push yourself enough to be a winner.

In both cases, you can only benefit from the method of 'will-power without effort'. So it is necessary to examine the way in which you behave, how you operate the different elements of will-power.

For each of these elements, two or three questions will be enough to serve as a 'test-standard', or initial indicators. These questions will require you to reflect a little beforehand, to know yourself as well as possible. Obviously you should reply with the utmost honesty, reflecting sufficiently in order to be as truthful as possible.

After each question, you will find a short commentary on the possible results. Don't read these until you have answered the questions!

DECISION

- **When you buy something:**

a. *You think about it for a certain time before deciding.*

b. *It takes you some time, because you hesitate. (Am I right, or not?)*

c. *It takes you some time because you read the information on the product . . .*

d. *You consider this purchase because you have seen a friend buy it or someone has advised you to.*

e. *You do it on the spur of the moment: you have seen it by chance in the shop-window and that sparks off your desire.*

COMMENTARY

a: You are 'secondary'; you always reflect before acting; you don't hesitate, but you consider logically the pros and cons.

b: You lack self-confidence because you do not create confidence in yourself or because you haven't sufficient dynamism for good self-assurance.

c: You are logical, rational and you have the internal force of your logic to back up your-decisions.

d: You are emotionally dependent, you need to feel yourself surrounded, in agreement with people around you, helped by their presence.

e: You are a 'primary' personality who acts immediately after the stimulation, which makes you an 'active' character. Your energy is such that your desires can set off an action.

- **Do you say to yourself: "I should . . ." without managing it:**

— *stop smoking*	*yes*	*no*
— *do some sport*	*yes*	*no*
— *watch what I eat and drink*	*yes*	*no*
— *do my personal accounts every day*	*yes*	*no*
— *something else . . .*	*yes*	*no*

- **Often:** *yes,* score 3
- **Sometimes:** *yes,* score 2
- **Never:** *yes,* score 1

COMMENTARY

- **Do your sums. If you have scored between 15 and 10,** you lack the spirit of decision-taking. Your situation is difficult, because you fall between two stools. You want to, but you can't decide. It would be better for you to make the choice between wanting and deciding, or not wanting!
- If you have scored **between 10 and 5,** you're not very forceful in your decision-taking. But is this through lack of desire or lack of dynamism?
- With **less than 5,** you are at ease with yourself. But is this because you have taken the route of not deciding to stop smoking, etc? Or is it because you keep to your decisions? Only in the latter case can you be proud of your spirit of decision-taking.

- **Are you late for meetings, getting to work, etc?**
  - a. *Always*
  - b. *Often*
  - c. *Never*

COMMENTARY

a: You clearly have a difficulty as far as decisions are concerned.
b: You are quite robust in your decision-taking, but perhaps lack dynamism when it comes to taking action.
c: You are firm in your decision-taking and have a a healthy energy in putting your decisions into action.

LAUNCHING

- **Do you realise your projects?**
  - a. *Very often*
  - b. *Rarely*
  - c. *Never*

COMMENTARY

a: You have a good capacity for launching the action, once you have decided.

b: There must be reasons which block your actions. Success from time to time shows that you have the ability to launch actions. But there must sometimes be something preventing you. Are you aware of any internal conflicts, for example, which sometimes block your performance?

c: You clearly have a tendency to dream (careful, this is good but shouldn't be abused). You take decisions but you are content to live them in your imagination.

- **When you have decided on a purchase:**
  a. *You go to buy it immediately.*
  b. *You wait for the opportunity when you will be passing the shop.*
  c. *You go no further than the decision and end up not buying it.*

COMMENTARY

a: You have a good capacity for getting yourself going. You are probably active and perhaps of a 'primary' temperament.

b: You clearly have a passive tendency. You decide, perhaps, but then you allow events to take their course, if they want to!

c: As for the commentary on the last reply in the previous question, this indicates a propensity for dreaming. If you have answered **c** on both occasions, it's time you got yourself into action and entered the real world.

TENACITY

- **Have you started and then abandoned (not for health or financial reasons):**
  — *a sport?*
  — *a course (foreign language; technical, such as needlework for example; art; musical instrument . . .)?*
  — *a charitable activity?*
  — *something else . . . ?*

COMMENTARY

If you have never undertaken anything, then this question is not for you! You can assess your tenacity as very good, average or weak according to the number of times you gave up (as a percentage of things undertaken) and the speed with which you gave up:
in less than 5 years – in less than 1 year – in less than 3 months.

41

- **If you set out on an excursion:**
  a. *You carry on right to the end, at any price.*
  b. *You give up before the end is reached, when you feel tired.*
  c. *You give up at the first minor difficulty.*

COMMENTARY

a: You are particularly tenacious.

b: You are tenacious, but mix this with common-sense. While answer **a** reveals a taste for 'forced' actions, you demonstrate here a taste for the choice of a pleasurable solution (still in the biological sense).

c: You have absolutely no tenacity. You can cope with immediate, spur-of-the-moment actions but collapse easily in the face of difficulties.

- **If you are looking to buy an object that is difficult to find:**
  a. *You persevere, you take whatever time is necessary and you find it.*
  b. *You go to all the obvious places where you think it might be. If you don't succeed, you give up the idea.*
  c. *You give up the idea after the first shop, even when you are told it can be ordered.*

COMMENTARY

a: As with the previous question, you are tenacious (even if people call you stubborn, don't let that put you off!). The important point is to be naturally gifted as regards the factors that make up will-power. You will find it easier than others to exercise effortless will-power since, as far as tenacity is concerned at any rate, you only have to follow your natural tendencies!

b: Your dynamism is not perhaps quite at its peak.

c: Not only do you not have any tenacity, but you also show pessimism. You don't even wait for someone to order the object for you! You abandon your desires a little too quickly, which can be a sign of depression.

SELF-CONFIDENCE

- **Have you been influenced in your important decisions?**
  — *professional choice*

  yes – a little – no – by whom – by what

— *choice of dwelling*   *yes – a little – no – by whom – by what*
— *choice of holidays*   *yes – a little – no – by whom – by what*
— *political opinions*   *yes – a little – no – by whom – by what*
— *style of clothes and behaviour*
                         yes – a little – no – by whom – by what
— *choice of cultural activity (films, theatre, books)*
                         yes – a little – no – by whom – by what
— *judgement of people (friends, colleagues)*
                         yes – a little – no – by whom – by what

COMMENTARY

A: Compare the number of *yes/a little/no* answers, which will give you an idea of how easily influenced you are. From this, you can deduce how self-confident you are.

B: Examine the *who* answers: who influences you most often? This will enable you to analyse the type of emotional relationship you have with others. Is it:

- someone you like?
- someone you admire?
- someone you fear (or have been afraid of)?

If you come up with the type of person who has been able to influence you the most, it will be in your interests to find someone who, for you, is of that same type (whom you like, admire or fear) to act as 'witness' for your training.

C: Examine the *what* answers: what is it that tends to influence you the most?

• Material contingencies, which you considered to be unavoidable: you need to work on your inventiveness.

• The opinion of others, in general or society: you don't have a very good opinion of yourself or see enough value in yourself. For you, the 'What will they say?' is more important than you think. You must have more confidence in yourself.

• The feeling of not being in a good position to make another choice. Perhaps you consider yourself too old (for certain studies, for example), too small or too big (choice of clothes), too weak, too slow, etc. All these 'too's show that you have a very poor opinion of yourself. You really do lack self-confidence. Perhaps you even have a depressive or pessimistic temperament.

MORALE

- **When you fail in a certain action, it makes you feel:**

  a. *Unhappy, with a desire to retire into your shell.*

  b. *Aggressive.*

  c. *The urge to start again, here or elsewhere.*

COMMENTARY

a: You have a fragile temperament. (Temperament here meaning the mechanism that automatically changes the colour around us, more or less easily, from clear to dull and vice-versa, from pessimism to optimism. A stable temperament only changes the colour of things in serious situations. If it is fragile, it can change on the least excuse.)

b: Your temperament is not very stable, but you have a good self-defence mechanism against the disruption such changes can bring. Aggression is an active way of avoiding feeling unhappy.

c: You have a sound morale, that is to say you protect yourself in a positive way against negative stimulation.

- **When you receive a bad shock, you recover:**

  a. *Immediately.*

  b. *After a moment or two, but you do it on your own.*

  c. *After a moment or two, but only if someone helps you.*

COMMENTARY

a: As for the previous answer **c**, you have a sound morale. If you have given this 'sound morale' reply in both cases, it is even sounder!

b: You lack really solid temperament at times, but you possess good inner dynamism which allows you to protect yourself.

c: You are dependent on others.

This questionnaire provides you with quite a detailed overall assessment of yourself, as far as the tendencies and capacities necessary for showing will-power are concerned. So, in order to act in a way that suits you, your choice of method, the rhythm of your exercising and so on should take your results into consideration, as they reveal your personality type:

- Particularly 'primary', active and immediate OR particularly 'secondary', reflective, meditative and needing to chew things over and consider all the arguments before deciding.
- Inner dynamism: this depends on your physical health, but also on a balanced temperament and self-confidence, as well as the role played by desires, wants and plans in your life.
- Particularly active and going into action voluntarily OR particularly passive, preferring to wait for the occasion or the incitement and with a tendency to let things work themselves out.
- Inclinations directed particularly towards realisation OR particularly towards dreams.
- Tenacity: this is in relation to inner drive and the factors on which this depends.
- Personal self-confidence and a good level of self-assurance OR a tendency to run yourself down.
- Particularly dependent on others, the need for their appreciation and, if possible, their support OR particularly independent with a taste for relying first and foremost on yourself.
- Morale: good with successful defence mechanism when under attack OR fragile.

▶ EXERCISES

These are aimed at making you competent in four areas:

I   The art of finding the right reasons for acting
II Inner drive
III Self-confidence
IV Tenacity

THE ART OF FINDING THE RIGHT REASONS FOR ACTING

▶ THE THEORY

In order to be able to exercise will-power effortlessly, voluntary actions must please you. The decision to act must be the result of a choice, from which you expect satisfaction. This expectation will quite naturally prompt your behaviour, your gestures or your approach.

An action can in itself bring immediate pleasure, which is enough to get you moving; or it can be the means of achieving contentment, gratification or even joy: we expect it, that is to say we want it, and this desire is a fundamental source of energy.

For something to seem desirable, whether immediately or in the near future, there have to be good reasons for it. These good reasons are not always obvious: we therefore have to learn to find them.

⋑ AN EXAMPLE

Imagine that you have a wardrobe that you basically use as a general dump – not because you have decided to but because, over the years, you have thrown in willy-nilly all the things you do not know where to put and you have not decided to throw away. It is in such chaos that it cannot be used. And, for good measure, you discover that cockroaches or similar little creepy-crawlies are well installed inside.

You would need lots of will-power to do something about it, to sacrifice a Saturday or Sunday morning . . . Don't push yourself. Launch Operation 'Instant Pleasure'!

"But how could I get satisfaction in making such a sacrifice?" you ask. Well, you will surely come across some interesting objects, things you bought while on holiday or with someone you love – and that will bring back memories . . . Perhaps you will come across something you can give your nephew for his birthday. Come to think of it, you remember a gadget you haven't used for years but you could now do with . . .

By thinking about all the things you could find in the wardrobe, it suddenly becomes like Ali Baba's treasure and you have just one desire and that is to start exploring! No need to force yourself. You can't wait until the coming Saturday to get started.

Let's continue our game of imagination. There you are, in the middle of a pile of junk . . . Everything has been taken out and is lying all over the floor. You have to arrange things rationally into groups . . . You are feeling rather discouraged. Still don't force yourself. You are going to launch Operation 'Future Pleasure'.

Start by stopping everything! Go and make a cup of tea and enjoy it quietly while you reflect: "Once I have put to one side all the 'presents' I can give away and all the things I need to throw away and have arranged what is left. I am going to have some welcome space. At last I will be able to sort out my stones and shells into a proper collection. I must borrow a book and find out all the names ... I'm going to ring Marion, who knows all about geology..."

Immediately you return to your arranging with enthusiasm. The following Saturday you are going to fix up a series of shelves to store your specimens and, once that's done, you are going to ring Marion. She will be surprised! You wish it were already done!

◪ THE PRACTICE

You must therefore get used to launching these operations – Instant Pleasure and Awaited Future Pleasure – while carrying on a series of everyday activities which requires will-power. Think about everything you do not manage to do or those things you do manage but only by forcing yourself more or less painfully.

Start with the rules of the requirements of domestic life (arranging, repairing, administration, accounts ...), of family necessity (visits, correspondence, children's education ...).

1. Make a list of those things that require a more or less painful effort of will-power. You can add to this list later, if your voluntary actions don't happen automatically and effortlessly after an initial series of exercises.
   • Regular hours of getting up in the morning and ways of avoiding the hustle and panic so that everyone is ready to leave on time. Perhaps it's necessary to get up a little earlier?
   • Regular hours for going to bed – even more essential if you have decided to get up a little earlier in order to start your day relaxed and not under pressure. You must obviously account for some evenings out, but make sure these are not so many as to exhaust you.
   • About 20 minutes of aerobics: find the right moment and stick to it. In fact, any time is good, between getting up and going to bed, with the exception of the hour following a meal.
   • Keeping an eye on your drinking. You must drink enough water (roughly a couple of litres of liquid per day in total); and

you must control the quantity of alcohol (wine, beer, spirits, etc.) according to your age, your way of life ... AND in addition to the obvious limits when driving a car!
- Keeping an eye on your diet: balanced meals (except on special occasions which shouldn't be too often!). No sweets and nibbles between meals ...
- Organising the family budget: frequency of purchase, accounts, maintenance, etc.
- Keeping an eye on the children's lessons and homework: precise and regular hours, etc.

2. Make a note against each item on your list, going from the easiest to the most painful or difficult.

Start by challenging yourself with the easiest action. When this becomes a pleasure, you can move on to the second and so on. The practice you put in on some of the everyday areas will bring about new mental habits and, without having to think about it, you will automatically launch into Operation Pleasure in any situation that involves a voluntary action on your part.

For your first exercise, you still won't be able to make the necessary long-term planning. After two or three exercises (two or three items on your list), however, you will be an expert and be able to allow yourself some delay before acting. Waiting for the moment when you feel mentally prepared to do something you dislike is a sort of challenge you throw out for yourself. It is a match with yourself, which produces a fresh outbreak of inner energy and helps with your training.

While waiting, prepare your reinforcements. To do that, you must anticipate your future success several stages before any given voluntary act becomes really easy. Imagine, for example, assessing yourself at the end of two weeks: if the system seems to be working, it is because your reasoning is good; you can be proud of yourself and have every right to be congratulated. Look forward to giving yourself a real material reward at the moment when you are sure you are completely victorious. Think about the reward and nurture your desire to have it, especially when you feel that you haven't yet got there.

Think also about punishments (not too heavy and always positive), some task (for which you can launch yourself into Operation Pleasure!), some sacrifice – but from which you can profit in a positive manner. For example, deny yourself a trip to the cinema, but in its place listen to some music that you normally never have the time to hear.

Imagine you have chosen, to begin with, **the hour of getting up.**

- Launch into *Operation Instant Pleasure*, taking the time to reflect well in order to find the good reason (or reasons) for getting up regularly at a certain time. It can take several days to find the pleasure you could get from this routine:

  — It can be the pleasure of getting up first in a house that's still sleeping.

  — Or that of rejoicing at the early morning atmosphere always full of promise because it has given you the nicest of presents: time!

  — It can be the pleasure of feeling strong inside.

  — Or the pleasure of looking forward to the admiration of others, etc.

  Make a note of all these good reasons as and when they come to mind, think about the moments you have lost and in the evening, when you go to bed, imagine hard your early mornings and the life and joy you feel in your veins. . . Quite quickly you will sense your desire growing and the trigger working. You will control your waking-up with a feeling of happy expectancy: tomorrow morning you have a meeting - with yourself!

- If the mechanism isn't working, launch into *Operation Future Pleasure*. Imagine everything that will be happening AFTER your early rising, all that you are going to be able to do with the extra time: a REAL breakfast, sitting down; even the time to talk with your partner and the children as if you were on holiday! Perhaps, if you calculate well, you could even do your famous aerobics, knowing the benefit you will get from them. . .

  And then think about leaving home without having to run, arriving at the office relaxed and almost two minutes early! What luxury! Nothing like starting work in a good mood; clearly everyone will notice it . . . if your image of a calm personality comes across, that will certainly be a plus – with colleagues but more especially with the bosses!

  Here again, make a note of all the satisfactions that await you, if only you have the courage to get up at a certain time every day. Before you go to sleep, daydream about these (the little inner cinema). And when your personal film show is over, don't forget to tell yourself: "But what's stopping me from doing it? Absolutely nothing! I have only to set my alarm and the rest will happen all by itself." When it rings in the morning, you think about all the things that are waiting for you if you get up straightaway. And hey presto, it's done!

Once your desire to get up at your chosen time is well-established and you have achieved it without even a thought that it might be hard, give yourself a pause of two weeks: are you going to continue to get up during all this time just for the pleasure? If you reply is affirmative, you have already achieved something important: you have given birth to a new skill – that of acting for the pleasure.

Make the most of all the positive reinforcements you can find. And don't be afraid to admire yourself. That will perhaps enable you to set a good example: you are doing a good deed by admiring yourself!

And if that doesn't work, if for example you continue only to keep to set times under sufferance and by forcing yourself, don't hesitate to tell yourself: "It's just a passing phase; I haven't yet found MY good reasons." Then resume your previous rhythm and actively look for pleasurable reasons you haven't thought about.

Perhaps by talking to close friends you will discover something about yourself that will force out the REALLY good reason. In any case, don't deny yourself this sufferance or feeling of being in a 'state of punishment'. Eventually, if you only have a slightly 'active' personality, give yourself a punishment task – on the subject of which you must find good reasons for getting satisfaction from it.

Once you have sufficiently developed your desire to start again, give it another go! There is a good chance it will work the second time round. Allow yourself one successful month – that is to say, once again, that for a whole a month you rise like a bird WITH PLEASURE (i.e. effortlessly) – to decide that this time you are absolutely comfortable with your new discipline: it suits you and you have no urge to change it. Now the round is won: it's the moment for the material reward!

After this, have a go at the next element on your list. You will find that with the third perhaps – or certainly the fourth – it will become a lot easier for you.

INNER DYNAMISM
■■■■■■■■■■■■■■■■■■■■■■■

◼ THE THEORY
....

Generally speaking, exercises on will-power, even 'for pleasure', require internal energy (just as all engines need power to work). You must always have your natural reserve ready to provide a supply.

The best energy comes from our desires (what psychologists call 'motivations'). We have all surely experienced that if we REALLY want something, we find the courage to do what is necessary to get it – and painlessly!

In fact, it has been proved scientifically that desire (ALL desire and not simply that of a sexual nature!) creates in us quite a mental and biological activity which releases our internal energies. Paradoxically, the majority of us allow ourselves to be carried along by life, we continue to RESPOND to its demands and many of us NO LONGER THINK ABOUT HAVING SPONTANEOUS DESIRES!

◼ AN EXAMPLE
....

For example, some well-made publicity has sparked off your 'desire' to go to Greece for your holidays. You contact the travel agents and send off a cheque; you know that on July 16 you have to meet up with a group at Gatwick Airport . . . In the meantime, you really don't have the time to think about it. You have done what is necessary and your mind's at rest.

But do you really WANT to go to Greece? When was the last time you really cherished an authentic desire, a wanting inside you, without it having to be created by some external stimulation?

◼ THE EXERCISE
....

In this area, the exercises concern your inner life, your dreams, your imagination: they work in parallel with the others. Their aim is to provide you with energy, which will be all the more welcome for your other exercises!

This is going to put a slight demand on your time – a little each day, but over quite a long period. It involves peering into your innermost recesses in search of all your spontaneous desires, the real ones, even those that you haven't thought about for a long time, as well as those you do consider or that are objectively unrealisable. As and when you find or rediscover a true desire, note it down.

When you feel you have a sufficient 'haul', take the time to examine it. Among all these desires, all these wants, choose something that can be realised. From this moment, it is no longer just a desire; it has become a PROJECT – even a long-term project is important.

And you are going to start putting the final touches to a plan of realisation. Think about it often, imagine a strategy for the various stages and partial results which will help you advance gently towards your goal. The mere fact of having a project that is near to your heart has an uplifting effect on your life in general, it maintains inside you those spontaneous discharges of energy from which all your activities will benefit. This will clearly be the ideal: for you to be able to start work on a plan to realise your project – especially if it reflects a very long held desire!

This work on yourself need not be too unpleasant . . . and you will be surprised at the dynamism it brings you. You will be taking giant steps towards an EASY mastery of yourself.

SELF-CONFIDENCE
■■■■■■■■■■■■■■■■■■■■■■■■■

◘ THE THEORY

Your inner dynamism also depends on the confidence you have in yourself. That begins with the feeling of being in agreement with yourself, that is to say acting according to your own convictions.

For example, you are convinced that the old boy passing the hat round on the pavement is going to use what people give him in order to buy some alcohol and get drunk, and you do not agree with being an accomplice to his self-destruction. So, if you drop some money in the hat, you are in disagreement with yourself! Perhaps you can transpose this trite example into something a lot more serious.

You must be completely in agreement with yourself in order to be sure of yourself and to have the self-confidence thanks to which you will not have to hesitate. Because in hesitating you lose all the energy that you should be using in the action!

◰ AN EXAMPLE

Imagine someone who lets himself be persuaded by a friend's kind words to join a choir. He has quite a good voice, but he is not mad on music and certainly the routine of rehearsals is misery for him. He didn't have the courage to say 'no' to his friend and now he continues to go along on the strength of his will-power and without any pleasure!

For this person, the exercising of will-power will not be supported by any search for good reasons to go to rehearsals: the reason for making music as an amateur is surely that of getting pleasure from it! And if this is not naturally the case, why force oneself?

So you must have the will-power to say 'no' which, as we have already said, can sometimes be a real effort. But you will do it without effort if you are sure of yourself.

You can exercise this self-confidence by learning to be in agreement with yourself at any given moment and especially where it concerns important elements of your existence.

◰ THE EXERCISES

A. This is going to start with **a real questioning of your essential options** (being capable of asking yourself questions and knowing how to answer them). Do this quietly, in writing, taking all the time you need. Plan some meetings with yourself, once or twice a week for example, for periods of ten to twenty minutes where you will be sure of not being disturbed.

- Make a list of what you are going to put under the microscope: job, home, political and religious opinions, etc. For each item, play the 'WHY?' game.
  For example, under JOB:
  Why do I have this job?
  — *Have you chosen it?* Why?
  — *Was it forced on you?* Why?
  — *Does it satisfy you?* Why?
  If it doesn't satisfy you:
  1. Prepare two columns:

— 1st column: note everything you criticise about it.

— 2nd column: note everything you expect of another job.

2. *Do you actually want to change jobs?*

If *no:* why?

If *yes:* is a plan of action for changing either realistic or possible?

Out of all that it follows that:

1. Either you are satisfied and clearly know why. The very fact of formulating this conviction strengthens you inside. Don't hesitate to remind yourself when something happens: "I have a job that pleases me and suits me."

2. Or you are dissatisfied but cannot change anything. Yes you can. Look for some good reasons to be satisfied! Suppress your criticisms and look on the bright side. Or look for satisfaction in some aspect quite separate from those that displease you at that particular moment. Psychologists call this 'secondary satisfaction': it's like: "I hate doing the washing-up, but at least I can say I'm a great housewife!"

As far as your job is concerned, you must manage to find the trick of being in agreement with yourself, of being able to tell yourself, and really think it: "At the end of the day, as things stand, it's still a minor evil! We'll see about changing it later!"

In every unpleasant situation where you cannot change anything, it is essential that you have confidence in the future, which can bring new elements into your life.

3. Or you are dissatisfied and you discover – perhaps thanks to this questioning – that with some will-power you could change something. Don't question your will-power. Establish your plan, get excited about your project. . . and the will-power will follow. Your pleasure in starting something constructive for yourself will provide an agreeable challenge.

• Whatever the result of the first exercise, practise it for all the items on your list. Clearly you must be in agreement with yourself as far as the principal choices in your life are concerned, before undertaking any important voluntary or long-term action.

B. Alongside this basic work on yourself, practise **asserting your authority easily** on all possible occasions during your daily life.

Consider situations where a discussion with your family or group can be foreseen: choice of purchases, outings, opinions on a book. Or even envisage the classical subjects of the dinner table: politics, society, the children's education, fashion ...

Prepare yourself for pleasure, already knowing what your position will be and making clear to yourself the reasons for your choice. When you are very sure of yourself, launch the offensive! If you express your arguments well, maybe others will come to agree with you. So much the better: that gives you a feeling of strength. But equally so much the worse: that doesn't allow you to argue!

If someone disagrees with you, make the most of this to bring your self-confidence into play and learn how not to let yourself be influenced by other people's point of view. That doesn't mean being stubborn, but developing your argument in order to support yourself in your choice or opinion.

TENACITY: LONG-TERM WILL-POWER WITH EASE

The thing that makes you lack tenacity is not necessarily the lack of will-power. Those who talk of 'tenacity' are talking about behaviour in relation to an action that has already been started: and, if you have started, it's because you are capable of exercising will-power! In reality, you give up because you have let yourself be discouraged, because you lack or no longer have the morale.

In order to carry on with a task, whatever it might be, you must hope for its result, believe in its success. In other words, you must be optimistic. Tenacity isn't so much the 'strength' of will-power as optimism! As we have already said, to believe in success is a form of faith and we all know that faith carries astonishing power, which displays itself in keeping going.

⇒ AN EXAMPLE

Let's take the example of a person who has undertaken to learn Spanish using language cassettes. For the first few weeks all goes well; he makes an encouraging start. Then, lo and behold, a Spanish client arrives in the office! It's the chance to put his work to the test (and impress his colleagues). But obviously one can feel at ease with the conversation proposed by a cassette after a few weeks ... without being able to decipher the torrent that emerges from a Spanish mouth at an unthinkable speed – and with an accent that has never appeared on the tape! It's a disaster (smiles from colleagues...); he must find an interpreter or, worse still, put up with the client's broken English! And he says to himself: "I'm never going to make it! I might as well give up immediately."

The person in question is forgetting that he had planned to spend a fortnight in Spain when he finished his cassette course (indispensable linguistic submersion!). He is also forgetting that he can register for an 'intensive course' with the basics he has already acquired.

◨ THE EXERCISES

The exercises will be based around the art of finding, here too, good reasons for hoping or good reasons for seeing something through to the end. In the example just given, these good reasons could in fact be the recourse to other methods. In other cases, it will perhaps be the satisfaction we can look forward to at the end of the task.

Now we can always make this satisfaction more real (in advance!) by living it in a daydream from time to time (the little inner cinema). We bring the dynamics of the project into play. The task that demands tenacity can be compared to a project, that is to say it includes the desire to achieve a goal. And this desire quite naturally creates the necessary energy – and painlessly!

To train yourself, make a list of long-term activities, those you have thought about at some time or another but the plan for which has escaped you even before being formulated. It isn't absolutely necessary for you to commit yourself to them, but they will provide an opportunity for you to form new automatic patterns of will-power quite painlessly.

Think about all those ideas that your have left floating, like cleaning and repainting certain rooms at home or at your parents' house, like arranging the family archives (photos, letters, etc.), like learning a foreign language, mechanics or art, like getting involved with a group (sport, amateur dramatics, charity, etc). Rank these tasks in order of difficulty – whether because of the time required (finding the time can demand reflection, imagination!) or because of the physical or mental effort involved.

So begin with what you feel is most accessible and establish your plan of action in a series of short stages. Look for arguments in order to fully convince yourself that you have EVERY chance of reaching at least the first stage. Keep your optimism right up to this initial success. If you feel it fading on the way, don't force yourself: the goal is not to get there at any price, but to get there PAINLESSLY.

In the event of a lapse, therefore, take the time to look again for some good reasons to regain your optimism. Think about other successes in other areas ("In reality, I am someone who succeeds quite often!"). Look to be even more deeply in agreement with yourself ("It suits me well to do that; it's very much up my street; it goes with my personality.").

When the first stage has been achieved, envisage the next with the same confidence, the same tactics of optimism and the same anticipation for pleasure. Don't forget, in this task, the system of your reinforcements.

Alongside this systematic training, do all you possibly can to maintain (or acquire) your optimism in life generally. It's not a question of forcing yourself. It's enough to make sure you always see the bottle *half-full* and not *half-empty*. After all, you have the choice to say either. But subconsciously it will do you good to look on the optimistic side!

It really is true that even the worst situations always have their bright side. Obviously you can feel overwhelmed and not see it. So it is absolutely essential that you implant in yourself the ability to look *automatically* on the bright side of everything. Even with the most serious events, you can always find a funny side; you mustn't feel ashamed about it, the very reverse.

There are lots of proverbs that tell us to look on the bright side. What this means is that doing so enables us naturally (without effort) to have the will-power to continue to act ... or to live.

SUGGESTED CARD INDEX FOR WILL POWER
■■■

- **On an index card, note:**

    1. *Results of the test-standard:*
        — Decision-taking : (one or two words)
        — Launching : ditto
        — Tenacity : ditto
        — Self-confidence : ditto
        — Morale : ditto

2. *My weak points:*
For example:
— Indecision
— Lack of tenacity
— Susceptibility to influence ...
For each area, make brief notes about what you have to do.
For example:
Indecision : exercises on making choices – agreement with myself – self-confidence

3. *To work on first:*
Note in YOUR order:
— Art of finding good reasons
— Search for inner dynamism (desires)
— Search for self-confidence
— Watching over good morale

4. *My reinforcements:*
Prepare in advance a list of rewards and punishments. You will refer to your index card when the time comes for a sanction. Make a list of purely morale elements (my satisfaction – X's admiration, etc.) and the rewards and punishments that materialised.

- **Sub-file concerning your first work theme (also card-mounted):**
For example: *To find some good reasons*
1. My list of items on which I will work :
2. The 1st item :
Note, over the days, the good reasons that came to mind:
Date: Reason:

- **On the back of your index card, prepare a calendar:**
CALENDAR
Example:

Day	Action	Success	Failure	Sanction
3.10	*do my card index*	+	–	–
16.10	*good sound reason*			
	for getting up	+	–	–
24.10	*getting up regularly*			*I am proud of*
	for a whole week	+	–	*myself; family*
				reaction +++

- In order to further your training, consult your files and find some new 'good reasons' in them!

THE PARTICULAR
CASE OF TOBACCO
■■■■■■■■■■■■■■■■■■■■■■■■

"I would like to give up smoking." Question of will-power? Yes. But... For each voluntary action you must have good reasons; you must be in agreement with yourself... This implies that you can change yourself using psychological methods.

For tobacco, as for alcohol and various drugs that threaten *dependence*, doctors, health experts and the media have widely circulated among the public explanations concerning the *biological* basis of dependence. This has put into many people's minds the conviction that, since it is biological and therefore physically implanted in us, we can do nothing about it, any more than we can change the colour of our eyes or the size of our feet. The battle against dependence is not a matter of will-power but of medical treatment!

It should also be said that this biological dependence is more or less strong according to the substance because of the mechanics within the nerve cells. And getting weaned off the product on which one is dependent is physically more or less painful. Thus biological conditions make the dependence on opiates (heroin) and cocaine (crack) very strong. Any drastic treatment can leave the patient ill for several weeks, while progressive treatment is always physically painful.

With alcohol, it has been shown that there are genetic differences: some people have a biological predisposition towards alcoholism and the medical treatment must be very carefully supervised because it does present risks. Others don't have this predisposition; they are 'psychological' alcoholics and can be treated without any worries.

As far as tobacco is concerned, the risks from total and immediate deprivation are non-existent from a physical point of view. Even animals, experimentally drugged for a certain time then totally deprived, only feel better. As for human beings, a very heavy smoker may give up totally and at once after an attack of angina pectoris. Such an attack, which is extremely painful, also produces a terrifying feeling of imminent death. The patient had been warned, perhaps over a number of years, by his doctor and family: "The tobacco is going to play a nasty trick on you!" And the nasty trick, when it happens, is such a shock that it automatically prompts total abstinence... which may sadly, only last a year or so! During this period the smoker, who has fully recovered, hasn't any sign of illness; on the contrary . . . If, one day, he starts smoking again, accepting the risk of another attack, it is because he has gradually regained a PSYCHOLOGICAL need.

Psychological dependence does exist and can be as strongly felt as physical dependence (that of opiates, for example). But while against the latter will-power alone can do nothing (at least without enormous help), in the case of psychological dependence it can do everything.

Tobacco creates psychological dependence. Some biological symptoms, which could be interpreted as signs of a dependence, can be directly modified through mental activities: each time we are enthusiastic, fed up or display other emotions of one sort or another, this is expressed through biological changes in the brain. Such alterations can, in their turn, change those that would have brought on smoking habits.

So why do some people suggest medical treatments (nicotine injections, for example), acupuncture or various medicines to try and reduce the need to smoke?

Everything can be worth trying . . . But it is not indispensable. The act of following a treatment, whatever it is, involves a voluntary decision (even if it is subconscious!) and it is this act of will-power that is at work in the case of a successful cure (of whatever sort). Even the most medical of treatments can fail (and often do). But it is not the fault of the treatment, since sometimes (rarely) it succeeds! It is the voluntary non-participation of the person undergoing treatment that is the cause of the failure.

Finally, after long clinical experiments endorsed by many serious anti-smoking clinicians, it is certain that, under the control of a sound technique, the action of will-power can release one from the need to smoke.

1st Stage: are you SURE you want to?

A. Write down YOUR good reasons
Reflect carefully, making certain that you are not simply repeating habitual arguments (without being REALLY convinced!): risk of cancer or heart-attacks . . . Do you really believe it could ever happen to you; or do such horrors only happen to others. . .? "I'm in good health!" you tell yourself. You are disturbed for a moment when a friend describes how his brother came to die of smoker's cancer . . . And you yourself are smoking at the time! As for cardio-

vascular risks, medicine has made such progress. Even the great fear of angina pectoris is quickly forgotten thanks to the many marvellous preventative medicines available today.

It is true that modern medical techniques are such that we should no longer die through heart problems. Nevertheless, along with road accidents and cancer, heart disease is high on the list of causes of premature death.

I repeat this out of habit because I am a doctor, but it is probable that nowadays neither cancer nor heart disease terrify people in the way they used to. And if you tell yourself it is this fear that will make you give up smoking, you have every chance of puffing on until you drop!

You must really look for what concerns YOU – and now. For example, aren't you fed up with having the taste of tobacco continually in your mouth, since it prevents you really appreciating what you eat and certainly spoils a good glass of something? Doesn't it bother you to inflict on a loved one your kisses complete with tobacco juice? Haven't you had enough of that nagging little cough or clearing of the throat, particularly in the morning, which stops you from speaking properly? Don't you find that, for your age (whatever that may be), you really are short of breath?

Search hard: to make a start, it is absolutely necessary that you find several *actual* reasons for being handicapped (or at least bothered) by symptoms which have every chance of being eliminated quite quickly once you have given up. (Clearly, if you smoke a packet a day, you will need to allow a bit of time before you no longer taste the tobacco!)

B. And you must, in addition, THROW YOURSELF A CHALLENGE

Adolescents often tease each other by saying: "You're not capable . . ." – which may well provoke the one who is teased into doing something stupid and dangerous just to prove that they can! An adult can, for better reasons, say something similar to himself and swear to prove to himself that he is capable!

Make this challenge a battle: who will be strongest, the filthiness or me? (Because smoking is a dirty habit: it chokes up the respiratory tracts, the ash and fag-ends dirty the house and to go on is cowardice, which amounts to a moral filthiness.)

Make it a sporty challenge of the kind: "I will get to Anapurna." Make it a moral vow – or even religious (for a believer, this can be an offering to God). On top of that, make it the condition for an important change in your life, a change that you wish for 'later on', like a special holiday, plans for moving or buying a caravan for weekends away.

If you succeed, you are certainly adding some extra years to your life. Acquiring this life-assurance definitely deserves to be crowned by something exceptional.

But let's be clear about it: this doesn't amount to a 'reward' in the same way as for the everyday exercises on will-power. There the image of the reward was an element in the drive behind your action. Here, THE reward – the only reward, the real reward – is LIBERATION from the different handicaps you have honestly listed and the assurance of adding a few extra years to your life. You should celebrate that like one celebrates the birth of a child!

2nd Stage

When you have YOUR good reasons clearly in front of you and have formulated your challenge, you must put together a practical plan.

A. If you have an active, unyielding, 'primary' type of temperament and if you sense the desire and capacity to stop smoking, do it, just like that. Don't replace the cigarette with little aids or tit-bits, like a match-stick to chew on, sweets or even an unlit cigarette between the lips. Get totally stuck into the struggle with yourself . . . And be the strongest! The dynamism of success is the pleasure of feeling stronger and not cheating with any props or crutches.

If you don't stick to it and succumb to smoking a cigarette, make a conscious note of your cowardice. Don't hesitate to consider yourself a 'wishy-washy' person and then drown yourself totally in your feeble cowardice for two or three days, just enough time to kick yourself into coming back up to the surface, and renewing the fight.

You can allow yourself, perhaps, two more tries . . . And if these fail, move on to the next method.

B. If you feel you don't have either the temperament or the strength for an 'all or nothing' plan, go at it progressively.

The first stage
- If you smoke 20 cigarettes or more a day, cut this immediately by half.
- Between 10 and 20 cigarettes a day, reduce this to eight.
- Less than 10 cigarettes a day, cut down by a half.

Each morning, prepare in a packet the number of cigarettes allowed for the day. And each time you go to take one out, think about waiting a little longer, to economise so that you don't find yourself without anything to smoke later. In no circumstances say to yourself: "I'll wait two hours and then I'll offer myself a reward cigarette." Just feel proud that you have held out for two hours: the pride is your reward.

Keep reminding yourself, however, that every cigarette – even within the number 'permitted' – is a FAILURE. Allowing yourself a certain number of cigarettes is allowing yourself a certain number of failures, because we can't manage to be strong right from the start!.

The second stage

After a fortnight of this system, change the brand or type of cigarette as follows:

* If you are used to smoking mild tipped cigarettes, buy some strong plain ones (without filters) or even small cigars. In this case smoke just a half of what was allowed before. You will enjoy them less because they are too strong and, what's more, they will make you cough. So much the better, since you will now have an even greater natural desire to stop! **But under no circumstances go back to your normal brand.**

* If you normally smoke strong cigarettes or cigars, change to filters and a mild type. So much the better if the taste puts you off, or if you feel as if you are smoking nothing! However, don't smoke more; keep to the required number. If they really do disgust you, you will smoke less – which is what you are trying to achieve!

The third stage

When you realise that you are managing to 'win' more and more often, that is to say you are smoking less than the amount prescribed, start reducing this number systematically: one cigarette less every two or three days. Until the day when you decide that IT IS FINISHED.

When it's finished, get rid of all the objects that are associated with tobacco (lighters, cigarette packets, ash-trays, etc). Sell them, give them away, throw them away ... Keep perhaps one ash-tray at the bottom of a cupboard in case one of your visitors is incapable of resisting the need to smoke! (It is preferable that you ask everyone to refrain from smoking in your home.)

If other members of your family or group continue to smoke at home, help them to find THEIR good reasons for stopping and imitate you. Insist that at least they don't smoke in the same room as yourself.

And continue POSITIVELY. Don't say to yourself: "I've given up for six months, so I can have just one cigarette. In any case, I have no desire to start again. There's absolutely no danger of that." Yes there is.

First, there is always the danger of 'letting go', even when you are strong. In order to preserve your integrity it is preferable not to take the risk. Also, it is illogical to 'offer yourself' a false pleasure. Smoking a cigarette is always a FAILURE as far as you are concerned (because you already decided to give up).

If you do let yourself go, don't forget to keep telling yourself that you are gaining the pleasure of a coward and a drip. That should destroy your idea of pleasure and so much the better! Having proved yourself by winning the anti-tobacco challenge, you are surely not going to let yourself be taken in and lower yourself with such a stupid little indulgence!

CHAPTER TWO

MEMORY

If we stop to think about it, the memory seems to be one of the most magical functions that the brain puts at our disposal. We are as astonished by its incomprehensible failures as by its successes ...

You are talking with a friend about a Japanese film that happened to impress you. "About the ... the ... those famous warriors of ancient Japan? Let's see, I know the name perfectly well! And, after that film, I can't stop thinking about it. The ... the ... Oh well, can't be helped. The name just won't come to me." You go on talking about something else, the rising cost of food perhaps, and then suddenly, in the middle of a sentence, you stop. "Samurai! Forgive me. It's the word I was looking for. What were we talking about? Oh yes, the price of meat ..."

So, why this mental block about something that had been more or less occupying your thoughts during the last few days? And how is it that, having given up searching for the word and started thinking and talking about something else, the word suddenly comes to you all on its own?

This mechanism of the memory has been playing us good and bad tricks since the day we were born. Since the first weeks of our life, it has been working and storing information. Why? The specialists continue to argue about it! It certainly worked right from the start because, quite soon, baby was capable of all sorts of performances: for example, recognising Mummy, then the other people around, deciphering the significance of certain facial expressions (which made him either laugh or cry . . .) and tones of voice. Such successes can only be achieved through memorised experiences during the first months of life.

This silent and discreet work of the memory goes on, hour after hour, from these early beginnings. Without noticing ourselves do it, we are constantly memorising a thousand and one different things in our daily lives. Thoughts and images continually roll round our heads, whether we are busy or resting, waiting for the bus or going to sleep. And what is this continual flow if not an intermingled chain of memories, of thoughts that come up from our memory to slide in front of our inner eye?

Moreover, don't most of our actions (writing our diary, lighting the gas-ring. . .) result from a sort of training, memorised at one moment or another and ready to emerge when we need them? Memories get scooped up, stockpiled and then re-emerge, without us having done anything. The brain has spontaneously started the 'memory' machine.

We can do a lot more with this extraordinarily complex mechanism if we don't let it work just under its own steam. It's like having a gift for music or painting . . . Certainly such gifts are more widespread than we might believe. But, as with a lot of things, they are not cultivated: perhaps we don't even realise they are there. As a result plenty of 'masterpieces' never see the light of day!

We all have the gift of memory; it's included in our human brain's machinery. But it's up to us to cultivate it for our greater efficiency and pleasure, and so doing brings many benefits. Not only is it an agreeable occupation in itself, but it also helps our other faculties to develop and that keeps us young.

What we tell ourselves

For several generations – perhaps since the start of compulsory education – we have passed on from father and mother to son and daughter a good number of false ideas about memory, which has obviously damaged its development.

The problem normally starts with school where, very often, memory involves mechanical repetition (multiplication tables and similar delights). The child who devotes himself to this irksome task and the next day can repeat his lesson parrot-fashion is a good little pupil! The one who doesn't is lazy and 'will have a poor memory'. But in fact, up to the age of eight or ten, everything goes in and a child can hang on to anything by simple retention without understanding it at all. Moreover, four or five-year-olds very often do not even need to bother with the repetition!

It's also said that memory is the result of the good habit of mechanical repetition – eventually without understanding what we are repeating, even when we are grown-ups, and that this conflicts with an intelligent approach: "You repeat like a machine, so you do not think." Thus we can separate, on the one hand, those with a good memory but who are not very sharp and, on the other hand, the intelligent people who can be forgiven their weakness in this dull witted ability!

Nothing is more false or misleading. It is true, as we have already said, that before the age of eight or ten the brain goes through such a growth surge that it indiscriminately swallows up all that is presented to it. A child of this age doesn't yet have the ability to pick and choose what it remembers. But once childhood is over, even if mechanical memorising is still possible, it becomes more and more painful and uncertain. And, even before puberty, the activity of memory through mental association starts – often before the child knows how to handle it. All mental association is an operation of the intelligence: the more 'intelligent' we are, the better we memorise.

It's also said that we lose our memory with age. There's nothing we can do; we have to resign ourselves to it. Hundreds or thousands of brain cells die every day and, as they don't reproduce themselves, it is clear that a time comes when we have no more of what makes the memory function.

This again is wrong. A little scientific knowledge is more harmful than total ignorance! It is true that, from the moment we are born, we lose what would appear to be impressive quantities of cells from our brain every day. But we have such a lot – too many at birth – that even if we were to reach the age of 120, we would still have enough of them to invent a mathematical theory such as that of Einstein or learn the lines of Shakespeare's *Hamlet*.

It is true that as we start to grow old (and this can happen at any time from our forties to past eighty, according to the individual . . .), we *seem* to have less memory. We forget everything and we ramble on because we no longer know what we have already said. But this is not due to a diminution of the *memory function*, which, as scientific work has proved, is potentially even greater with the advancement of years. However, for the memory to work effectively, we must continue to be interested and attend to what is going on. And it is this interest, this curiosity in life, that declines with age – not through lack of nerve cells but because, psychologically, we let it decline . . . Once again, it is not a physical failure that lets us down: it is our morale that grows old and carries with it the functioning of the brain. *We can very easily avoid this.* We are obviously going to change with age, but not decay!

People also often say to themselves: "Someone the same age as me has a good memory. I often wonder how he does it. I'm not so lucky. I have to jot everything down and then I forget where I put my list!" One hears talk that this is a question of unequal distribution of talent, like beauty . . . Of course there are differences in mental aptitude between some and others. But this simply reflects the *use* each makes of a brain WHICH, IN THE MAIN, IS THE SAME FOR EVERYONE.

Effectively, some people know better than others how to use their little grey cells, like Hercule Poirot, because they have learnt to and because they have found out how all on their own. Others don't know how to: they let their brain lie fallow, so obviously it produces less.

But everyone can learn to make the brain work better. And at any age.

WHAT IS MEMORY?

T The first answer to this question is that memory is what we use to remember. For example. If in a game someone says to you "Battle of Hastings?", you would reply "1066", just as you know that the capital of Italy is Rome . . . Memory enables you to relive in your mind a piece of countryside you visited on your last holiday or a particular smile of your grandmother, who passed away some years ago. Memory is our personal luggage.

But also, if we think about it for a moment, we realise that most of our actions last a certain time. Reading a newspaper article or even a simple sentence is not instantaneous; it requires us to recall what we have read prior to the word we are on, otherwise the sentence doesn't make sense!

When you do your shopping at the market, you have a look round the various stalls when you arrive to see what's on offer, and to work out which, for you, represents the best value in terms of quality and price. Without even noticing it, you have marked down in your memory a large quantity of information which provides you with all you need to know when, for example, you decide to buy a pound of carrots.

It is clear that someone a bit doddery who always tells you the same story when she meets you has forgotten that she has already related it to you. Are you sure that hasn't happened to you? Why? Because, when you have said something to a given person, that is automatically noted in your memory: you don't have to make any effort to do it, since you KNOW you have already said it. The memory is like a cash register except that you don't need to press the buttons: once registered, it goes off on its own, prompted by the requirements of what we are doing.

But it is also a reservoir that we can fill up voluntarily. Right through our time at school, most certainly, we spend a certain amount of time each day learning voluntarily – or because we are made to! But afterwards, in adult life, we may still need to learn the words of a song, a theatrical part, a foreign language, the names of colleagues, pupils, preparatory notes for a meeting, sometimes with lists of numbers ... There are plenty of occasions when an adult says to himself: "I must learn that", and with more or less good humour he tackles the task of putting into his memory a series of sentences, numbers or even gestures.

How does it happen?

Even when this happens all by itself and we are not aware of it, the work the brain does to put some things into the memory and bring others out is carried out in several stages.

THE IMMEDIATE MEMORY

The first stage is that of the IMMEDIATE MEMORY. This is the mechanism that enables us to know automatically what we have just done. I call it the 'telephone memory', because it is the same one that functions when we read a telephone number just before dialling it. It's possible that if we need to recall the number two hours later, we are pleasantly surprised to find it still in the memory. But, on most occasions this type of memorising only lasts for as long as it takes to dial the number.

While this immediate memory is, indeed, automatic, it does have limits (with which we must learn to play in order to improve it . . .).

• The 7 seconds rule

The time during which you can automatically memorise some-thing you are going to use IMMEDIATELY cannot exceed 7 seconds – and that is a maximum; usually it varies between 4 and 5 seconds. Thus, provided you can easily read the telephone num-ber you want to call, you remember it without any problem. But if you have forgotten your glasses or you are in a poorly lit call-box, you start to dial the number and then realise you've forgotten the final numbers! Your reading took more than the 5 seconds of your immediate memory.

• The 30 seconds rule

Thirty seconds is the maximum interval between the moment memorisation occurs and when you can repeat it or use the immediate memory . . . at least if, during these 30 seconds, you do not repeat what you have just learned. If you repeat your number, for example, a dozen times, thinking that you will have to redial it a little bit later, this increases the length of memorisation!

But we are already entering the stockpiling mechanism. Stay-ing with the immediate memory, you can rely on being able to repeat after up to 25 or 30 seconds without thinking about it. That is to say, provided you have read your number in less than 5 seconds, you still have up to 30 seconds to dial it without having to repeat it to yourself during that time.

However, don't be surprised if the number doesn't stick in your mind for this length of time: it means you've suffered an *interference!* That is to say, straight after your immediate memori-sation, you went on to think of something else – "I mustn't forget to ring Laurence after I've made this call." In a flash, your brain is automatically concentrating on 'Laurence' and has wiped off what had just happened (the immediate learning of the tele-phone number).

An active thought thus creates an interference. For the 30 seconds that follow the immediate memorisation, you must keep your mind 'clear' so that it can function properly.

• *The interest rule*

Every stage of the memory works much better when you are more interested in the subjects you are handling. Of course, with the strength of will-power, you can take in ideas that you consider uninteresting, but the work involved is proportionately that much greater and can take longer!

On the other hand, when you are interested by something, you recall it automatically. As far as the immediate memory is concerned, it functions much better when there is an immediate use, as in the example of the telephone number. But don't start to look at yourself with a critical eye to see whether you really are automatically retaining everything that happens. At any given moment, we are plunged into hundreds of situations with the potential for entering the memory: dozens of noises, words, objects both animated and otherwise pass before our eyes, sensations, ideas, images that come to mind . . . Happily not all this is marked down in the memory, even for an 'immediate memory'! We only memorise for a few seconds what interests us at the time, when it happens via the automatic mechanism about which we don't need to think.

CONSOLIDATION
■■■■■■■■■■■■■■■■■■■■■

All memorising necessarily begins with the preceding phase of the immediate memory. But, again fortunately, not all that we use from the permanent memory throughout the length of each day is permanently registered! The majority of impressions are just passing ones . . . Nevertheless, it would often be more helpful if some were a little less so!

We must therefore consolidate those we want to keep so that we can put them into our inner stock. The time for this phase varies according to the individual and what has to be retained, but also according to whether we are aiming for the short or long term.

• **The short term** (a few hours to a few days) requires that, during the period of consolidation:

    1. You avoid interferences: for a moment, you must make yourself think of nothing else but what you want to remember.

    2. You adopt an attitude of positive attention, that is to say you not only don't think of anything else, but you also think actively about and concentrate on the thing to be retained.

3. You associate the item to be remembered with things you already know and which are safely installed in your memory's stock-pile.

4. Finally, you repeat not only the thing to be retained but also the associations you have made with it.

For example, you want to remember a telephone number (for argument's sake in Inner London, which starts with 0171) – 344 3945. So you can use the following associations: 344 is your month and year of birth (March 1944) and 3945 is the period of the Second World War (1939 to 1945).

Once you have found your associations, all you have to do is repeat them, thinking about them a dozen or so times. This way, the number will be locked in for several days.

• **The long term** (for years, all your life):

Moving from the short to the long term happens through repetition – but of use, not parrot fashion. Each time you dial this number it will register a little more . . . How come doctors remember those uncivilised names of medicines so well? Simply because of the repeated occasions on which they talk about them and write them down on prescriptions!

RECALL
■■■■■■■■■

We are searching for a word or an image, which sometimes arrives on its own . . . and sometimes not! We have often experienced this 'failure': the thing is there, 'on the tip of our tongue', and by continuing to look for it, we eventually find it. Sometimes after we have summoned it, it comes on its own when we've given up waiting for it. This clearly shows us that summoning a memory sets in motion all the mechanics of the brain, which are quite capable of functioning automatically – and usually do – but can also be made to work by our actively searching. Most importantly, we can exercise the brain and help it to work a little better.

The following is a BIOLOGICAL law of the memory, which you will experience if you work at it a little: *The more one makes this marvellous machine work, the more it strengthens and extends itself.*

What the memory needs

For the memory to work efficiently, we must master the three operations whose links constitutes its mechanism:

- **Perception**
- **Stockpiling**
- **Recall**

PERCEPTION
■■■■■■■■■■■■■■■

As the word indicates, the act of perceiving – or noticing – implies more than simply glimpsing. Since our daily life is a constant to and fro between the information from outside and our responses (and vice-versa), it is usually sufficient for us to cast a glance in order to respond and then continue on our way . . . But how do we remember things that we haven't really noticed? All memorisation must start with a perception: children do it quite naturally; but as adults we 'already know': a glance, a little bell ringing is enough for us. But that is not the way to help us remember. We must rediscover the attitudes of our childhood – to look closely, to listen hard . . .

STOCKPILING
■■■■■■■■■■■■■■■

In order to stockpile something in our memory, we must button-hole it, that is to say establish a link between what we have perceived (and want to keep) and what we have already put in our memory. That means *making an association* or even several. The more old memories we find with which to associate the one we want to retain, the more firmly the new item will be installed in our memory.

For example, imagine I want to remember the name of the poet Coleridge. I have read the name, then re-read it and pronounced it out loud. The perception has been made.

Now, what can that make me think of? Cole? Perhaps 'coal' . . . And then the 'ridge'? I remember reading some of his poetry when I was on holiday in the Welsh Valleys some years ago . . . That's it! If I think about my Welsh holidays and the coal mines I saw in the valleys, that will remind me of my poet Coleridge!

But that alone is not enough. You must *classify* it in order to be able to find it again, like a book in a library! Otherwise you will have stored it but without the ability to recall it. How would you find one book among thousands on the shelves if it wasn't classified? And your memory already contains hundreds of millions of pieces of information . . .

Without even thinking about it, we automatically form categories, for our perceptions as much as our actions: the easy and the difficult, those tasks we do particularly in the morning or the evening, with friends or on our own, etc. Since this is already natural to us, thinking about it will be enough to make it happen!

Finally – and we cannot repeat it too often – we must *repeat it!* Not in a mechanical way like a child learning his tables, but by telling other people or ourselves, by thinking it over in connection with something it evokes. The oldest memories are the deepest rooted, because after all those years we have had numerous occasions for recalling them, in other words, repeating them.

RECALLING
■■■■■■■■■■■■■■■

This does not always happen by itself and sometimes we dig through our memory for something to emerge. But very often we rummage about and throw everything 'up in the air' without order or method. The mechanism is so extraordinary that it can often respond all the same! Like a car moving off in second gear ... But there are failures and when we do recall correctly we have the feeling that it is only by chance – which doesn't help in reprinting the memory.

Let's consider the follow image. Memorised objects are provided with cords; to recall them, we must pull on the right cord. These cords are in effect associations: the more associations we make at the moment of stockpiling, the more chance we have of finding an appropriate cord! And if, in addition, these cords correspond to the levels of classification, by reviewing these levels it would be very surprising if we did not come across a cord.

For example, you are looking for the name of a fabulous animal ... which does not exist but is mentioned in stories ... It's an animal (1st classification level). It's not a bird or a fish ... it's a four-legged animal (2nd level). With four legs? It's like a mouse? a cat? a lion? a horse? Yes, that's it, it's like a horse (3rd level). A horse that doesn't exist: because it has five legs? two heads? horns? No! One horn! That's it ... a something horn ... A single horn ... a uni horn ... Of course, a UNICORN!

Finally, to train your memory is to know how to perceive or notice, to be curious, to regard, to listen ... thoroughly. And it is to be cunning: to prepare the associations and cords and follow Ariane's thread to find the right cord to leave by.

HOW GOOD IS YOUR MEMORY?

Before starting to train yourself, it can be interesting to know if you already have a memory that functions well or if you are totally dependent on little notebooks, lists and other 'memory-joggers'. I am not suggesting a real psychological 'test', but a **method** for interrogating or observing yourself in a way that will give you a better way of understanding yourself.

- Decide one evening, before going to sleep and without having pre-planned the exercise, to recall the whole of your day, hour by hour, in the greatest possible detail. Jot down in a notebook how your memory fared:
  - *remembered everything:* 3 points
  - *remembered overall, but gaps in the detail:* 2 points
  - *one or several complete gaps (for example: impossible to remember the time I went out to see someone):* 1 point

  The following day, decide in the morning that in the evening you will be looking to remember your day (but don't write anything down!). Do your exercise in the evening and make a note of your performance:
  - *remembered everything:* 3 points
  - *remembered overall, but gaps in the detail:* 2 points
  - *one or several complete gaps:* 1 point

- In the same way, decide one evening to think of three people you met during the day (colleagues, clients, shopkeepers . . .) and try to remember in the greatest possible detail how each was dressed. Note down your performance:
  - *no recall difficulty, all came to mind easily:* 3 points
  - *not completely sure of details (tie, scarf . . .):* 2 points
  - *important lapses (colour of suit, skirt or dress . . .):* 1 point
  - *practically no memory:* 0 points

  The following day, decide to look at three people whose dress you will try to remember in the evening. Do your exercise in the evening and note your score:
  - *no recall difficulty, all came easily to mind:* 3 points

- *not completely sure of details:* 2 points
- *important lapses:* 1 point
- *practically no memory:* 0 points

- In the same way, try to remember in the evening before going to bed what was in the newspaper you read or on the television news you watched. Note your score:
  - *everything came back to you:* 3 points
  - *all the headlines, but not all their contents:* 2 points
  - *impression that you missed a headline or, for one topic, absolutely no memory:* 1 point

The following day, whether reading the newspaper or watching the television news, remind yourself that you are going to ask yourself some questions in the evening. Do your questioning in the evening and note your performance:
  - *everything came back to you:* 3 points
  - *all the headlines, but not all their contents:* 2 points
  - *impression that you missed a headline or, for one of them, absolutely no memory:* 1 point

- One or two days after completing these three groups of questions, look at the scores you noted down at the time:
  - There is a clear difference between your spontaneous memories and those when you are pre-warned: this implies that if you don't think about paying attention, you will live like an automaton! But attention is enough to make you memorise: your brain is asking to function better.
  - There is hardly any difference between one situation or another: your memory mechanisms are clogged up. It may be that you don't know how to look or hear properly, even when you decide to do it, or perhaps you allow interferences to wipe out immediately what you have just noticed, or you don't keep your attention fixed on things for long enough.

QUESTIONNAIRE
■■■■■■■■■■■■■■■■■■■■■

- **Do you look for a word without finding it?**
  - proper nouns: *never* – 4; *sometimes* – 3; *often* – 2; *very often* – 1; *every time* – 0
  - common nouns, verbs, adjectives: *never* – 3; *sometimes* – 2; *often* – 1; *continually* – 0
- **Do you have to re-read the previous sentence because you have forgotten it?**

never – 3; *sometimes* – 2; *often* – 1; *every time* – 0
- ***Do you forget the name of someone you have just been introduced to?***
  never – 3; *sometimes* – 2; *when I'm tired* – 1; *practically always* – 0
- ***Do you have to re-read a telephone number at least once before dialling it?***
  never – 3; *sometimes* – 2; *often* – 1; *always* – 0
- ***Do you know the birthdays of your parents, spouse, children, close friends?***
  Score 1 point for each date (maximum 4)
- ***Do you forget where you have put useful but not everyday things (photos, bills, special tools . . .)?***
  never – 3; *sometimes* – 2; *often* – 1; *always* (I must note everything down!) – 0
- ***How many current government ministers can you name immediately?***
  Score 1 point for each name (maximum 4)

Add up your scores:

25 or more: you have a good memory; you can aspire to excellence.

Between 16 and 24: your memory is good but it is misused.

Under 16: your memory mechanism is clogged up; exercises are imperative!

➡ EXERCISES

Memory exercises must be thought of as games that you play with yourself. And it is important that as well as gaining pleasure from watching your growing success, you find them amusing. The aim is to change your way of being in contact with what surrounds you (people and situations) – or, if your contact is already close and concentrated, to make it even more effective.

You must reach a point where you see clearly, hear well and feel fully everything that happens to you, everything you do, and not let yourself be overcome by the apparent ease of being an 'automaton'. Live your life while being totally CONSCIOUS of the moment – every moment.

You must also live in constant contact with yourself: use and evoke your memories and your knowledge, make them resonate with the present moment ("That reminds me . . . That makes me think of such and such a moment, book, person . . . It's different from last year; it's better . . . it's worse . . .").

In order for things to enter your memory without you having to make the least effort, you have to live them fully. As a general rule, you must know how to interest yourself in more or less anything, be in touch with everything, be curious about everything... in short, know how to LIVE!

PERCEPTION
■■■■■■■■■■■■■■■■

A first exercise, to warm up, concerns the **immediate memory.**

You have less than 7 seconds for registering everything you can perceive in this time and retaining it for several minutes. In such a short period you can only register a limited number of units, for example, but the shape of these units can vary. You could compare this limit to that of a purse that only holds ten coins. If these are 10p pieces, then it contains £1; if they are of £1 coins, then it contains £10!

Take a telephone number. It is not particularly easy to remember a sequence of 11 numbers (0171-344 3945). Certainly it is extremely hard to retain them individually as 0-1-7-1-3-4-4-3-9-4-5! But if you group them into twos or threes, it becomes that much easier. Thus: 01-71-344-39-45.

The same principle applies with words too. You will find it hard to retain a list of 12 words in less than 7 seconds, unless you use a sentence to group them together. Thus: 'All the family spends the Christmas holidays at the grand-parents' country house', will be retained as if by magic!

So, when you've got some spare moments, you can play the following game:

Underline at random a series of 8 words in your newspaper or a publicity handout. Try grouping them into two or three units (words which will go together for one reason or another: they start with the same letter or syllable, they concern the same area, etc.). For example: live – house, summer – heat, government – social – economise – parties ... Think about your groups for about a minute, trying to block everything else out of your head. Now try to find your words.

You will probably succeed first time! If not, try again. After two or three of these little games, it will surely work. Then increase the number of words – to 10, then 12 ...

Even when you are completely satisfied with your memory, play this game from time to time when you have a few minutes to spare.

Some themes

• **Colours**

Decide one day that you are going to look systematically, throughout the day, at everything that is either wholly or partly RED. In the evening, note down everything you can remember. The following day check, in the same places as the day before, and see whether you have forgotten anything. You will notice that not only have you forgotten things, but that there are also a number of things you did not see on the first day. Try to quantify (an approximate number will do):

- what you did not see
- what you forgot during the day.

Several days later, carry out the same exercise with another colour. You will certainly notice a slight improvement.

• **Shapes**

A few days later, decide that you are going to look systematically at everything that is SQUARE or CUBED. In the evening, note down what you remembered seeing.

The following day, check and quantify:

- what you did not see
- what you forgot.

Several days later, carry out the same exercise with SPHERES or OVALS.

According to your improvement and the amusement you get from these games, go back another day to the colour test, then a little later to the shape test (cylinders, triangles, cones, etc). Make sure you leave at least two or three days between each series, since the brain cells need to 'digest' this kind of softening-up exercise!

Don't forget your reward when you have reached a suitably elevated performance compared to the way you began. For punishment, continue the exercises until you get better!

• **People**

It's not obvious how to observe EVERYTHING about a person in front of you, even given periods of a quarter-of-an-hour or more (the time of a short journey, for example). You will only attempt it after the previous training. The method of observation acquired by your brain can then be used for subjects other than those in these exercises.

But you must design your plan of observation beforehand: to

look at an object as complex as a human being without any plan is like looking for a needle in a haystack. If you go at it in any old order, you can leave large areas unexplored without even realising it.

– You can, for example, start with the general silhouette: tall, fat, upright, round-shouldered, etc.

– Then you can examine the clothes: shape, colour, texture ...

– Then the hands and the feet.

– Then all that concerns the face: make a detailed plan of the subject (shape of features, skin, hair, eyes, mouth ...).

Write down your plan and re-read it, trying to use it in order to imagine certain people, someone close to you, for example. Is it sufficient? Is it precise enough? Read it again several times during the following two or three days and, when you have it well fixed in your head, give it a try.

Decide one day that you are going to look at two people. In the evening, consult your plan and reply to each item. There will almost certainly be gaps. Note down how many.

The following day, start again: you will surely notice an improvement. Let two or three days go by, then try once more, always with two people. When you are perfectly successful with these, move on to three and then four people.

When you find you are capable of describing four people you have met during the day without any errors or gaps, you can certainly feel proud of yourself.

• **Listening**

Decide at some moment in your day to give yourself 3 minutes (or a little more if you can) to be attentive to all the noises you can hear at the time: a conversation, street noises (especially cars, pedestrians, voices...), telephones ringing, etc. Note them down in the evening.

The following day, try to repeat the exercise at the same time. Are there some changes? Are these real changes or just things you didn't notice the day before?

Over the next few days, repeat the exercise several times but at different moments in the day. By including this exercise with repetitions of the previous ones, you will have quite a detailed survey of your whole day. In the evening, when you can relate to yourself the story of the noises of your whole day, you will definitely deserve a reward.

Don't let this skill for hearing die away. Continue living with the sounds around you. It doesn't hinder reflection. On the contrary, it promotes it.

Virtuosity

You are now ready for exercises based on attentive observation without effort. As always, do them at moments when you have time to kill (waiting, on a journey, etc.), as some people do their crosswords.

- **Crossing out letters**

Take a newspaper and decide to cross out a certain letter – the 'a's, the 'e's, etc. – in a half-column, for example. Do this by reading the words as quickly as possible without going back to check. Afterwards you can check more slowly and note down the number of letters you have missed.

Repeat the exercise with a different letter.

Once you have succeeded two or three times without error, you can then cross out a syllable – *con, in, le,* etc.

- **Divided attention**

There are plenty of occasions when we are obliged to pay attention to several things at once: that needs practising, too.

Again reading quickly, you can decide to cross out at the same time a letter and a syllable that does not contain that letter (for example, the 'b's and the syllable *de*).

A little more difficult: still reading quickly, count in your head the number of times you find a certain syllable, for example *ge.* Note down the number after reading a half-column of a newspaper. Then re-read the section slowly, writing down the frequency of the syllable. How many did you miss?

Once you can claim total success each time you try this last exercise, you can consider yourself to have acquired a good aptitude for perception. You should still, however, continue to play one or other of these games from time to time for the pleasure. And one evening or on a Sunday, why not play them with the family or some friends?

Multiplying the signs

You have already practised noticing automatically those elements to which you have decided to pay attention: such and such a colour, shape, syllable . . . This perception of detail was only an initial softener: you have already practised multiplying these details in relation to a complex subject, when you made your plan of observing a particular person.

These exercises have started to change your habits, your way of living with what's around you. You are now ready for a new stage, another change. The aim is to systematically increase your attention to everything without you having to think about it! You must get into the habit of multiple perception on every occasion and for every sentence, situation, place, object . . .

'Multiple' perception is that by which we all started to know the world. Watch a baby to whom you have given, for example, a box with a marble inside. He seizes it, passes it between his hands, turns it, looks at it from every angle, shakes it, puts it to his ear (because of the noise the marble makes when he shakes the box . . .), bangs it on the table, nibbles at it. In short, he explores all the possible aspects. He doesn't yet know what it is, but he has gained all the information the object can offer him. An adult doesn't do so much: a moment's glance tells him it's a box; that's enough for him. A single visual characteristic, a 'sign' enables him to reconstruct the whole of the object in his head. As it is a box, he knows that there could be something inside: he doesn't need to shake it to assure himself of that.

How many times does a moustache, a movement of the hand, the sound of a voice make us say with certainty: "It's so-and-so!" Look at the silhouette of a bald chubby head with a large cigar and you would almost certainly say straight away: "That's Churchill!"

This perception 'by one or two signs' is so frequent that it becomes widespread and we have no more need to be attentive. . . but we can be mistaken. If I draw you a certain little black moustache, you will perhaps say: "That's Hitler", while I'm trying to evoke Charlie Chaplin.

Back to the box. If you do not open it or shake it, you will not know whether it contains anything; your perception is incomplete. And as we have already said, there is little chance of remembering something if we haven't really perceived it. How could you remind yourself of someone you'd seen only once, if the only thing you noticed was the colour of the tie or scarf?

If you knew that person well and that he or she was particularly fond of blue and grey stripes, then a tie or scarf carrying such colours could evoke that person. But if it is a question of a single meeting, then this one sign would not be enough, since so many other people could have the same taste in colours and patterns!

The baby knows nothing, so he looks, he listens, he sucks, he sniffs, he feels the weight ... We are too blasé about things; we think we know everything; so we don't look and we don't listen. This is what we must change. Unless you belong to the quite small category of true creators, who spontaneously have this multi-sign perception of the world, which is also that of the child, then you are going to have to train yourself ...

• **Objects**

When you have a few minutes' rest during the day, decide to carry out a multi-sign perception of an object near you – a lamp, a vase, a knick-knack – which you are aware that you have always seen without paying any attention to it.

Don't hesitate to pick it up to get an idea of its weight and how it feels in the hand – different for the base and the shade of the lamp for example – turn it in every direction to see all its different sides and how the light is created. When you have finished, stop looking at it and jot down in a few words all the features that you have picked out.

The following day or a little later, take a few minutes to try to describe the object (either to some sympathetic listener or in writing). You will be surprised to learn that this simple exercise is already enough for you to see the object as if it were there in front of your eyes, even more clearly than before!

Obviously, this can only be medium-term memorisation and involve just a single object. Before automatically remembering all you want, you must train yourself further!

Play this type of game as often as possible and, when it starts to work well, take more complicated objects and multiply them.

• **Sentences**

Have you noticed that when you are reading your newspaper, or even a book, you never read all the sentences completely? As soon as we have really learnt to read – and it is all the more marked when we read a lot – a few words are enough for our brain to reconstruct the whole of the sentence. Since this reconstruction is quicker than reading every word that is written, it enables us to go faster.

Exercises in this area are not intended to change your general way of reading in the way that the previous exercises were intended to change your habits. While with the perception of objects, situations, etc., you have nothing to lose by adopting the habit of being more attentive, with reading, it is true that it can often be useful to read as quickly as possible. But it can also be nice to memorise certain passages without effort, whether for professional reasons or for the pleasure of repeating them at suitable moments ... poetry, for example. If you have the ability to read quickly, you also need to have that of reading to retain information automatically when you want. (This exercise is not enough for that: it only concerns the first stage, that of perception!)

As always, in a spare moment, a journey, while you're waiting ... decide to read for multi-signs two or three paragraphs from your newspaper or book. Imagine that you are a teacher about to mark an essay. You are going to read all the words properly, all the articles, all the conjunctions, etc. You are also going to pull the text to pieces: are the sentences too short or too long? Are there a lot of adjectives or adverbs? Is it clear or is it confused and badly explained? Is it simple or pretentious? Is it imaginative? Does it express well what it means? Are there repetitions? Is it just verbose nonsense?

A little later, jot down in a few words your personal commentary (one word for each comment ... this word is the 'sign' which will eventually help you memorise). The following day or the day after, try to write down from memory what you remember of the text. You will almost certainly be astonished by the results!

- **Images**

We live surrounded by images: news photos in magazines, illustrations in books, reproductions of paintings ... But have you ever studied one of these images in real detail, multiplying the signs? Have you really seen all the objects and people represented, the colours, the light and the shade, the movements, the relations between objects, the plan (foreground and background), the significance of what is represented, anger, violence (and what it is directed at), peace ...? Is there something that arouses feelings in you? What? Why?

You are going to train yourself in this systematic attention as soon as the opportunity arises.

Choose a picture and give yourself a few minutes to collect the maximum number of details possible. Then hide the image and, a little later, jot down in a word each of the details you noticed – not just a list of objects represented, but also your remarks: sombre, exciting, light, etc.

One or two days later, try to describe this picture. You will recapture not only the whole, but also a surprising number of details!

Detail gymnastics, or the art of perceiving as many aspects as possible of everything that surrounds you, must be continued for a long period and renewed from time to time if you detect that you have forgotten to do it automatically; because it must become a new way of life. This is the basis of stockpiling techniques and also of the art of retrieving memories and past knowledge: each detail is a cord which makes the rest come back, automatically. But it is particularly the art of living while being attentive to our lives, the art of not being blasé. We will come back to this: it is the best source of youthfulness and dynamism.

ASSOCIATION
■■■■■■■■■■■■■■■■■■

In learning to perceive well, you have tested your abilities and discovered that a simple perception, well made, almost enables you to memorise spontaneously! It's quite simply that, without being conscious of it, you have not been able to prevent yourself from *associating* your perception with some memory or knowledge already installed in your mind. This is because the act of associating results from a programme that is built into our brain function and which has been working away since we were very young.

When a baby learns to put his hand in his mouth (he has to learn it because this voluntary command of the muscles in his arm is not inborn), when he learns this gesture, his memory is going to guard it thanks to the fact that he has associated something new with something already inscribed in him. The new thing to memorise is the arm movement (later, in learning to play a sport or a musical instrument, one memorises lots of gestures), which is associated with the pleasure felt from sucking.

In effect, association is at the bottom of all memorising. We possess the mechanism in an inbred way and we use it at every turn without even thinking about it. All we have to do is be conscious of it and exercise it in order to reinforce it.

In order to do this, we don't need to go in for training sessions, which would take up our time. We need simply to THINK ABOUT IT, think about consciously making associations at every possible moment.

There are several types of association and the ideal is to work on several levels at the same time.

Personal Associations

Logically, these are the strongest. In effect, an association is a link between two segments, what is new and what is already known. The more strongly the already known is marked in us, the better the chance of the association holding. And things that concerns us personally are practically unforgettable. We do not forget that we like carrots but not spinach, that we have a mother-in-law called Mary who lives in Norwich, that we go cycling on a Saturday afternoon . . . Each time we can say 'I' about something new, there is a good chance that we will remember it.

For example, imagine that you want to remember the route in a town that you do not know at all well. In driving through it for the first time, you find that you turn right at the spot where you pass in front of the first baker's shop ("I like cakes, but I must watch my weight: turn but do not go into the baker's."). Then you turn left after a shop "painted in just the colour green I like" ("I turn beside the colour I like."). After that you turn left again just past a gateway "with the type of brass handles I would like for my house". Thus, your route becomes a tracking game between the points that you like: the baker's shop, the colour green and the brass handles. Easy to remember, isn't it?

From now on, play this little game with everything that comes to hand: an object, the title of a book or article, a professional item . . . something that involves you. Do this repeatedly throughout the day without jotting anything down. Before going to sleep at night, think back on your associations. Do they come to you easily? Practice must make this exercise easier and easier.

Try to recall as many as you can, although there is no point in marking yourself on this. You will know if you feel you have recalled everything or, on the other hand, that you have forgotten a lot. Just jot down in your notebook from time to time:

* *ease of association: very good* – +++; *average* – ++; *poor* – +.
* *memories: very numerous* – +++; *average* – ++; *few* – +.

Thus you can follow your progress through a period of days and then months.

Repeat this game at your leisure: it is going to become a sort of inner reflex. Above all, do not get annoyed about thinking to yourself systematically in this way. Each time you evoke in yourself something that concerns you – a taste, a personal memory, one of your characteristics – you are living it, making it real. This prevents the humdrum of daily life from trapping you in self-forgetfulness.

Virtuosity

When you feel that these associations come to you spontaneously, challenge yourself to a more exacting exercise. Look around you for an object on which you are going to concentrate your attention, to study its entire range of different characteristics (an object, an image, a place, a piece of writing . . .). And, for each characteristic, find a personal association.

For example: "It is heavy: I am only small and I only like light things. It is bright: I like half-tones, shadows, uncertainties which allow me to dream. It is useful: I hate useful things; I like useless things!" And so on.

With this little game, you multiply the reasons for liking or not liking the object in question. Far from being destructive, it is useful to know the personal reasons behind your choice.

Association by resemblance 'It's like . . .'

These associations come very easily. When visiting a foreign town, who hasn't thought or said: "That looks like such-and-such a spot back home."

Resemblances can be visual, based on sound or be based on more than one sense. For example, a child could tell you: "I easily remember the number 2468: it's like a staircase!" Even when we have lost this natural child's astuteness, we have a thousand and one reasons for saying "It's like . . ." at any given moment.

For example, if you are learning French, the word 'maison' meaning 'house' is like the word 'maisonette', which is used for a small terraced house. Get used to finding resemblances for everything you stumble across during your day and don't forget to tell yourself as often as possible: "Wait a minute, that makes me think of . . ."

In reality, what an object makes you think about is no other than your memories, something you know. By saying "That makes me think of such and such", you are recalling it and repeating it and this sets it firmly in your memory for the future!

So, with this type of association, you are killing two birds with one stone. You are noting some new knowledge by associating it, while at the same time reinforcing some existing knowledge!

Association in pairs

Our brain is so organised that one thing – an idea, a mental image, a memory . . . – leads automatically to another with which it is linked, either because we are accustomed to seeing them together (these are **pairs by contiguity**) or because one derives logically from the other (these are **logical pairs**).

So when we think of the kings of England, the name Henry makes us think automatically of the number VIII, the one with all the wives. To recall someone's name, it is easier to start with the first name: first names are relatively common and easy to remember and very often it is the Christian name which prompts us to recall the surname that goes with it – or makes a pair.

Pairs are ever-present in the daily world around us. The time is often a pair (12.15), as are prices (£3.50) or information (the London-New York flight) . . .

Practise registering pairs in your mind and do this in order to reduce the number of things to memorise, for example while making a shopping list: newspaper-matches ("To light the fire I need some paper and matches") or notebook-pencil ("To jot things down I need a notebook and a pencil").

Logical pairs are of several kinds:
- One part is linked to the whole (and vice-versa): nose-face.
- One element is the cause – or effect – of the other: catch cold-have a chill.
- One thing is contrary to the other: hot-cold, girls-boys.

To practise, you can look at a picture of a public event. Take, for example, the Prime Minister next to a visiting foreign diplomat (one pair). Next take the Prime Minister in his armchair (another pair). When thinking about it later, you will easily remember the known image of the Prime Minister, and that will almost certainly bring on the image of the armchair.

Carry on from there: the armchair-Prime Minister seated, so

you see his knees: crossed or not? And further: knees of the Prime Minister-knees of his guest . . .

Briefly, in an instant you have memorised – for a short moment – a certain number of elements in the image.

Chains

With this type of little game, you will discover that pairs link together easily. This starts by a known thing (here the image of the Prime Minister) which makes a pair with something unknown (here the armchair). And this in turn makes a pair with something else, either unknown or variable . . . Each second element of one pair becomes the first of another pair: the chain is formed and develops easily.

The system of chains is a marvellously associative one, which functions admirably provided that the link between the two elements of each pair is, for you, obvious. It will come in useful when you want to remember groups (objects in an image, pupils in a classroom, a succession of words and sentences of a text you have to learn . . .). It is equally useful to use those associations which enable you to recall memories and knowledge.

To master the technique, you must do some real gymnastics: systematic exercises several times a week.

Choose a group, image or extract from a newspaper article or the page of a book . . . Look for associations capable of forming a chain, always starting with a known item that is easy to evoke. To start with, make a chain of ten items, which will certainly stretch the brain. Reflect carefully on each association and repeat the previous ones each time you find the next. When you have reached your tenth item, go back over your memory chain: it should unfold all on its own.

Wait until you have been successful several times before increasing the number of pairs in your chain. And when you have reached the moment when your mental agility is well established, you can move on to other games. But come back to these chain exercises from time to time.

CLASSIFICATION
■■■■■■■■■■■■■■■■■■■■■

The world around us is made up of a mass of different elements: objects, people, sentences read or heard, various movements, sounds, light … However, we continue to orientate ourselves without too much apparent effort within this junk-room, thanks to the fact that implicitly we never cease to classify whatever presents itself and whatever we have to do.

The simplest example of this is when we decide immediately what is urgent or essential, what can wait or is of secondary interest, what we keep on one side to enjoy at leisure.

The best way of demonstrating this is to play the game of *Twenty Questions* with one or two partners.

One player thinks of an object which the others have to find. They ask if possible less than twenty questions, to which the first player only replies 'yes' or 'no'. If you are one of those asking the questions, think about an order of questions going from the general to the particular, starting with groups like "Is it animal, vegetable or mineral?" If it is animal, imagine two more groups, those that live in water and those that live on land. If it lives on land, think whether it has fur, feathers or scales? If it has scales, are they large or small? If small, does it have legs? And if it is legless, then you have found the answer. It's a snake! By working through the groups you are able to arrive at the right answer in less than twenty questions, having started off completely in the dark!

This game is an excellent exercise, so try to play it as often as possible, each time making it that little bit harder.

Decide, for example, that the object will be a person. If you start by running through the names of all the people you know, your allocation of questions must surely be used up before you find the answer! You have to find pertinent groups, such as man or woman, young or middle-aged or old, of the family, or a friend, or in the public domain and so on. In the last case, is it someone living or dead? Politician, artist …?

You can also choose to include in things to find, the titles of films or famous events, for example. This requires a real skill for grouping by means of which, starting as always with no clues, each question will enable you to eliminate large categories of objects.

The capacity for grouping is essential because, as with chains, this is a strategy with the help of which you can recall memories. You should therefore use this as an exercise as often as possible. And since you will not always have the time or the partners available to play *Twenty Questions*, make up groups on your own whenever you have the chance.

Take, for example, a television programme. Is it a game, a variety show, a magazine, a film, a documentary? If it is a variety show, group the contents: presenter, type of songs, type of guests, type of dancing, type of sets . . . At whom is it aimed: children, the general public, adults only? What time is it on: afternoon, peak viewing time, late in the evening? And how often does it appear: regularly, every week, each month?

In the same way, give yourself some extra hard work: "If I should come across the word 'cephalopod', into which group should I put it?" Play the same little game with a government minister, a musical tune, a sentence from a book and so on.

When you have made a mental note of your group, repeat it so that you can clearly see it in its entirety. Then ask yourself the following question: "If I had to find it later in my memory, with what association would I begin?"

To answer your question, if you automatically follow the plan of your grouping, you will have the agreeable impression of a thread that unravels itself all alone right to the end, where you will find attached the memory you are searching for.

If you stop this unravelling, for example by saying: "It's a vegetable; yes but then what . . .? Where is this leading me?" If in other words the association does not come all on its own, it is because a stage in your grouping is missing. For example, with the vegetable, you have passed on to the method of cooking when you first needed to envisage the groups of roots, leaves, fruit, etc.

So you have to test your groupings to make sure that you choose those that will always do the job.

For example, if you want to remember a television programme, it is probable that you will start by asking yourself when you saw it . . . It was therefore important to begin your classification with 'regular transmission, every Friday . . .' So it was a Friday . . . but not the last one, because you weren't at home then . . . It was the day when so-and-so was there . . . You told him . . . And there you have it! Working from the beginning of your groupings, everything has unravelled and the contents of the programme come back to you.

Groupings and structures

There are numerous occasions when we want to grab hold of and guard in our memory a complex whole – a landscape, for example, or the atmosphere of an evening out . . . In such cases, groupings are difficult and not directly helpful, or at least they are insufficient. But one needs to put all the information in order, that's definite: the brain only functions correctly with order.

The technique in such cases consists of associating and eventually classifying all the items in such a way as to enable them to go into groups that signify something, for you at least. When they come together to form a whole that will stick, you have a structure – and the brain can easily manipulate structures. It classes them, anchors them in its luggage and easily sends them back on demand.

The best example is the **transposition of a disparate list** (of purchases, for example) into a story, and a personal story, which is the easiest for our little grey cells to handle.

So, think about what you have to bring home this evening: shoe polish, coat-hangers, newspaper, margarine, biro refills, light bulbs and plant food. It's simple. Tell yourself the story of your return home:

"When I arrive, I'm going to hang up my coat *(coat-hanger)* and have a brief read *(newspaper)*. Yes, but the lamp next to the armchair doesn't work *(light bulbs)*. Talking of light, I need to move the house plants *(plant food)*. Afterwards I'm going to make myself some salad and an omelette *(margarine)*. When I've eaten, I need to write to my mother *(biro refills)* and before going to bed I must get my clothes ready for the morning and clean my shoes *(shoe polish)*."

Recount this story to yourself once or twice and it will automatically provide you with your shopping list.

From now on, forbid yourself all written lists: shopping, things to do, meetings ... The evening before, put everything you have to do the next day – and particularly the 'little things', phone calls and so on – in a structured story that you recount to yourself before going to sleep and again the next day when you wake up.

Perhaps to start with you will have to put up with forgetting one or two items. But don't give in; don't go back to the notebook. Very quickly the system will function on its own.

To practise, as always, choose those spare moments, those journey or waiting periods ... Take a book or a newspaper and, to start with, select at random ten words. Write them down in your notebook and consider your selection. You can, for the fun of it, make a quick initial grouping: the list of verbs, that of nouns, that of adjectives, of adverbs ... Chose one of your categories and group the words in it in a structured manner, that is to say make up a story adding as few additional words as possible.

Imagine, for example, that you have in front of you a list of three verbs: talk, sleep, envisage. You could make up from these the following: "When I want to *talk*, my parents (or my children) go to *sleep*. So I can *envisage* my evening."

Do the same with the category of nouns, then adjectives and then adverbs. And, for the fun of it, make up a whole story that incorporates all the categories. That is a real exercise in cunning.

And don't worry if it's a little far-fetched, particularly if this makes it funnier. Because funny things, like emotionally moving things, stick in the mind better than anything neutral. And, above all, don't be surprised if, that evening, you remember your ten words as if you had 'learned them by heart'!

REPETITION: THE LONG-TERM ROUTE

Certainly these stockpiling exercises, brilliant as they are at getting you to remember those items with which you have been exercising, without having learned them, two or three days later, these precisely targeted exercises are not sufficient for your memory to retain the information in the long term.

For a long-term memory, you will need *repetition*. But repetition is an art: it does not consist just of going over something tediously and mechanically.

YOU MUST NOT REPEAT
TEDIOUSLY AND MECHANICALLY!

You have to find the time to repeat the exercise in its entirety, the associations, the groupings, the little structured stories, whether it is to distract yourself in a slack moment or whether it concerns something else to which this exercise can be connected. You must play with what you are going to learn as the miser plays with his pieces of gold.

Each time you recall you can add a little something, an extra association, a new look. And above all look for every situation where you can use your new training: tell your story to others, put it into practice . . .

This is how someone learns, for example, how to play bridge. He buys a book and learns the rules of the game. If he plays regularly, he can put these rules into practice and, with each game, they fix themselves more firmly in his head. If, on the other hand, after reading the rules he does not have the opportunity to play, even if he has learned the essentials of what he must know parrot-fashion for hours on end, you can be sure that six months later he will have forgotten everything.

If you have played a lot over a period of your life, even with an interruption of a few years you will find you have lost virtually nothing. Recall and use your acquisitions, live with them and play with them.

An actor once told me: "When I learn a role, I sing it, I dance it, I eat it, I breathe it, I spit it ..." He is quite safe from tedious repetition! It is a wonderful game for him.

RECALL
■■■■■■■■■

When you tackle the work of this last stage in the memory's processes, you may perhaps be saying to yourself that it is pointless: you have practised so well at having an attentive and systematic perception, at cunning storage, that spontaneous recall is too easy! Any additional effort seems to you superfluous!

True, but you have an enormous amount of luggage, which you acquired long before you learned a way of memorising and which is therefore perhaps not well classified in your memory. It is, however, luggage that you could well have a use for at any moment and which you must know how to get at on demand.

We tend to tell ourselves a little too quickly: "I've forgotten that. Never mind! In any case it's old so it's surely lost!" and we give up looking for it. In reality, specialists have proved that *we forget a lot less than we think.*

You may already have experienced this. For example, you learned French at school and totally 'forgot' it when you finished your studies. Then, approaching your forties, you register for evening classes in French and are surprised to find that your progress is much quicker than your colleagues who have never come across a word of the language. Indeed, during this course, words and phrases come to you of their own accord, before your teacher has even mentioned them! This quite simply means that your brain has not forgotten what you learned at school. But, as an adult, you do not know how to pull on the right cords to bring it back to life.

Often it's the other way round. The older a memory gets, the more easily one recalls it. We have already mentioned that it is with each recall of a memory, whatever it is, a personal experience, technical knowledge or whatever, that we reprint it in our memory. And the repetition of these reprints over a period of years makes an indelible mark. They stay very close to our consciousness and are easy to extract.

However good our memory, we must exercise it using systematic recall methods. These methods are the opposite of the storage cells.

Associations

You are looking for the name of a person, a British general during the Second World War. What personal association can you make – or have you been able to make on a previous occasion – with this name?

Look for your old school memories: "I made a joke that my teacher didn't appreciate ..." Let your memories turn around your class: you see again the friend who sat next to you, the teacher's head ... Everyone had laughed when you said in a loud voice: "Monty Python!", because of your favourite comedy series on the television. And there's the link: Monty was the nickname of General Montgomery.

Set yourself some teasers in those spare moments, just for the fun of playing with your associations. Look not only for names but also events, notions, a recipe, a route, the story of a film seen a long time ago. . . To begin with, it will be quite difficult. But, little by little, like the sun chasing away the mist, the memories will start to come rushing back.

Scanning: the chain

You have certainly been using chains of thought in a spontaneous way for a long time. For example, one day it was impossible to find your car keys at the moment you were due to leave. Having searched in vain here, there and everywhere, you stopped to think:

"Let's see, when I came home last night, I had them in my hand . . . No, because I'd taken out the house keys in order to get in. In order to do that, I'd put the car keys in my left-hand pocket.

Yes, but I forgot that my coat pocket has a hole in it. So they must be in the lining! No, the lining isn't attached to the coat. So they fell on the doorstep . . . but surely I would have heard them falling on the tiles . . . Perhaps not, since I was right beside the door and they might have dropped on the mat."

You rushed to the front door and there, of course, were the keys waiting for you on the mat!

Using this method, one thing leads to another and you arrive at what you were looking for. The real 'key' here is to find the right starting point. For example, if you are searching for the contents of a film apparently forgotten, a good starting point would be to ask yourself: "Where and when did I see it?" That leads to the next question: "With whom?" and from there: "I said such-and-such to my friend about the principal actor . . ." then "He (or she) didn't agree, he found that . . . but both of us liked the setting . . ."

Slowly but surely the film starts to turn again in front of your eyes!

In those spare moments, give yourself the chance to rediscover some more or less complex memories using the chain of association. This can often be quite entertaining since, at various moments in the chain, all sorts of additional memories can suddenly appear.

On the subject of the film, for example, your friend was wearing a tie that surprised you: "It's the first time I had seen this type of tie, which has become such a fashion. It's funny. I'd never thought of that before."

Thus you will discover along the way numerous treasures from your memory that you didn't even know you had. Clearly, all these recollections reinforce their impression in your head and enrich the available space. Don't forget that the richer this memory bank is, the easier and more subtle the associations become and so the better the storage of everything you want to retain.

Equally, the more associations you create, the greater the chance of finding quickly the cord that leads to a particular memory.

**THE RICHER YOUR MEMORY,
THE EASIER IT WILL BE TO ENRICH IT FURTHER
AND THE BETTER YOU WILL KNOW
HOW TO USE IT!**

Scanning: the groups

Making up a group from a forgotten memory is certainly a skilful exercise. But it is a game with oneself that can often be so enjoyable that it is worth practising.

How do you classify something that is totally unknown – at least apparently so, since you have forgotten it? You should start off as for the game of *Twenty Questions*. You can only perhaps answer approximately, but you will see that gradually you will be able to tighten up your questions until you arrive at the solution.

Imagine, for example, you are looking for the period when Joan of Arc was burned at the stake. First question: "She was burned at Orleans? No, that was the scene of her great triumph. Then Reims? No, that was where the kings of France were crowned. But which king? Louis XI? No, Joan of Arc had nothing to do with him. Then perhaps Saint Louis? No, that was the Crusades, long before her . . . Er, Charles? Charles VII? Yes, that's it!"

Now you're getting there . . . Joan of Arc fought to get Charles crowned, which he wasn't able to be. Why? Because of the English occupation . . . That's it! It was the time of the Hundred Years' War between England and France.

It's now up to you to play. Your training so far will enable you to cope with these games. Practise them to enjoy and profit from your personal treasure of memories.

MEMORY FILE SUGGESTION
■■■■■■■■■■■■■■■■■■■■■■■■■■■■■■■■■■■■■■

My weak points: (from test on pages 76 and 77) ....

....

My strong points: ....

....

WORK PLAN
- **Spare moments** (journeys, waiting periods . . .): ....
  ....
- **a preplanned schedule** for memory games (of up to 15 minutes):
  ....
  ....

Perception
- the range of senses to test (sight, hearing, etc.): ....
....
....
- plan for observing a person: ....
....
- exercises to increase your skill in finding associations to help
you remember things: ....
....
- multiple sense perception exercises: ....
....

Stockpiling
- personal assocations: ....
    making pairs to assist your memory
- chains of linked pairs: ....
....
    groups which together form a complex memory ....
....
    structures created to unify a complex memory ....
....
long-term: occasions for repeating: ....
....

Recall
- games of association
- scanning: chains: ....
               groups: ....

Reinforcements
- what will the signs of progress be: ....
....
- rewards: ....
- punishments: ....

On the back: calendar (see page 58)

NB: It may be difficult in to plan a calendar. If so, keep a diary that
lists your successes and failures instead.

CHAPTER THREE

RESOLVING PROBLEMS

Every day, or nearly, we are faced with having to 'resolve a problem' in our personal lives, our professional lives, or perhaps in the context of working with an association or in the local community ... It can happen with even quite everyday decisions. For example, should you entertain your friends at home or take them to a restaurant? There are both pros and cons: the cost incurred, the work involved, the comfort, what the friends might think about it and so on.

Our existence is thus sown with choice and decisions, and our school, or even university education has taught us absolutely nothing about how to choose well or make the right decision. Sometimes we are conscious that something is wrong and we say: "I have a problem", but we do not know how to tackle it and less still how to solve it.

For example, your children – and particularly the oldest who is well into adolescence – are always in a bad mood; what's more, you could say that they were spoilt! Their school work is not too bad and they are in good health; at least they don't really trouble the doctor. So, where can you go for advice? You sometimes discuss your problem with other parents, but the responsibility comes back on to your shoulders, and you end up losing sleep about it.

Or again, in many professional situations, you have to go to meetings whose aim is to find ways of improving efficiency, reducing costs, increasing work satisfaction and so on. Clearly you want to find the solution that will earn you the admiration of your colleagues and give your career prospects a boost! But where and how are you going to find that brilliant idea?

What we tell ourselves

Very often we tell ourselves that we don't know how to find a way out, that it's better to wait and let chance make the decision for us. Or we may tell ourselves that we are 'deciders', we opt immediately for the first answer that comes into our head; we look no further than the end of our nose! Alternatively we ask for all the advice possible, all of which is naturally different, and we end up back at square one!

We can, of course, adopt the optimism of the ostrich, decide that there is no problem and bury our heads in the sand. Or we can seek refuge in taking the traditional route: "In this type of situation, I have always done so and so. It's a proven choice, so I will do the same thing here." Only here, although the problem may be the same, the context has changed. What was right in 1950 is not at all relevant now as we approach the year 2000.

Imagine that you have a power cut. Are you going to light the candles and say: "Before electricity, people used to live all right with light like this"? Of course not! You are going to go through a series of logical procedures to resolve your problem:

1) Check the trip-switch; if it is still ON, the problem is a general one and you will ring the electricity people for information.
2) If it is OFF, you will switch it back on again.

Here there are two possibilities:

a) The light comes back on and stays on. Something happened, that's certain, but you now have the time to look for the cause. I – a circuit overload (too many appliances working at the same time). II – an accidental short circuit: an appliance whose wiring was not properly isolated and the wires touched accidentally ...

b) The trip-switch 'trips' continually. You need to find the cause urgently. You check as per stages I and II above and here there are again two possibilities: a') you find the reason or b') you don't, in which case you call the electrician.

This strategy can be presented in a graphical way, as shown below.

Certainly in the case of a power cut, you are not going to draw yourself a chart like this! You're not even going to formulate the different stages of your plan of attack. Quite simply, you will follow the strategy without even being conscious that it exists.

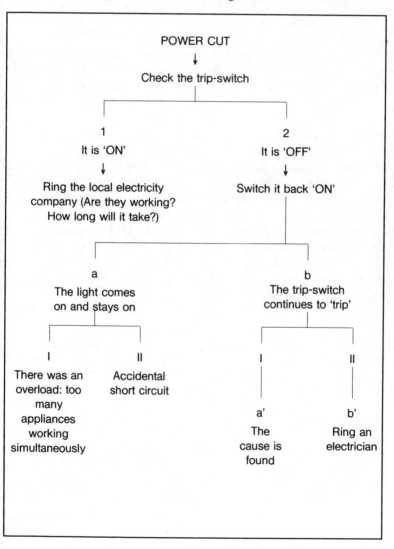

WHAT IS 'RESOLVING THE PROBLEM'?

Resolving problems comes back to mastering – overcoming or diverting – obstacles that we meet with in our daily lives. Action, anything we 'do', is indispensable for carrying on life and for all that makes for the continuation of our species and its progressive evolution. The art of resolving problems goes back to the dawn of humanity. Without a real capacity for outwitting traps of all sorts, our human species would have probably disappeared, a prey without great natural defences against the large predators and natural disasters. So our brains always had an idea of all the necessary tricks to pull us through the most thorny situations. And even today we are continually finding solutions to our problems without being conscious of applying ourselves to the task. Each time the little cog-wheels inside our skull are doing their extraordinary work like a computer.

Nevertheless the challenges that confront us now at the end of the century often demand more than the brain has been handling on its own, in an inbred way, for thousands of years. Even our personal lives become more difficult to manage, from one year to the next, thanks to the dizzy evolution of society.

Of course, to find his way through the primeval forest a caveman had to analyse, classify a range of information and plan appropriate strategies. And our ancestors have spent thousands of years adopting the same principles and passing on this skill to their descendants, both genetically and through education.

Today we are experiencing a rapid break with all our traditions. Certain skills, even those genetically transmitted, are perhaps less necessary to us than the ability to adapt ourselves as quickly as we can to continually new situations.

For example, we know very well the route to take between one town and another . . . But, in the space of a few months, all is disrupted by new motorways, new ring roads. And we find ourselves on a bypass we don't know how to get off, even though we can see very close on our right the town we want to get to! And there's no question of slowing down at a junction: the impatience of the other drivers forces us to maintain our speed!

Previous generations had the time to prepare their journeys with a map, stopping a moment at the side of the road by a junction to check they were on the right route.. Today, with the way in which the major roads are built, we can't stop wherever we like and we can only exit at certain fixed points. We are faced with problems that were unknown twenty years ago.

Today we continually have to invent new solutions and new methods for everything. Models that serve as references become obsolete almost as soon as they are created!

The computer is certainly there, inside our skull, ready to apply itself to these new tasks. But its inbuilt programs are today not sufficient. We have to furnish it with more complex ones. This means that, when faced with a problem, we cannot be content to let our internal computer do the work on its own, that is to say we mustn't be satisfied to look only as far as the end of our nose for the solution. We have to work consciously at finding strategies and plans for resolving problems, and exercises which will be a new departure for the brain, like a second 'running-in'.

Once this change to a higher level in the art of overcoming obstacles has been well installed, the brain will cope effortlessly on its own, just as we are mastering the numerous problems that confront us in everyday life without even thinking about them.

What is a 'problem'?

Before starting out on any training in problem solving, we need to know what a problem really is. It has nothing to do with the puzzles of our schooldays, which involved maths problems: those we learned how to resolve, because they have a solution – and only one. In contrast, those problems of life that concern us cannot be resolved using a formula, right or wrong. Their solution lies in making the problem disappear. And, usually, there is not just one way of achieving this, but several possible solutions.

Life's problems are sometimes quite obvious to us because we are conscious of them and say: "I have a problem." But all too frequently we live through a difficult situation without recognising it as a problem requiring a solution. Such situations arise in many different guises. However, in examining the daily life of a number of different people, we discover that they all belong to one or other of the following five categories:

- **CHOICES**
  These can be of a very basic nature, such as "With or without

sugar?" In general, we opt for one or the other without asking ourselves too many questions. However, this apparently spontaneous choice in fact relates to our attitude towards health, budgeting and so on. More serious are the choices such as "car or train" for a particular journey or "take a job in London, up North or abroad". In such cases, we are conscious of having to find arguments to put on the imaginary weighing-scales. But how can we be sure that we have properly considered all the relevant factors?

- **DECISIONS**
These often boil down to a choice: when we have chosen, we opt for one of the competing elements. But sometimes necessity imposes an answer straightaway. Should we move home or job ... or quite simply put up with it? Sometimes our job demands almost daily decision-taking. When that happens on its own, it's because the brain silently links up all the necessary logical operations. But, from time to time, it is very difficult; we hesitate and we are considered 'indecisive'. But it isn't a character trait. It's a lack of training in resolving problems.

- **JUDGEMENTS**
These are necessary for making both choices and decisions. And they are often delicate to formulate ... Have you ever watched ice-skating championships on television? And have you never asked yourself how the judges attribute their marks? It's a great shame that they don't give their reasons, because often the differences of appreciation can be astonishing ... and have led to disputes! We all have numerous occasions on which to make a judgement about people, situations, objects and so on. And sometimes the consequences that stem from that judgement can be quite serious. How can we be sure we have made the right assessment?

- **PERSONAL OR PROFESSIONAL CHANGES**
The basis of our activities lies in habits. We adapt to our environment, our work, our family life, so well that in many cases we behave in an automatic way and we know quite naturally how to react and what we can expect. There is no problem! On the other hand, any change requires us to readapt: we have to find another way of seeing what is around us, other actions, other solutions.

- **DISCOMFORT, DISSATISFACTION, PREOCCUPATION**
This is when we feel uncomfortable, personally or professionally. It happens, for example, when we are obliged to
wear a tie although we hate doing it or when we feel that there is
absolutely nothing in common between us and the people we
are with. How do we remedy such a situation?

   It should, however, be stressed here that any problem, in
whatever category it falls, gives us that uncomfortable or
uneasy feeling.

⬛ EXERCISE

Plan a good quarter-of-an-hour of peace and quiet and prepare in
your notebook a page for each of these categories. Alternatively
mark five columns on a large piece of paper, one for each
category. Think about your problems, whether current or recent,
and jot them down in one or other of the five groups.

   This first exercise, which is uncontroversial, will get you used
to characterising your problems and handling the method of
grouping. Looking at your classification, you will realise that you
can go even further: in every case, the problem boils down to
two elements:

1. It is an uncomfortable situation which affects the flow of
   activities, slowing them down or stopping them: it's a
   blockage.
2. It's a situation for which you do not have a ready-made solution, already tried and ready to be implemented to overcome
   the problem and re-establish a harmonious flow of activities.

   In effect, our life is made up of a continuous chain of
exchanges with what surrounds us. It is like a succession of questions and answers, from which we learn the rules and regulations
from our childhood onwards. We know what to ask of others, what
to expect from difficult situations and how to ask and get. In the
same way, we know how to react to situations that present themselves because we can more or less predict what will happen. In
general, from childhood to adulthood, parents, teachers and
society provide models which train us in this dialogue and in what
we must know in order to predict outcomes. It follows that,
although life's conditions often become more complicated, this
happens sufficiently gradually for us to be able to adapt without
too many problems. These problems pose themselves each time

we are short of a reply and when we have no model to which we can refer. We have to build up and invent new types of behaviour, new ways of considering situations. It's there that the problem lies!

STRATEGY FOR RESOLVING PROBLEMS

The strategy for resolving problems is made up of several stages:

- The perception of the problem.
- The analysis of the situation.
- The search for solutions.
- The choice of solution.

PERCEPTION OF WHAT IS POSING A PROBLEM

The perception must end in clearly posing the problem. And you must remember the golden rule:

'A PROBLEM WELL POSED IS MORE THAN HALF RESOLVED'

For this first stage, the method consists of asking yourself a large number of questions to which you can reply. You thus receive a mass of information that quite often you don't know you have. And you organise this according to a plan that enables you to extract valuable clues in order to reach a solution.

- First of all, you are faced with an obstacle: the problem. It exists. But are you sure you don't already have an adequate solution? Have you already met with this type of obstacle? How did you overcome it? Sometimes that is sufficient to force out the "But yes, of course!" and you have the course of action to follow.
- Next, you must differentiate between what the problem is and what it is not. For example, you live in a flat in a large town and

you cannot leave your bicycle in the hallway because it is bound to be pinched straightaway. However, the staircase is narrow and to carry the bike up and down each time you want to use it presents a real challenge. Problem. Yes, but when will you be cycling in town? Probably never!

- You must also know where the problem lies. For example, your child works badly in class. What must you do to remedy his laziness and inattention? In fact, a medical check-up reveals – in the nick of time – that he is short-sighted and needs glasses.

- You must also not forget that a problem doesn't exist 'in itself': it exists for the person who is troubled. For example, you are the mother of a family and have a professional job outside the home. How are you going to do all the household shopping? Doing the shopping is not a problem in itself, but it becomes one if you do not know how to find the time between leaving the office and picking the children up from school.

- Then, quite often, you are not the only one to be concerned by a given problem. For example, the father of a family is in the habit, since before he got married, of spending Sundays with his parents. It is a problem, because he would like to do other things ... But it is also a problem for his wife ... and the children!

- Finally, you sometimes have a tendency to interpret facts before actually looking at them. And by doing this you formulate a 'side problem'! Let's take as an example the little story of the flea and the technician.

A technician is watching a flea jump. He says to it: "Jump" and it leaps 500 times its height. He removes one of its legs and says to it: "Jump" and it leaps 400 times its height. He removes another leg and so on. When he has removed all its legs and says "Jump", it doesn't move at all. Then he writes in his notebook: "The removal of the legs of a flea makes it deaf. How can one remove its legs without making it deaf?"

To pose the problem in the best possible way, you must study it from every angle and, to do that, **follow a plan**.

Studying the difficulty

A good way of studying the difficulty or discomfort you feel is to pose yourself the following series of 'key questions':

- **WHO?**
  Who are the people concerned by my problem? For example, I have a problem finding a day nursery for my child: the person concerned is my child. Or again, I have a problem with the sound-proofing of my flat, because my neighbour plays a clarinet: the person concerned is my neighbour ... If you are involved in work in the community, the problem may be the transport of old people, with no individual directly concerned: but the minibus company that serves the community? And so on.

- **WHERE?**
  In exactly what place does my problem lie? It can be, for example, in the place I live or in the transport I use to get to work. If it's a question of work, perhaps it's in the entrance hall ...

- **WHEN?**
  At what moment (or moments) does my discomfort or concern reveal itself? It may be on weekdays or at the weekend. Perhaps it's in the evening, the morning, all the day, on certain days, etc.

- **WHAT?**
  During what kind of action or in what situation do I feel my discomfort or concern? It can be the washing-up, tidying up, collecting from school, the atmosphere at home or in the office ...

- **HOW MANY?**
  What is the number of people (possibly approximate) concerned by this problem? How many times does this discomfort arise each day, each week, etc? How much does this difficulty cost me? How many people (approximately) would a possible solution affect?

- **BUT**
  What are the constraints I would have to take into account during my efforts to find a solution? These could be time, lack of money, the rearrangement of a place where I can't alter the walls or doorways, hygiene requirements ...

- **WHY?**
  It is essential to ask yourself: "Why do I have this problem?",

clearly distinguishing between the subjective and the objective aspects.

– The objective aspect of the problem is represented by what would be a problem for anyone. For example, everyone is annoyed by the office's faulty air-conditioning system. And anyone suffering from asthma would be actively searching for a solution!

– The subjective aspect is not only unique to each one of us depending on our tastes, our character and so on, but also according to the moment. Our subjectivity can make us view the world in a way totally different from others. Take, for example, some students who have been shown a series of abstract designs, made up of lines and curves mixed in every possible way. One group saw lots of different loaves of bread within the pattern, while the other group didn't see the food at all!

Among the 'why's, you must always think about matters relating to change. In many cases, you can be conscious of feeling uncomfortable without being able to explain it very well. You continue to live as you have always lived and then, suddenly, with everything being all right one moment, now it's not any more! Why? This question can arise in your personal life or with your work. Now it is possible that the problem arises from the fact that a lot of things have changed, that you have not seen them change and that one fine day you find the ground has gone from under your feet. When your 'why's' put you in this situation, it is useful to have recourse to a precise technique to see things more clearly: the construction of a **'family tree'**.

1. Formulate as succinctly as possible the situation surrounding the problem and the solution that you have always been using up to now but which no longer proves satisfactory.

2. List everything that has changed in your world (new values, new needs of the young and others . . .)

3. List the discoveries and technical and social applications over the last few years.

Now put all that information on a tree (see overleaf).

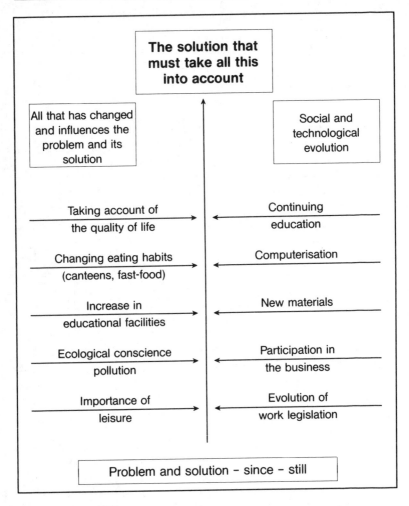

EXERCISE

Find a quiet moment and look for a situation in the life you are now leading which could be the origin of the problem. Formulate it succinctly. Then ask yourself the key questions and make a note of your answers.

When you arrive at the 'why's', make a clear distinction between the subjective and objective aspects. And then try to construct a 'family tree'.

If your current problem doesn't lend itself to this, imagine posing the questions twenty years ago and try to put on your tree all that could have changed the information since that time and could therefore influence the search for a solution.

Studying the environment

A concern or problem is not isolated. Imagine it in the centre of a circle made up of people, objects, various conditions, all of which are more or less affected by the problem – and affect it in their turn.

In this circle that surrounds our problem, we have to distinguish:

1. What can play a causal role in our problem. Therefore we will begin with the 'BECAUSE'.

For example, you have a problem seeing your daughter off to school, BECAUSE she gets cold waiting for the bus and BECAUSE it is not safe for her to wait on her own.

Let's continue the 'because' probes around the problem. She gets cold BECAUSE she always has to wait, at least a little while, and it is a very windy spot.

She waits BECAUSE the children before her on the route are not always exactly on time and, for each group, the bus can take an extra two to five minutes. But it is never certain. Therefore she must be there on time!

You can start the BECAUSE process even further back and, to see the problem more clearly, put down all these facts in the form of a chart – a BECAUSE tree (see overleaf).

This chart enables you to see immediately that the problem essentially involves accepting the possibility that your daughter will have to wait for the bus. As far as the bus is concerned, you can do nothing. Therefore it is up to you to find a way of staying with her, armed with an extra coat that you can take back when she gets on the bus, or of finding someone who can take your place. Alternatively, you will have to teach her to:
1) Keep her extra coat with her.
2) Not cross the road for any reasons (despite any temptation to play games, etc.).
3) Not to speak with anyone she doesn't know.
   . . . and wait for the moment when you can trust her to do as she has been told.

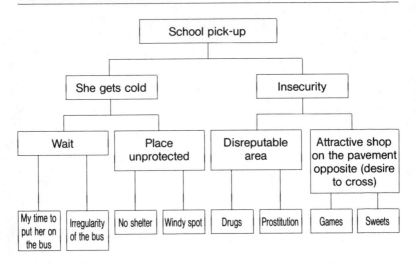

2. What the STRUCTURES are from which the concern stems. The structures are made up of objects and things, as well as the overall situation surrounding the problem.

A problem of a 'family' nature is obviously different from a professional one. For example, we tolerate disrespect (that's not a problem . . .) from our children or spouse that we would not put up with from our colleagues. In this sort of way we must get into the habit of always making a note of the elements of the structure. And in noting them, be it directly or in the form of a chart, we can extract those that have a direct causal role in our concern.

So put down for each one of these: "Can be changed" or "Cannot be changed". For example, you have a problem over alterations in your house. Some non load-bearing walls can be knocked down, while others can't be touched. You need to find a solution for these walls!

3. Who the PEOPLE are around our concern. They can have a causal role in the problem; they can be concerned more or less as we are; they can have a different point of view from ours about the problem, the way of tackling it, the consequences it involves and so on.

For example, you carry with you a problem you have failed to resolve for years, that of your weekends. You aren't sure what you would like. But one thing is certain. It's Monday and you have started the week feeling frustrated because you haven't made the most of your two days off!

Examine the structures
1. Possible travel options: by car, train, coach, bicycle . . .
2. Destination: near or far, towards the water (sea, river, lake . . .), towards forests, towards mountains . . .
3. Accommodation: with parents, with friends, in a hotel, camping
4. Activity: cultural (visiting churches, museums . . .), sporting (cycling, tennis, rock-climbing . . .), rambling . . .

You can present these elements **graphically**:

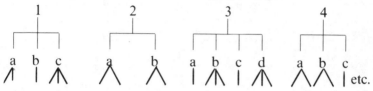

You can see more clearly from this what you want and what is possible.

But there are people
Make a list of the people concerned: your spouse, your three children, your parents. Each has his or her tastes, point of view, etc. For example, if you want to spend your Saturdays playing tennis, what are the others going to do? Even if they can organise themselves very well without you, won't you be sad at not seeing them?

Doesn't the problem boil down to one of choice: to be with your family or not? But perhaps also everyone's tastes are different. In this case, in order to see the problem more clearly, you can make a chart in the form of a **'double-entry table'**.

Horizontally, you put down the structures you have defined (in our example there are four categories). Vertically, you list the people concerned. Then, under each category and for each person, you note down what you feel is suitable, as follows:

	1	2	3	4
me	car	far, sea	camping	rambling
spouse	car	near, forest	hotel	walking
child (3 yrs)	?	?	with grandparents	playing in sand
child (5 yrs)	car	far, lake	with grandparents	playing with others
child (8 yrs)	bike	far, sea	camping	sport/cycling
parents	train	near, countryside	at home	walking

This is a clear table but it still doesn't give you a conclusion! But remind yourself that it is only a stage. You now have to go back to your overall reflection on what your problem really is.

Organising the information

Now reorganise your notes in the form of a presentation, if possible using a tree or chart, along the following lines:

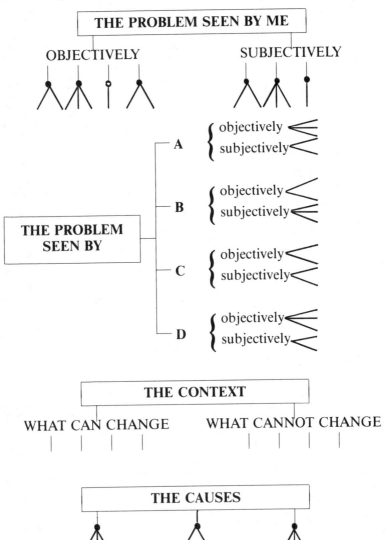

◪ EXERCISES

You can exercise yourself directly on one of your problems, although it is preferable to work on imaginary ones. After several exercises, you will be surprised to discover the ease with which you can resolve your own difficulties! And this satisfaction will be the best reinforcement of the method.

So imagine the problems that can arise: the car, the television; someone in an old people's home; the creation of a pedestrian area in the town ...

Begin with the key questions. Then study the environment of the problem: the 'because', the 'structures', the 'people'. And finally organise your information. Try as far as possible to use graphics. Each time some essential element appears, note it down to one side.

It's not impossible that this method of 'posing the problem' will present you with a solution all on its own, as if by magic. But this won't always be the case. Plenty of problems are complex and their solution cannot be found from this first global approach. A greater and more effective analysis of the situation may well be required.

FUNCTION ANALYSIS

A problem becomes a concern because it results from the fact that something doesn't work as we would wish or expect it to. It's concerning because there is an underlying problem resulting in our having unsatisfied needs and we don't know how to satisfy them ... And, very often, we don't say: "I have such-and-such a problem" but "I need such-and-such ...".

For example, the ink flows erratically from my pen; sometimes I get a great splodge and other times I have to shake it to get the ink to come out – and I splatter it all over my desk! I tell myself: "I need a new pen." But, in effect, what do I really need? I need to write easily, consistently and without the fear of ink blotches. What are the FUNCTIONS that I expect from the instrument that meets my NEEDS?

1. Consistent writing.
2. No loss of time refilling my pen.
3. Reasonably fine and legible writing.

4. Possible to erase easily.

Have I really posed all the relevant questions? No. There is still one essential question: what is going to be done with what I am writing? Answer: it is going to be typed. So, as well as my requirements, I can make a note of a non-requirement: I don't have to write with a pen. I don't even need to write in ink!

So it appears that the functions that respond to my needs are perfectly fulfilled by ... a sharp pencil!

Formulating a problem by saying: "I need such-and-such" is like putting the cart in front of the horse. It's giving a solution before posing the problem!

Therefore you must POSE THE PROBLEM IN TERMS OF NEEDS, then FORMULATE THESE NEEDS IN TERMS OF FUNCTIONS before thinking about the object or the solution that will make the concern disappear. So you shouldn't say: "I'm going to have to do such-and-such ... take such-and-such decision ..." before having properly considered: "I am annoyed because ... I need ..." and found what will stop the annoyance or respond to the needs.

The two key questions
Faced with any problem or difficulty, you must take the few minutes necessary to reply first to the question:

• **WHAT DO I NEED?**
Force yourself to formulate the functions that you need to fulfil, as we have seen in the previous example. Then let the solutions – or bits of the solution – come to mind. For example, "I need a car" or "I need a course in computer studies"... And, for each one, ask yourself the question:

• **WHAT USE IS THAT TO ME?**
For example, your friends are surprised: "What? You haven't got a computer? They solve all one's problems ..." Perhaps ... But what problems could YOU resolve with a computer? What use would this new toy be to you?

Let's go back to our example of the pen. What use is it? What are its functions?
1. To write with.
2. To write in ink: lasting, usable documents.
3. To write with a nib: quality of calligraphy.

4. Needs to be filled regularly.
5. Needs to be cleaned from time to time.
6. Produces writing which is difficult to correct: need for special erasers, correction fluid . . .

■ EXERCISE

Make a list of worries or problems encountered by the caretaker of a block of flats, by a visiting nurse, in classifying business or private documents, by the installation of a chimney . . .

Then, having studied these problems in whichever order you like and taking no more than ten minutes for each exercise, answer the key questions for each one of them and establish:
1. The list of expected functions, through which the problem can be solved.
2. The list of solutions or objectives that come to mind.
3. For each of these solutions or objectives, the list of functions they fulfil.

The first two lists must be made independently of each other. When an objective comes to mind as an eventual solution to the problem, consider its functions without thinking about the problem.

For example, if you think about the functions of a pen, without taking into account the problem in the example above, you are going to find that: 1) it serves to write; 2) it serves to write in ink, etc. But you will be able to add additional functions, like for example: it is an object of prestige when it's a famous make; it can make a nice present; or it can be part of an image for impressing the client . . .

■ PRACTICAL METHOD

When, through these exercises, you have properly familiarised yourself with the idea of function, make a note of your personal plan for analysing functions. What is suggested here is not the only one!

Write it down in your notebook or in the blank pages left at the back of this book for your convenience so that you can consult it quickly the moment you come across a problem. It won't be long, however, before you'll have no more need of it. This strategy will become part of your personal luggage and will unfold quite automatically. Look at the outline overleaf.

117

1. My objective

I should write it down, formulating it in a precise and succinct way.

2. My expectations and needs

a. I will make a list of these – written – giving myself time for the ideas to come to mind. If the problem is important, it's worth the effort to tell myself: "I'll give myself two or three days." During this time, I will jot down each idea the moment it comes to me ...

b. When I am satisfied that everything that could have come to mind has been noted, I will give myself a moment to consider the list, then group the items in categories and, if possible, in each category find a classification in groups.

For example:
My objective: successful holidays
My expectations and needs: rest, distraction, cultural activities, sport, getting back into physical shape, meeting people, changing environment ...

These can be grouped as follows:
A: Those that concern the physique.
B: Those that concern the mind.
C: Those that concern relations with other people.

Within each category, I can group again:
a. What involves pleasure.
b. What involves health.
c. What involves interest.
d. What involves cost, etc.

And, as always, all will become clear if you make a chart in which to include all the information. For example, you can put it down in the form of a tree or prepare a double-entry table.

- **The tree of needs and expectations**

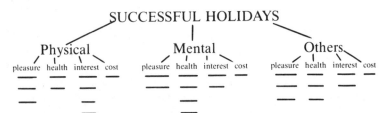

SUCCESSFUL HOLIDAYS

Physical — Mental — Others

pleasure health interest cost   pleasure health interest cost   pleasure health interest cost

• The double-entry table

	A Physical	B Mental	C Others
a. Pleasure	Sofa	Reading	New friends
b. Health	Regular sleep Exercise Diet	No professional problems	Someone who trains me in sport
c. Interest	Rambling; discoveries	Personal improvement	Interesting professional encounters
d. Cost	To be calculated	To be calculated	To be calculated

Formulating your thoughts in this way enables you to highlight the priorities and clarify the relationships, for example between 'health' and 'interest': what is good for your health is not necessarily boring! So, by linking up the priorities in each column, you can more easily discern your expectations: what situation is going to offer you at the same time 'regular sleep, exercise, diet, time to read your favourite book and the possibility of meeting new people'. It could be a spa town, for example. "What if I asked my doctor if some therapy would do me some good? And what type of therapy? ..."

3. What the solution must provide me with

Just as for the expectations and needs, you must make a list, a classification, if possible in the form of a chart of those functions which the solution must fulfil. Comparing the expectations with what such-and-such a solution would bring, will reveal valuable clues.

For example, we have already seen that my expectations of successful holidays start with 'rest'. So we will start by asking ourselves what solutions contain the function: 'ability to rest'. We can then make a list, for example as follows:

1. Staying at home.
2. Going to my parents to be pampered.
3. Going to a hotel.
4. Going to a club ...

Next, we go back to the double-entry table containing the expectations and write in what would result from the second solution – going to my parents.

119

	A Physical	B Mental	C Others
a. Pleasure	No effort Bed and sofa	Time to read	Nothing new
b. Health	Diet Good conditions for exercise	Risk of boredom	Mother's health habits
c. Interest	Nothing new	Parents' library	?
d. Cost	Expenses reduced	Expenses reduced	Expenses reduced

Go through the same exercise with the other three options ...
Then repeat this with your other expectations: distractions, cultural activities, physical fitness, new friends ...

By comparing all your tables, you will necessarily see those points that are essential for you. By grouping them, THE ideal solution will appear 'magically' in front of your very eyes!

Of course, this does seem rather a tedious process for a not very serious problem. And it is quite complicated when you do it systematically and perhaps a little difficult to settle down to consciously. But once you are well used to this strategy and how it works, your brain will do it on its own, without you knowing it and with a surprising ease and speed.

To get to this stage, practise using it as a starting-point for all your personal problems, even those that seem simple to resolve. Go through all the various operations, even when you are sure you have the ideal solution. It's a form of mental gymnastics to improve logical suppleness, but it's also a game, like the puzzles you find in some magazines.

And if you are short of problems, invent some! For example, the layout of your kitchen, the best school for your children, joining a particular association; or imagine professional problems: promoting a product, working out schedules or work rotas ...

At this stage, you will be well experienced in the treatment of all the elements necessary for understanding a problem. You will have analysed the concern:

- Reply to the key questions – What do I need? What use is that to me?
- Study what 'surrounds' the problem:
  - the 'because'

– the structures and environment within which you must work to find a solution
– the people involved.

You have defined the expected functions and the functions of the solutions to be found. Now it's time to practise putting all that together, if possible in graphical form. The brain proceeds in this way: you help it by consciously deciding to use this method of operation.

The comparison between expected functions and those presented by possible solutions boils down to what is an 'advantage' and what is a 'disadvantage'. Your synthesis will thus present itself in this form: advantages/disadvantages.

Let's take the example of the problem posed by the choice between a job in London or one in the North. You can simplify and present it with a tree of the functions of the 'North' solution, as follows:

JOB UP NORTH

JOURNEYS	HOUSING	LOCATION	FAMILY
Shorter – easier – more agreeable More free time – superior quality of life	Garden – easy access to shops – near to schools Quality of life – children's security	Near to sea – mountains . . . Health (sports) – facility for agreeable weekends	Near to my parents – my in-laws Emotional satisfaction – practical advantages (children)

Make a list of the people concerned:
• *Me*
• *Me – spouse – children – parents . . .*

And build up for each person a tree of some advantages and disadvantages.

SEARCH FOR SOLUTIONS
■■■■■■■■■■■■■■■■■■■■■■■■■■■■■■■■■■

The search for solutions can only be undertaken after you have studied the problems. However, as we have already seen, such a study often prompts ideas about solutions. But don't let yourself be influenced by this (to the point of relying on the automatic work of your brain!) while you are still in the process of practising.

The 'solution search' strategy can generate other ideas, perhaps better ones.

According to your personality, your tastes and the kind of problem to be resolved, you can choose between two types of method for this strategy: logical and creative.

Principles of the logical method

Here we will give you the main principles of this type of method. It is up to you, when practising, to adapt them to best suit your own needs.

After having properly studied your problem and perhaps got some ideas for a solution, you are going to imagine what would be the ideal, probably unrealisable, solution without really taking into account what is likely to prevent its realisation: it is **UTOPIA**.

1. Describe this utopia by replying to the key questions for studying the problem. Try to draw up the same type of graphical representation that you used for your study of the problem.

2. Then juxtapose, point by point, each element of the 'problem' situation with that of the 'utopia' solution. For example: on one side the insecurity elements and on the other the guaranteed security elements. Or, again, on one side the reason for an exorbitant cost and on the other the means of incurring almost no cost, etc.

3. Think for each of these pairs: how to get as close as possible to the conditions of utopia.

For example:

- **The problem side**

Insecurity because
- accidents because
  - narrow pavements
  - heavy traffic
- fights because
  - prostitution
  - drug dealers

- **The utopian side**

Security because
- no accidents because: pedestrian zones
- no fights because: small town where everyone knows each other

122

How to pass from one situation to the other? An idea springs to mind: move home and leave the large town for a smaller one with pedestrian zones.

4.   The answer that can emerge from a single pair is clearly not sufficient. In the previous example, it may be simply impossible to move home! You must therefore look for another solution ...

It is in any case necessary to make a list of all the solution ideas that appear from the juxtaposition of all the pairs, because even if a solution seems acceptable, you cannot be sure that you won't find a better one by going through your information again.

5.   The grouping: you will very quickly get used to handling this type of information and will end up with quite a long list which you will have difficulty finding your way around. You must therefore practise grouping these ideas into categories.

For example, A: all that involves a change of location; B: all that involves a change of hours; C: all that involves a change of people, etc.

Then, within each category, try to distinguish groups. For example, for A: 1) all those which involve a change in work location; 2) all those which involve a change in home location; 3) all those which involve a change in district (town centre, outskirts ...); 4) all those which involve a change in town, etc.

Finally, try to extract two or three main classes of solutions. For example: I – all the changes; II – the family, if the solutions can be divided between those that involve a change and those that involve the family situation.

List of solutions	categories	groups	classes
}	A		
		} 1	
}	B		} I
}	C	} 2	
}	D		
}	E }	.... 3	II

In this way you may find yourself faced with two or three types of solution from which you will have to make your choice.

6. The specifications: studying the pairs: the problem element/ equivalent utopian element enables you to set out a series of snags and obligations which will make the utopian element unachievable. Make a list and eventually – if it is a long one – a classification of all the snags and constraints.

Build up a certain number of possible solutions from the elements that emerge from your group of solutions and eliminate from it the impossibilities or sift through them in relation to those constraints that you have already defined.

◧ EXERCISE

Take the information from one of the problems covered during the previous exercises.

- Create the UTOPIA.
- Make up equivalent pairs of problem and utopian elements.
- Extract a list of solutions. Group them.
- Establish the specifications.
- Formulate between four and six solutions.

Principles of the creative method

The essential of these principles for solving problems lies in what we call **BRAIN-STORMING.**

Brain-storming is a method of creativity and inventiveness which has proved itself in workgroup situations. In consists of encouraging and stimulating the outpouring of ideas and images more or less buried in our unconscious. The principle lies in the fact that one word leads directly to another without knowing why ... Most of the time we automatically repress this kind of association, which has no rhyme or reason. We stop ourselves from saying whatever comes into our heads! But this 'it doesn't matter what', which escapes the control of reason, belongs to our unconscious world and can contain some treasures.

When we are in a group, we can stimulate ourselves to say the first thing that comes into our head; there is a communicating warmth in the game and we end up bringing out things that are often quite astonishing. For that to happen depends on the encouragement that the participants give one another and the length of the sessions. Tiredness weakens our control over our rational side, which blocks the unconscious. When we are alone, the dynamics are clearly not the same! We have to play the game with ourselves. We have posed the problem and we start to think about any solution under the sun just to amuse ourselves – even, and particularly, the most absurd. And we let one solution produce another even more crazy ...

When playing this 'game' it is imperative that you note down everything that passes through your head for ten minutes or a quarter of an hour. Afterwards, think no more about it and then, the following day, read back what you have written. That will stir up other ideas that are going to develop, ever more hair-brained.

After several days, you will have the impression of going round in a circle: the mad ideas will cease!

• The classification
When you feel you are exhausted, go back over everything you have written, pull out the essential ideas and classify the material you have gathered in categories.

• The functions
Each major theme that appears has a certain number of functions. These functions throw out in their turn some ideas for solutions.

Let's take the example of the problem: **journeys to work.** You have extracted the following solution: a little folding helicopter, which can be carried like a rucksack, that will take me from my house, over all the traffic jams to the window of my office.

What are the functions of such a gadget? 1) to avoid other people; 2) to avoid traffic lights and cross-roads, etc. What else can transport me in such a way that I do not have to think about anything? The train, the bus, the underground!

This example is not so far fetched as it seems: ideas that come from the unconscious thanks to the little game of wild imaginings (the brain-storming) can bring you some conscious thoughts which will help you see a clear solution that had up till then escaped you.

⬛ EXERCISE

....

It isn't easy to conquer the control exercised by our habit of being reasonable: you have to practise it tenaciously, but also with pleasure. Look to surprise yourself with those ridiculous ideas that you dare to let emerge! In those spare moments, get used to 'finding solutions' to everything and for everything, but crazy solutions! That's essential ...

Make the most of those moments in your daily life, like the queue at a check-out, a colleague's silent mood, the obligatory evening walk with the dog ...

THE CHOICE OF SOLUTION
■■■■■■■■■■■■■■■■■■■■■■■■■■■■■■■■■■■■■

The logical method, like the creative one, usually provides you with several solutions, maybe up to four or five, among which you will still have to choose THE BEST – knowing only too well that no solution is perfect!

To prepare yourself, when the time comes for this final stage, the safest way is to use graphic presentation.

● **The double-entry table**

A. Go back to the list of essential functions which the solution you require must fulfil (between two and five functions).

B. Make a list of the solutions that remain in contention (between two and five).

On the vertical axis of the table, make a note of the functions. And, on the horizontal axis, put down the solutions.

For solution A you therefore have between two and five vertical boxes corresponding to functions 1, 2, 3 etc. Mark in the relevant box a + if the solution contains this function and a 0 if it doesn't. Do the same for the other solutions – B, C etc.

Example:

	A	B	C	D	Solutions
Functions					
1	+	0	0	+	
2	+	0	+	+	
3	0	+	0	0	
4	+	+	0	0	
5	+	+	+	0	

So, in this example, solution A seems the most satisfactory.

• The silhouette graph

This method enables you to fine-tune your appraisal of the various solutions you are considering. A solution can fulfil certain functions more or less fully. For example, certain food can be very good to taste, of average cost and particularly inadvisable for your health, while another food will fulfil all three functions to a reasonable degree.

Let's take another example. A bicycle gives you average freedom of movement – average because you cannot do more than X miles a day. If you are scoring the function 'freedom of movement' from 0 to 5, you will probably mark it down as 3. With a car, this will be 4 and for a plane 5. On the other hand, you can leave a bicycle anywhere, so for the 'ease of use' function it will score 5, while the car would be maybe 3 and the plane 2 ...

To draw this graph, you will have to establish a list of functions which the solution must satisfy, which you will mark down on the vertical axis. On the horizontal axis, you will write in the scores from 0 to 5 or 6. Then, with crayons of different colours for each solution, put a dot in the boxes corresponding to each of them. Finally join up the dots of each of the colours in turn which will give you a series of silhouettes positioned differently between 0 and 5 or 6.

	1	2	3	4	5	6	Notes
Functions							
1							
2							
3							
4							
5							

_____ Solution A.
.... Solution B.

It is quite clear from this graph that solution A is better than solution B.

SUMMARY
■■■■■■■■■■■■■

So this is the strategy for resolving problems, which your brain will follow automatically once you have properly trained it to do so. Let's remind ourselves of the various stages that we have to go through:

1. Defining the problem: describing the concern.
2. Studying everything that surrounds the problem: environment, people, etc.
3. Studying the functions which the solution must contain.
4. Finding some solutions: logical method and creative method.
5. Choosing the best solution.

QUICK METHOD
■■■■■■■■■■■■■■■■■■■■■■

This method could be useful in an urgent situation, but only for those who can already manipulate the resolution of problems easily, those who are used to drawing up lists, appreciating the functions, using graphs . . .

It is made up of **four stages:**

1. Highlighting the problem and formulating it.

2. Looking for the causes: by making a list of them and putting them down in chart form, for example as a 'tree of causes'.

3. Looking for the ways of eliminating the causes, by examining each one in turn. For each, you can find a list of methods. In combining these methods, you will formulate a certain number of solutions.

4. Constructing the solutions. At this stage, it will be useful to create a double-entry table, carrying on the vertical axis the list of causes and on the horizontal axis the list of solutions, even partial ones. If, for example, you have a list of eight causes (marked 1 to 8) and five solutions (marked A to E), you will easily be able to see that solution A deals with causes 1-3-4-7, while solution B deals with causes 2-3-4-6-7, etc. And you will have found the best choice.

CHAPTER FOUR

SELF-CONTROL

S elf-control is the power of mastering impulses, such as sudden changes in temper. So we assume that it exists rather than that we are carried along by external influences, like a stone that rolls along the road. But it's not that easy. The well-known French tragic author Corneille wrote the following words for Emperor Augustus to speak, when he learned of the treason of all those whom he loved and trusted in: "I am master of myself like I am master of the Universe". Is it really as difficult to control oneself as it is to master the world? It certainly seems that when we feel an irresistible urge inside us for revenge, or suffer a sense of despair, we have more difficulty in containing our own impulses that in dominating the world!

In fact we often lose our tempers, allow ourselves to panic, become weighed down with anguish or are tempted to wallow in depression. It is the ultimate refuge, that of curling up in a corner so that we no longer see or know anything.

To other people the incidents which make us lose our control appear quite minor. And that doesn't normally instil sympathetic understanding, even less the indulgence of those who are the cause of or witness to our frailty – even if it is only passing! And the consequences of this, as much in our emotional or personal life as in a work situation, can be more serious than the original offence. It is certainly unfair because we really should be forgiven the occasional bit of spilt blood, the odd angry word or loss of control... But at such moments we are both deaf and blind to the consequences and we can inadvertently wound somebody or drop a serious clanger. And particularly, in showing ourselves to lack full control of ourselves, we lose the confidence of others. We run the risk that one day our boss will turn round to someone and say: "He certainly has some good qualities, but it's a pity we can't rely on him. He gets carried away for no particular reason and allows himself to be upset far too easily!" And that's a big career handicap ...

What we tell ourselves

We often say to ourselves that it's not very important: displays of anger don't mean anything, it's what is deep down inside that counts! So we give our grandson a slap. It's not serious, because we know only too well we love him more than anything... And what's more, we cannot feel guilty because that revealing little phrase is there at the ready: "I couldn't stop myself...". But others don't have the same tolerance of "what we can't stop ourselves doing". And for them, displays of behaviour count as much as what is there inside!

We also tell ourselves: "I always let myself be driven by my first impulse... even if I regret it later!" as if regret was able to repair the damage that we had perhaps caused!

We may even say: "I cry about nothing at all" or "I burst out laughing all the time, particularly when I shouldn't!"; and then we have the feeling, even if we don't put it into words, of being like a weathercock or straw blown about in the wind. The lack of firmness about which "we can do nothing" is like a disability, a congenital weakness! We cannot rely on ourselves and that undermines all attempts at self-assurance.

WHAT DOES LACK OF SELF-CONTROL SIGNIFY?

We blame external causes, the thing that angers us, the event that makes us cry and so on. But in fact it is inside ourselves that all this happens. It's an internal force which, prompted by a signal, suddenly lets itself go and leads us, just for a short while, to behave completely automatically. It's not we who are blushing or going pale, trembling or shouting ... It's happening all on its own.

This force is the expression of a very specific mechanism in the brain: that of EMOTION. When it is released, all sorts of reactions occur in our bodies and minds without us apparently being able to control them. Emotion can sometimes show itself as an impulse: then we act under the effect of an inner impulse which shuts us off from all doubt.

In fact the state of emotion unfolds along a path written in the brain before we were born which blindly follows a progression right to the end, which is the return to the normal, pre-emotion state.

So lacking self-control is, in a biological sense, the fact of being in an emotional state.

But it is also true that emotion shows itself more or less easily, depending on whether we are in a good or bad mood. And, conversely, agreeable emotions lead to optimism and good temper, just as disagreeable emotions lead to pessimism and bad temper. In other words self-control, which boils down to emotional control, is intimately linked with mastering our temper.

Last but not least, we are all familiar with the common problem of anxiety. It is the most painful of conditions because it produces repeated rages which are simply emotions, super charged. When we suffer from anxiety, all our internal energy is stretched, ready to erupt at the slightest prompting. That is to say it is already, in itself, a form of continual emotion that encourages super charged outbursts.

The common expression is that 'we let ourselves be overcome with anxiety', which implies an unconscious admission: anxiety is a clear expression of lack of self-control.

So everything rests on mastery of emotion:

1. Its outbursts which include anger, panic, tears...
2. Its expression in actions that are impulses.
3. Its chronic state represented by anxiety.
4. The inner state which underlies mood.

What is emotion?

The mechanism of emotion is installed in us like a magnificent wild beast. This image comes to us from the publicity of a famous brand of petrol: the tiger in the tank! We must certainly not destroy it or cage it because it is our life source; it's what brings relief to our existence. But we must tame it and enable it to be master of its excesses. And, to do that, we must understand it properly.

Emotion is due to the intense activation of several parts of the brain which together make up what is called the rhinencephalon. When this system is stimulated, it influences in its turn all of the rest of the brain. Everything picks up the rhythm of the emotion and ideas flow rapidly but remain unaffected by anything that is foreign to the cause of the emotion. It would almost be true to say that when we are carried away by emotion; a thunderbolt could strike next to us and we wouldn't hear it. At the same time, reserves of energy are suddenly released, supplying the body (muscles and organs) with the necessary conditions and fuel for powerful and rapid action.

In effect this rhinencephalon, which is also present in the brain of the most inferior of vertebra like fish (which existed on earth before man), is the instrument of survival *par excellence*. It activates itself automatically when under threat and prompts the individual's response. Whether this response is frantic escape or ferocious attack, it will be powerful.

It is thanks to the fact that at the first threatening sign the rhinencephalon activates the 'Orsec' plan of flight or struggle, providing the surplus of energetic fuel necessary for such extreme behaviour, that our ancient ancestors were able to survive in their hostile environment thousands of years ago.

We still have the same mechanism, but what sets it going is clearly no longer the same! The causes of emotion in the western world as we approach the year 2000 are very different from those which affected people in the Middle Ages or even those that today disturb the tribes of deepest Africa or the Eskimos of the frozen North.

The tiger within us is certainly still there however, always the same. But it is ready to spring (and us with it) at those signals that are specific to the world in which we live; and, to our own individual experiences and personality...

With today's technical developments in all areas we are, without realising it, more and more 'programmed from outside'. Our life is spent encountering a variety of demands, certainly, but they are known, predictable, and they themselves control the form of our response to them. Since childhood we have thus learned to react in an automatic way and our response leads to a predictable and therefore expected result, which in its turn brings a new demand. And so it goes on: demands and responses between the world and ourselves continue harmoniously – up to the point when there is a 'failure': and that's emotion.

For example:

I feel my mouth is dry (not that it's really the thirst which will be the emotion, but the having of the thirst), which is the incentive for me to go into the kitchen where the cold water tap will enable me to fill a glass. I drink and I resume my activities with a minimum of interruption. The pleasure of the cold water is hardly a display of emotion!

But let's imagine that, when I turn on the tap, nothing comes out: there's no water! I certainly wasn't expecting that! *Now* it's emotion. Depending on the circumstances, I can go off more or less irritated in search of the cause of this absence of water; or I can resign myself to waiting for some eventual help from another member of the family. Whatever happens, the resumption of my activities will be disturbed for good while.

Storm in a teacup, you might say? Certainly, this example involves a minor emotion. But even in such a modest dose, all the ingredients are there – with the marked disruption to my activities.

The signal: it's an unexpected situation. I am appealing to my environment, asking for some water. I am expecting a favourable response, since running water in the home is a perfectly well established comfort in our society. The environment responded with a failure!

The response to this signal is immediate: a liberation of energy. This either drives me frantically to look for the cause of the failure, or it locks me in resigned withdrawal, because this withdrawal (or blockage), which is one of the reactions of

133

emotion, requires a surplus of energy just like an action does.

The emotion's mental response is also present. For a while, I lose interest in my other activities. I can only think about looking for the cause of the failure or about my thirst which is going to get worse.

Another example:
This is provided for us by chess players. A good player knows exactly, from the first move, what his opponent's and his own following five or six moves will be, provided that his opponent is as good a player as he is. But if his opponent is a beginner who improvises all his moves, the exchanges on the board will become incoherent for our champion. He will start by being distracted and these unexpected moves will make him irritated. In the end he will win quite quickly, of course, but at the expense of a certain exasperation which stretches him more than the orderly, predictable competition he is used to with a player of his own level.

THE EMOTION SIGNAL COMES FROM SOMETHING OR SOME SITUATION THAT IS UNEXPECTED

Faced with the unexpected, we suddenly find ourselves without the prepared plan of action that enables us to respond automatically. We have been thrown completely off-track and are DISCONNECTED. We are put on alert. Since the body can no longer cope, it seeks recourse to the oldest form of defence: emotion.

For example, imagine a person who has been tied up in a chair by some crooks: it's terrifying! He cannot think calmly to find a way of undoing the cords. The admirable computer in his brain could surely resolve this practical problem, if only the victim would let it go to work! But he wriggles about in all directions, which only tightens the knots and risks strangling him! In fact, his panic has liberated a surge of brute force to enable him to make his desperate escape. The 'escape' urge is starting, but it is blind to the fact that the muscular programming hasn't taken the situation into proper consideration and his gestures are useless.

When we are swept along on the wave of emotional automatism, we are more or less cut off from contact with the world around us. We live our emotion all alone and stumble about in the dark.

THE UNEXPECTED is the principle which releases emotion and it can assume a number of forms.

It can be, paradoxically, **waiting** for something or someone. If, for example, I am waiting for a loved one at eight o'clock in the evening, I have thought about him or her all day. In my imagination, that person has become a part of my interaction with the world around me. But it's just imagination. In reality, I cannot hear or see that person. And the nearer the time gets when I will actually be able to touch them, the more their absence contrasts with my imaginings. I was used to talking with their imaginary presence, but it is no longer possible and their absence becomes unexpected!

Any **failure** is also quite unexpected. While we may well have *said* that we expected it, the body never really expects to fail. When we undertake an action, with an objective in sight, the body forsees acting right up the achievement of that goal. Failure takes it by surprise. However difficult the task, the brain cannot automatically prepare itself to abandon the action or accept defeat. So when we decide: "It's a failure", the brain sees this as the signal for launching into the automatic drive – the emotion – which takes over from the manual control which hasn't been able to achieve success.

For example, two people can be teasing each other or be involved in a quite aggressive exchange, while their emotions are only moderately aroused, in proportion to the situation. This can continue with no difficulty so long as the two are level pegging. However, when one of them finds himself short on replies or arguments, he will start to get angry and raise his voice. This behaviour only expresses crude and ineffective aggression because it no longer means anything. Because he has found himself lacking answers he feels a failure, a signal for super charged emotion, which will 'disconnect' him. The anger is poured out blindly and all control is lost.

An **inner conflict** is an excellent example of the unexpected. We are well programmed so that our relationships with the world are 'nicely oiled', so when we find we are at odds with ourselves or with the world because we have diverged from the usual pattern, we feel we have gone 'off the rails' and become ill adjusted to our situation.

Again, it's the signal for emotion, the survival drive that masks the conflict.

Here is a situation which is a caricature but a perfect example of this automatic recourse to emotion. I have planned a journey which takes me via a charming little road . . . but when I arrive at the turning, I find there is a barrier with a 'road closed' sign. I'm furious. I get out of my car and go to kick the barrier! I really should be kicking myself for not having foreseen such a possibility. I should always have another route to turn to if needed. I thus find I am in disagreement with myself, but I hide this conflict by taking my anger out on the barrier.

This anger is a diversion thanks to which I avoid looking at my conflict, which clearly does not help me to deal with it. Because if, having accepted that I couldn't do what I wanted I had knuckled down to correcting my stupidity by looking straightaway for another pleasant route, I would not have had any reason to lose my temper.

What is anxiety?

This is a state of permanent emotion. Biologically it corresponds to the continuous activity of the fear system. Psychologically, it is a condition which makes us live in a state of perpetual expectancy.

When we are anxious, we believe that "anything can happen", just anything: the unimaginable, the worst, the unforeseen. We forget that our demands on and responses to the world around us continue in a quite harmonious way ("Life goes on!"). We only make ourselves think about what could happen if the mechanism was to seize up. We wait for the catastrophe that clearly doesn't happen. And this is the worst part about it, because therein lies the unexpected!

The great worriers are the most effective people in the event of a drama: finally something they have been waiting for! That reduces their anxiety and makes them perform better.

This kind of obsession clearly upsets our contact with the surrounding world: the emotional tension isolates the worrier. Normally we need to be constantly in touch with reality. Anxiety upsets this rapport, which in turn often leads the worrier into inappropriate behaviour. When we start to think that the moon is made of green cheese, we are in serious danger of being locked up!

What is mood?

Our good or bad moods also depend on a mechanism of the brain. Certain parts of the brain discharge certain chemical substances which make us either optimists or pessimists. But also, when we decide to see the good or bad side of things, that makes those cerebral zones concerned in the regulation of mood operate in one direction or the other.

When we are 'in a black mood' (or grey or pink), for us the whole world has that shade of colour. It's as if nothing is intrinsically pleasant or unpleasant, good or bad; it's one or the other for each individual, according to the way we feel at the time. Clearly we mustn't exaggerate this relativist philosophy: there are certainly some situations which are objectively, for some of us, desirable or repellent.

Wallowing in our moods, of joy and even more of sadness, increases the number of occasions when we are taken over by emotion. Pessimism is doubled by anxiety. We can't manage an easy relationship with our surroundings and expect catastrophe around every corner: whatever happens spells disaster.

A certain kind of exaggerated optimism brings on a sense of elation that pushes us to distort reality, to deny failure – which does nothing to help us avoid it. A mood is normal when it is not exaggerated, one way or the other. And especially when it changes in accordance with the hazards of life. It oscillates, without extremes, between optimism and depression, at the mercy of any serious incidents we may encounter; but it automatically recovers its equilibrium as soon as it has taken the shock on board.

Mood is called unstable when it swings a little too easily, at a little scratch or a flicker of sunlight ...

We cannot master either emotion or mood by trying to confront them head-on. We don't control them with force, as we saw when we talked of acquiring will-power. It's important to emphasise that emotion, in its chronic form of anxiety, and mood depend on the brain's biological mechanisms. Even if these are in their turn altered by what we are feeling, we cannot direct them simply by saying: "I want". They are the 'wild beasts' in us and we cannot tame them with a cudgel. We have to distract their attention, subdue them and then discipline them bit by bit – with their full agreement!

We mustn't try to suppress these emotions. They not only give us our spark, but even more importantly they produce the surges of energy which renew everything inside us (like a tonic!) both biologically and psychologically.

Charles Darwin, whose work on the theory of evolution needs little introduction, said that before settling down to work he sometimes began by looking through his papers to find a phrase that would make him angry. It must have been easy, since his work had met with a lot of opposition and his correspondence provided all the stimulation he needed! This always stirred up his temper. We can do the same thing ourselves just by having our own argument! Then, as we have all experienced, the period of emotion only lasts a short time; after a few minutes the calm returns of its own accord. So, after these few minutes of excitement, Darwin felt himself suitably stirred and ready to apply himself to his work – saving himself the expense of a cup of coffee!

All the same, we mustn't try to invent moods from nothing: that would be a tragic indifference, a non-life. True mastery of oneself has, for its goal, the knowledge and power to harmonise the phenomena of mood and emotion in real-life circumstances, in order to draw from them the maximum benefit (interest, dynamism . . .) without letting them become sources of failure or reasons for annoyance either for us or others.

QUESTIONNAIRE
■■■■■■■■■■■■■■■■■■■■

We are all more or less emotional, but each of us in different ways. Before starting training on the mastery of your inner self, you will need to take some time for a little introspection to highlight your particular weaknesses in order to know better how to direct your efforts.

	always 2	sometimes 1	never 0
1. *Do sudden noises (telephone, doors . . .) make you jump?*			
2. *Do you lose sleep when you have serious worries?*			
3. *Do you feel you are a failure?*			

	always 2	sometimes 1	never 0
4. Do you speak without thinking and regret it afterwards?			
5. Do you cry in moments of emotion, sadness, anger?			
6. Do you feel your heart beats in a worrying manner?			
7. Are you discouraged and give up at the first hurdle?			
8. Do you make impulse purchases as the fancy takes you?			
9. Do you lose your temper?			
10. If someone close to you is late for a meeting, do you think immediately of an accident?			
11. Do you believe catastrophes await us that we can do nothing about (war, hole in the ozone layer, epidemics . . .)?			
12. Do you have an immediate sympathy or antipathy for someone at a first meeting?			
13. Do you suddenly lose your thread in moments of emotion (mental blockage, clumsiness . . .)?			
14. Do you watch your health in fear of a heart-attack or cancer?			
15. Do you have highs and lows of mood that nothing can change?			
16. Have you broken an emotional or professional relationship in a fit of anger?			

COMMENTARY

These questions explore – but very superficially, because their main aim is to get you to take an objective look at yourself – the four elements on which your personal control exercises will be based.

- Begin by adding up your score. You will find:
- **20+:** you are particularly lacking in control, super-emotional. It's time to get a hold of yourself!
- **15-19:** you are certainly suffering from a troublesome instability.
- **8-14:** your reactions are average for most people today.
- **less than 8:** you possess a remarkable calmness. One question to be asked here: is it natural? And, in this case, is it due to the fact that you have found nothing worth getting emotional about? Or are you automatically master of yourself?

- Differentiate between the scores obtained in your search for the four elements you must know how to control:

Questions 1 – 5 – 9 – 13: emotion
- **5-8:** you display emotion too easily.
- **2-4:** you display average emotion.
- **less than 2:** you have too little emotion. Such indifference is suspect. Perhaps you have problems that you should open up to someone . . .

Questions 4 – 8 – 12 – 16: impulsiveness
- **5-8:** dangerous impulsiveness.
- **3-4:** impulsiveness to be watched.
- **less than 3:** good control over impulse.

Questions 2 – 6 – 10 – 14: anxiety
- **5-8:** extreme anxiety. You should speak to your doctor.
- **2-4:** your basic level of anxiety is relatively high and normal if it is accompanied by a fighting spirit.
- **less than 2:** this is serenity. If you have scored 0, this indifference is suspect.

Questions 3 – 7 – 11 – 15: mood
- **5-8:** changeable mood. Instability – depressive tendency. If you are not sure about being able to master this, seek advice from your doctor.

- **2-4:** mood can be better controlled.
- **less than 2:** good control of mood.

It should be repeated that these results are only an indication. Take time to think about the way you live, how you have been living over the last few years. As far as emotion is concerned, have you experienced a lot, a little or none at all?

Do you remember individual impulsive actions? Do you suffer from moments of unbearable anxiety? Do you take, or have you felt like taking tranquillisers, or sleeping pills? Do you feel that you never know in advance what your mood will be?

Ask yourself all the possible questions so that you will get to know your weaknesses better. This self-assessment will give you the urge and the energy to practise controlling and mastering yourself better.

This mastery depends on education, which some societies took pride in giving from childhood. Today it has gone out of fashion almost everywhere! True, it is a demanding exercise for children too young to understand the reasons for it. But if, when we reach adulthood, we do not learn how to control ourselves, the result will be a degree of disorder ... We're not advocating iron control at all times, but between the superman myth and a total free-for-all, there is room for a harmonious balance of self-mastery and spontaneity, the basis for true freedom ...

Below are some pointers to help you achieve, naturally and without forcing, a good mastery of your emotion, your impulsiveness, your anxiety and your mood.

EMOTION
■■■■■■■■■■■

Emotion is released by any break in the interaction, which is normally predictable, between a person and his or her environment. It is released by the UNEXPECTED. So, to control emotion, we have to **COPE WITH THE UNEXPECTED.**

We must be clear, however, on one very important point: we must never confuse the unexpected with the unknown, the fact of being taken by surprise by the unexpected and the pleasure of exercising our curiosity to explore the unknown.

Of course, we cannot predict what will be a novelty and it is just the going to meet this unknown that is the pleasure of curiosity. It arouses an agreeable sense of excitement, an emotion certainly but not an upset. Emotion that remains within limits that don't upset us is like a breath of fresh air. It produces a little burst of internal energy that can only be favourable (remember Darwin . . .). And this difference of intensity from that of an upsetting emotion is in fact a difference of nature: the latter is caused by the unexpected producing a break in our pattern of life.

Naturally the unknown can be unexpected and produce major emotion. For example, we expect when walking into a room we know to find certain pieces of furniture, certain objects and so on in certain places. If everything has changed without us knowing it, we are entering into the unknown . . . which we were not expecting! And this throws us. But, for the curious who go in search of the unknown, travelling to a distant country for example, the unknown is expected, programmed!

So we can make clear the distinction between two qualities of emotion: those of an intensity within the limits of normal behaviour (even if disagreeable, they are not harmful either to the person affected or those around him) and those devastating emotions that disturb both the person experiencing them and everyone around.

Self-mastery enables us to mitigate the occurrences of this second category, to keep them within normal limits. Anger, for example, can be reduced to an irritation pushing us to put right what is annoying us. Panic can be reduced to the knowledge of a threat, implying that we need to increase our attention. . . For this to happen, it is necessary that nothing in our daily life be totally unexpected, only a little different to what we have predicted. . .

So how do we cope with the unexpected in such a way as not to be thrown by it? The principle is self-evident: we must reduce the share of the unexpected in our life in general and more especially on those occasions when we might stand in fear of emotional shocks. . .

Watch how children live. They are always to a greater or lesser degree in a state of emotion. It doesn't take much for them to burst out crying or laughing. What makes them cry when they fall over, for example, is not the pain but the emotional impact of the fall. What makes them laugh is not a particularly funny situation but quite simply something new around them: father's unaccustomed gesture or a word from mother that they have never heard before . . . It's that they don't yet know a lot, about anything, even their own reactions. They live in a world of constant surprises for a good five or six years of their life! We know that the little lad running across a pebbly beach is going to fall over; but he's not expecting it! That's why he cries.

Moreover, when it comes to falling over, we often do the same. When, for example, we put on our skis, we are expecting the occasional tumble; it's not very pleasant but as long as we don't break anything we don't turn it into a drama. However, a fall in the hotel (albeit painless) because we have missed the last step on the stairs can throw us completely, despite the fact that we were earlier laughing about the sensational cartwheel we did on the ski slope. On the snow, it was expected; on the staircase, it was unexpected.

We must therefore learn to be ready for anything. What is not expected awaits everyone – and therein lies the anxiety. The hero in a John Wayne western is not emotional. For him, anything is possible and he is completely confident. He knows that he will get out of every situation. So, nothing unexpected! It's the audience who tremble in his place – and how enjoyably!

In real life, of course, no-one can actually expect EVERY-THING. But those who have control over themselves are ready for *anything that might happen in the circumstances of the moment.* In other words, they have observed and they KNOW what to expect. This is the position of the adult, as opposed to that of the child who hasn't yet learned . . .

The first rule consists of always knowing how to **programme** what might happen. That involves foreseeing – further or less far ahead, depending on the situation – anything that could happen (at least the most likely) and the way in which we will be able to react for the best, given different eventualities. Then we imagine what this reaction will in its turn produce and so on.

Of course, what happens in reality can differ from our predictions. But if we have carefully reviewed several possibilities, there will always be one that comes close enough to the reality so that we are not left in a void. The important thing is not to know *exactly* what we are expecting, but *to be expecting something.* After that, it's a question of knowing *what kind of thing we are expecting.*

The second rule stems from the first. In order that this programming can continue, we must really be aware of what we are doing, that is to say **be conscious** of ourselves and what is around us. It may sound silly to say that, but most of the time we react without really being there! This is the bad side of that marvellous computer which is our brain; because it allows us to behave in a sometimes quite complicated way as if it were automatically!

How many times has someone talking to you said: "Are you listening to me?". You reply: "But of course" and you repeat what he has said ... but like a robot, because you haven't *really* been listening!

We go to have a wash, do the cooking, often even do the daily shopping without thinking about it. We manage to carry out a number of professional tasks while we ourselves are 'miles away'.

It is clear that if we are not sufficiently attentive to our own life, we will be swept along by it and therefore be vulnerable to its surprises. If, on the other hand, we get a grip on ourselves, we will know at any given time what is happening and we will be ready for what follows.

The third rule in its turn stems from the previous one. When we are aware of what we are doing, we really notice it and register it automatically. Every moment is an experience that adds to the immense store of knowledge we possess. Now, **the more we know** about everything, about life in fact, **the less we meet with the unexpected.** We joke about the person who has seen everything, knows everything and has done everything – and is therefore surprised by nothing. But this is, of course, not true, because there is always something ready to arouse the curiosity of even the most blasé! But without going as far as this, we know that one of the reasons why an adult doesn't suffer the quick changes of emotion that come with the innocence of childhood is HE KNOWS! And it is from on-going observation that experienced people are less susceptible to the risks of any given situation than are the innocent. So we must, at every opportunity, enrich our lives, amass knowledge and live life as an adventure that should leave its mark. This is one way (and agreeable at that) of acquiring the most effective mastery of ourselves.

The fourth rule, finally, emanates from the others: **self-assurance reduces the impact of the unexpected,** whatever it might be. When it is absolutely certain that, whatever happens, we will not be caught on the hop, it is clear that we can expect anything with complete peace of mind.

Let's go back to the example of our friend strapped to the chair. If he does not control himself, his fear and anger will lead him to struggle to free himself in vain. If, on the other hand, he 1) knows (because he has seen it in the cinema, because he has already lived the situation, even in play. . .) that with certain tricks he can free himself, and if he 2) is sure he will manage it (because this certitude is deep-rooted in him), then he stops panicking and reflects on the situation. It's a problem to be resolved and one thing that is very far from being unexpected is the fact that life poses us problems! This one at least has the merit of being original (a little humour does no harm!). Our prisoner looks calmly for a solution ... and he is certain to find it.

◧ ESSENTIAL EXERCISES

Mastering ourselves carries a comforting feeling of reassurance. Our experience tells us that when we are sure we can exercise self-control in any given situation, we can approach it with self-confidence.

The links between mastery of oneself and personal assurance start from around the second year of life. When the young child 'learns' to control his bladder (he asks for the pot and *waits* to be installed on it before releasing what used to arrive on its own!), he feels very proud and happy. But then, a few days later, he displays a degree of self-assurance that upsets family life. He discovers that he can say 'no' and abuses this. He imposes his will (or at least tries to) to see just how far he can go.

I am not proposing exercises in self-assurance; the gain in composure comes with the acquisition of self-control! As for the need always to know more and to safeguard the wealth of all our experiences, I hope that the chapter devoted to memory has trained you in the art of always gathering more information and using the treasures of your knowledge.

It remains for you to acquire 1) the habit of always programming the immediate future; and 2) of 'living consciously', fully, taking account of everything at every moment.

◧ PROGRAMMING EXERCISES

1. Before going to sleep, programme what you are going to do the next day. Invite yourself to live the day in advance, by creating for yourself a little cinema of how things will go. It's a scenario in which you are at one and the same time both actor and audience. With your eyes closed, you are seeing yourself behave and hearing yourself speak.

Try to live several possibilities, even during those dull moments (like: "I meet the big boss in the lift: he says to me ... I say to him..." and "The baker's is shut, so I am going to ...", etc.).

The aim is to get the little cogs in your brain used to these predictions, to the idea of several possibilities, so that during the following day, in the real situation, the programming will occur of its own accord and you will never be taken by surprise. To manage that, you must allow enough time. The best discipline is to play your little programming game systematically every evening before going to sleep, in the same way as you clean your teeth!

2. Make the most of those daily moments of emotional tension to practise.

For example, *waiting times:* while you are waiting for something or someone, practise imagining all that could happen to affect your wait, creating a delay, making what happens different from what you were expecting, etc.

When you have found a cause for the delay or the upset ...., change everything around and 'play with it'. Ask yourself what is the percentage of chances that it will come about, what conditions will make it happen, when and on what occasion have you heard talk of such an eventuality, why it might have taken place and so on.

Fill up your waiting times with an active dialogue with yourself. You will see how the time passes more quickly and, most importantly, that you are waiting in a relaxed mood.

3. Make use of your *failures.* If you have not succeeded in achieving something you wanted, immediately programme yourself that it should be done another time. Analyse what has lead to the failure; and certainly don't start by saying: "I should have ..." but look for the 'because': "That didn't work because ..." and go through what, the next time, you must not do ... and what you should try to do!

Our daily life provides us with its crop of little failures ... once again, we must look on them as such. For example, a missed train, a forgotten letter left in a pocket, toast burned ... The programming effort needed to ensure that these failures don't repeat themselves is very modest! But, to repeat, it is effective and once the brain has got into the habit it will use the method spontaneously in more important situations.

Don't forget that if you can have confidence in yourself not to miss the train, not to forget to post the letter, etc..., you will unconsciously draw from that a feeling of self-assurance, which is the key to self-mastery.

4. Finally, each time you find yourself in a situation of internal conflict, for example, faced with a difficult choice, having to do something you don't agree with, or when you have made a mistake, think of the person strapped to the chair. Don't let yourself be overcome with emotion. Your conflict can be compared to a knot inside you: you are a prisoner of yourself, just like the man in his chair!

Consider the situation as a problem to resolve. Look for solutions, several if possible, and create your programming for each of them: "If I do such-and-such, then that, that and that will happen. I should then do this and this, etc..."

Not only will this help you to find your solution but, killing two birds with one stone, you will have benefited from the advantages of a programming exercise.

◪ 'CONSCIOUSISATION' EXERCISES

Let's remember that with this dreadful sounding word we want to express the fact of living this present moment in a conscious and non-automatic manner.

We say that consciousness is the 'peculiarity of man'. This means that animals don't have it. When they are hungry, they go and hunt for food; fear makes them flee or fight. The sensation produces the action. The human being not only gets hungry and looks for food, but what's more he KNOWS he is hungry and IS CONSCIOUS that what he is doing is looking for food.

We are given this 'bonus' ... but, thanks to automation in every area of today's society, we have less and less need to pay attention during our different activities; so much so that this gift is tending to become superfluous! This awareness of each gesture had a vital role to play when a deadly trap could be waiting behind every tree or rock for our prehistoric ancestors, those poor, defenceless little people. But today, even if the pitfalls are numerous, they don't put our life in danger. So we can let ourselves be guided, led, lifted, carried, protected, fed and even be put to sleep or woken up by the wonders of mechanics, electronics, social organisations or medicines. And so well is this done that we no longer have much need to foresee anything, be attentive or even really be aware of what we are doing!

Of course, this is a bit of an exaggeration; but it is not that far from reality ... And it must stir us into not being seduced by the temptations of technology. We should use these advances, but not be 'ruled' by them. We must continue our completely separate lives as human beings.

What's more, thinking about what we do and how we live is not an exclusive occupation. We can think about what we are doing while we are brushing our teeth, for example: this doesn't stop us from planning our day at the same time. Our brain allows us to THINK about several things at once. Napoleon is said to have written letters, dictated a memo and carried on a conversation all at the same time. And, contrary to what some people like to think, he had no bigger a brain than you or I. Perhaps he knew better how to use the little computer inside the skull?

So we can think about several things at once, but it is necessary that one of these things is exactly what we are in the middle of doing or living at the time. And we must practise this, because it is becoming less and less natural!

1. To begin with, become conscious of your emotional life. Emotions are not always the great shocks that leave us 'disturbed' sometimes for hours after they have first hit us. They can be little upsets, the little moments of joy or irritation . . .

Use a small notepad to jot down in the evening the emotions you felt during the day, even the slightest ones. A few words will suffice for you to remember them again. Also make a note of your reactions: "I shook for a moment . . . I caught my breath . . . I felt myself blushing . . . For a moment I lost the thread of the conversation . . ."

Then, ask yourself why: "Why did I jump? There was apparently no reason at all to be afraid . . .", etc.

2. When you feel you are well 'run-in' with this first exercise, you will discover that already you are spontaneously living your emotions in a more conscious way. You no longer put up with jumping. You say to yourself: "Look! I'm jumping!". And, at the same time, you realise that the feeling of being alarmed diminishes . . .

So try, for at least a couple of weeks, to keep a diary of each day – as complete as possible. One word can suffice for each item, but try hard to recall EVERYTHING you have done and lived – even those visits to the toilet!

Here again you will make some discoveries. After a few days your brain, foreseeing the evening's exercise, will make a note for you of everything that happens. It will be automatically attentive.

And you will be conscious of what you are doing without even having to decide to do it!

ANXIETY
■■■■■■■■■■■

Mastering anxiety starts with work on your body. Even if you do not consciously feel it, physical tension leads to mental tension and blocks any psychological approach to it. So you must force yourself to have a session of relaxation at least once a day (if you know that it is anxiety which dominates you).

In the morning, wake up a quarter-of-an-hour earlier than usual to practise this 'cure'. And if you feel very tense, repeat it in the evening before going to sleep.

↘ RELAXATION
....

Relaxation is a truly psychosomatic exercise, a mental technique that allows you to relax the muscles. This muscular relaxation in its turn affects your mental life. Moreover, you can do it the next time you feel your temper rising: without thinking of anything, force yourself to smile, a real smile and not just a grimace with your lips. You will be surprised to feel an immediate easing and your irritation could even disappear! So, it was only an actor's smile, without any feeling behind it; but the play of muscles was enough to calm you down.

You must prepare your relaxation by first reading carefully the method given here. If you are afraid you might forget all the stages during the session, dictate them into a tape-recorder. You must not interrupt the sequence to go and check the rest of the stages in your notebook.

 – Stretch yourself out completely flat on a comfortable mattress, with a small soft cushion under your head if you feel you need it. Loosen your clothes and take off your shoes. (If you are doing your session in the morning or evening, your dressing-gown is the most appropriate clothing).

 – When you are ready, shut your eyes. Do you feel yourself comfortably settled? Be conscious of the contact between your whole body and the mattress, with your arms stretched out flat and palms of the hands downwards. Start by telling yourself that you feel well.

 – Then concentrate your thoughts on your right foot and

leg. Without making any movement, contract all the muscles in that foot and leg and keep the contraction going to the count of five. Feel all your contracted muscles one after the other. After five good seconds, release the contraction. Feel as much as possible how agreeable it is to relax yourself after the tension. Concentrate your thoughts on this leg, totally soft and relaxed. Try not to feel it at all any more: little by little it no longer weighs on the mattress ... Then stretch your leg as far as possible as if you were trying to reach something at the end of your toes. Maintain this stretching to a slow count of five. Concentrate your thoughts on this leg which is stretching, stretching ... Then release the effort and let the leg become limp and lifeless. You will now feel a gentle heat spread through it, like a kind of well-being in your blood-vessels. This warmth is the sign of successful relaxation, although you may not experience it for the first two or three times ... But once you do, it will happen regularly afterwards.

- Make the most of this feeling of well-being in your right foot and leg for a moment or two. Then do the same thing with the left foot and leg. Concentrate your thoughts on them ... Contract your muscles, foot, leg, as hard as possible while counting slowly up to five ... Relax ... try not to feel them any more ... Then stretch them for a good five seconds. Relax ... Enjoy your sense of well-being.

- Next move on to your upper limbs: first the right arm. Clench the right hand for a good five seconds. Release it. Feel the well-being. Contract all the arm muscles, right up to the shoulder (always remaining motionless). Maintain this contraction while you count up to five, then relax. Feel the pleasure and wait for the sensation of warmth.

- Now do the same with your left arm. Clench the left hand: contract ... Relax ... Feel the pleasure ... Contract all the arm muscles. Hold this contraction for five seconds ... Release ... Feel the well-being and the warmth ...

- Move on now to your trunk. Contract your back and stomach muscles, as if to sink your bottom deep into the mattress (still without moving). Hold the contraction five seconds, then let yourself go all limp like a rag-doll. You will feel a well-being in the pit of your stomach. Make the most of this to breathe gently, enjoying the warmth which runs through you.

- To finish up, move on to the neck. Concentrate your thoughts on the muscles in your neck, so often painfully strained ... You are going to contract your shoulder muscles as if shrugging them and your neck muscles as if you were sinking your head into the pillow. Keep the contraction going for a good five seconds, then relax and roll your head gently from left to right to feel the well-being of this relaxation.

This manoeuvre alone can stop certain types of headache.

Now you have experienced the sensation produced by the contraction and relaxation of your principal body muscles. You are feeling particularly relaxed. With the gentle warmth that accompanies this relaxation, you feel the blood flowing in your muscles and the oxygen reviving them.

You will probably need a week of daily exercising to feel the complete sense of well-being brought about through this method.

Very soon afterwards you will discover that something has happened, as if by magic. You can consider calmly the reasons for your anxiety, formulate them as problems ... and find the solution!

Of course, even if you do manage to master your anxiety effectively, this will not stop it from hitting you at an unexpected moment ... But you have at your disposal two techniques to use during the day, and without anyone noticing provided that you have trained yourself suitably: abdominal breathing and 'mini-relaxation'.

ABDOMINAL BREATHING

Most of us don't know how to breathe. Of course we breathe, but badly! It's a little like insisting on driving a car in second gear, whatever the road conditions, while saying: "I know how to drive, because my car is running." But what does the engine think about it?

Breathing consists of drawing air into the lungs by increasing the capacity of the thoracic cage: that is inhaling; then of releasing this air by compressing the thoracic cage: that is exhaling. For breathing, we have three possibilities:

- **Breathing from the shoulders**
  By shrugging our shoulders, we increase in height the capacity of the thorax. It is a sharp movement accompanying a sudden emotion and is linked with another type of breathing to reinforce the action.

- **Thoracic breathing**
  The distension of the top of the thoracic cage, this is a relatively

rapid and shallow movement. It's the breathing of urgency, of a state of alert (of stress!). And actually, in our western world, it's the normal method of breathing. When the individual's level of tension mounts, the rhythm of movements accelerates without in any way satisfying the physiological needs because these movements are incomplete. This can lead to a sensation of sickness and vertigo – if the accelerated breathing is very marked.

- **Abdominal breathing**
  This type of breathing increases the capacity of the thorax from the bottom. If we push out our stomach, the viscera (internal organs) drop, pulling down the membrane that closes the thoracic cage; this considerably increase its capacity. It is a slow, deep movement, corresponding to a 'cruising' state for those who know how to breathe properly.

Normally, the different types of breathing are programmed to occur according to the individual's needs. But most people strain this system and leave it in a permanent state of 'second gear'! We therefore have to learn how to restore abdominal breathing – first as a practice, when there is no cause for tension, but also consciously to ease our tension. It is, moreover, the first stage in Yoga and Zen meditation training.

To train yourself, take a few minutes several times a day (if not every day, then at least several times a week) until you have mastered the following technique:

  – Lie down flat on your back and put a telephone directory on your stomach on top of your navel. Breathe gently, pushing on your stomach, which will cause the directory to rise with each inhalation. To begin with, you will think about making fuller movements (without exaggeration) than normal. Then, gradually, you will find your rhythm and capacity. When you are quite used to this exercise in a stretched-out position, practise this type of breathing for a minute or two when sitting down and standing up. And you will immediately start feeling the benefit.

Afterwards, as soon as you feel tension coming on, force yourself to breathe like this for a minute or two. No-one will notice it and you will recover your calm.

◨ MINI RELAXATION

This will only work if you have already trained yourself properly to relax, according to the method described above. The aim is to produce, in an 'express' fashion, a feeling of relaxation and physical well-being which will in turn lead automatically to clear thinking.

At work, for example, you can 'switch off' for a few minutes while remaining at your desk – or when you are sitting waiting for a meeting that worries you . . .

– Shut your eyes and concentrate your thoughts on one or other part of your body: the neck, the shoulders and afterwards the hands give the best results. Contract the muscles, leaving the rest of your body relaxed, and maintain this contraction for a good five seconds. Then relax and, still with your eyes shut, enjoy as much as possible the sense of well-being that flows through the part of the body you have contracted. As a result, your whole body will feel relaxed.

– If this is difficult to do, shut your eyes and contract your eyelids as tightly as possible, which will normally induce an overall contraction of your face (rest this in your hands, if necessary, to hide what you are doing!). Hold this contraction for five seconds, thinking as hard as possible about your grimace. Then release it and gently massage your face, especially above and below the eyelids, for a moment or two. This can be enough to ease an apparently irreducible tension. Particularly recommended before an interview or a meeting that promises to be difficult . . .

TEMPERAMENT

Contrary to what people often believe, we are not helpless against our own temperament. We can influence it by knowing how to tackle it.

A lot of parents do this automatically with their children when they repeat to them, for example: "Look how happy you are! You really are lucky! You have Mummy and Daddy next to you and you've got your sandpit and swing! Everything's fine! You can run about and play with the ball! Everyone's happy!" And the little boy (or girl) who was about to burst out crying, is carried along with this and starts instead to laugh and clap his hands in glee, singing to himself: "I'm happy, I'm happy". How could he possibly cry when he says: "I'm happy"? Without realising it, the parents have adopted a LOGICAL method of affecting the child's mood. They have made him CONSCIOUS of the REASONS he has to be happy.

In effect, our mood adapts automatically to the way we are living or to what we are giving to what we are living.

If, for example, I believe that I am a failure, that I will never be successful, this is a quite natural reason for being in a grumpy mood! Moreover, if I feel myself to be a failure, I only see failures around me. The whole world is in distress and that only increases my pessimism.

On the other hand, if I tell myself it's a real achievement at my age to cycle 30 miles every Sunday morning, then my humour is well set on the right path. It's good to look on the bright side from time to time. We all have a lot to be positive about, but we find these things so natural that we forget they exist!

MASTERY OF MOOD LIES WITH THE ART OF FINDING REASONS TO BE IN A GOOD HUMOUR

(Here we are only considering the ways of getting back into a good mood. Controlling an over-optimistic or excessively exuberant humour is a question for the medical specialists.)

When you feel low or even in a really foul mood, there are several ways of recovering your humour.

▰ GENTLE METHODS FOR THOSE A LITTLE CHEESED OFF

• **The miser and his treasure**
I make reference to this, because it's a question of looking on the bright side, at what's 'good'. This can be material things, but what gives the most pleasure are moral possessions: qualities ("Those no-one can take from me!"), past successes, actual abilities – sporting, intellectual, social, etc.

It's true that we must think about them consciously and even force ourselves to look for this 'treasure' because, particularly when we are feeling a little bit depressed, we have a tendency to black out all the good things. We can even make ourselves write a list of all the good things we have! And when we have all these positive things in front of us, we can give ourselves a moment for feeding on them, to enjoy a good session of self-satisfaction.

There is nothing immoral in enjoying (privately) the good side of ourselves. That can only reinforce the positive elements. What is conceited is to refuse to see them; because this amounts to false modesty.

- **The mote and the beam**

Compare your situation with that of a serious event (earthquake, deadly disease . . .). Certainly none of our reasons for being in a bad mood bear comparison with what inhabitants of some other countries, whether near or far, are suffering. Such a comparison puts the finger on how lucky we are to be protected from such disasters. And that makes us feel a lot better!

I can cite the example of someone who has overcome an irrepressible tendency to depression by working for Amnesty International. The documents with which she is regularly confronted release in her the most powerful indignation you could imagine. This translates itself like an injection of the clear dynamism of the struggle which has swept away all her earlier uncertainty of mood!

- **Humour**

Humour is an excellent therapy, particularly against bad things. Stand back from yourself and think about how many of your sad recriminations could make you laugh if they were mimicked by a comedian. With a little bit of will-power, you can make yourself laugh at them as if you were watching a comedy act on television.

◪ A MORE ELABORATE METHOD

If your pessimism is really deeply rooted and the gentle methods already mentioned have left you shrugging your shoulders, then you must really get down to the question.

The principle is to consider this bad humour as **a problem** and to set yourself the task, eventually stretching over several weeks, of **resolving the problem**.

- Look for all the reasons for this attitude (list, eventual grouping of items) and formulate the discomfort in terms of the problem to be resolved: "I am depressed, pessimistic, etc. What is the problem?"

- Study what surrounds the discomfort:
  - situations and people involved in the causes of my discomfort.
  - situations and people suffering because of my discomfort.

- Create a UTOPIA, which will be a situation in which I should feel optimistic:
  - make a list of the functions of such a situation (I expect such-and-such a thing ...).
  - compare the actual situation, element by element, with that of the utopia.

- Look for some solutions:
  - choose the best solution.
  - devise a plan for putting it into operation.

CHAPTER FIVE

COPING
WITH
STRESS

C an we really say when stress entered our modern way of life? The age of stress imposed itself too quickly for us to really know what was happening or even realise to what degree our everyday life was upset compared to what it had been ten or even five years ago ...

We certainly talk about it. The word 'stress' is used more and more in the media and in everyday conversation. But we still don't really know what lies beneath this word. We defend ourselves against it as best we can, sometimes successfully and other times not.

The 'stress-related' illnesses that were a novelty for doctors fifty years ago are already very different from those of that period and affect more than half today's active population. It is therefore certainly time to face up to this curse and to take effective measures against it. Even before we understood about microbes, when a plague threatened we knew what measures to take to minimise the disastrous consequences. In cold countries, all the houses are fitted with double-glazing, while in the desert the Berbers protect themselves from the heat by wearing the heavy woollen burnous. Those societies that have been victims of disasters have succeeded in defending themselves – even if not completely, then at least partially.

Stress is, for our civilisation, like a plague or a famine was for our ancestors! Some people manage somehow or other so that it doesn't destroy them. We are starting to find ways of defending ourselves. We must know what they are, use them and spread the word!

What we tell ourselves

We say very readily and at any opportunity: "I'm under stress." Whether it's a child who can't cope with the test in class, someone having an argument with a colleague at work, a housewife letting her cake burn in the oven or a person fed up with taking public transport to go to work every day, we say: "It's stress".

But by using THE WORD so commonly in this way, we end up forgetting that it can have a precise significance. Emotions, which we spoke about in the previous chapter, are clearly not stresses. The schoolchild's 2 out of 20, or the burnt cake, can only be unexpected hiccups which create a state of emotion that lasts minutes rather than hours! But we are so used to being 'on the rails', driven by the automation of today's society which is so marvellously ruled by technology, that the slightest emotion – that unexpected little event which can in an instant plunge us into a feeling of uncertainty – becomes a real threat. What ten years ago provoked a slight overheating is today felt as completely destabilising!

We also say that the whole world is under stress. We can see it, we can hear it; the problem is universal, so there's no reason why we should escape it. So let's resign ourselves to it. What's more, there are so many things we have to resign ourselves to today in order to survive, that one more isn't going to make any difference!

We can add that there is every reason in the world to be stressed. The competition for survival is becoming harder and harder. Our needs grow and the conditions we have to fulfil to satisfy them are more and more unattainable. Changes, in every aspect of life, take place more and more rapidly. We don't have the time to adjust or to get used to things. We have to adapt to different techniques, different situations. We now have to be for ever on the go ...

And, what's more, the media make us live all the world's catastrophes the moment they happen. Gone are the days when we would only be disturbed once a week by the weekend's road casualty figures! Now we have to share our supper every evening with a helping of murderous guerrilla attacks somewhere in the world, the latest figures on the victims of an earthquake ...

In brief, we tell ourselves: "It's an inescapable sickness of our civilisation." And we reflect how fortunate we are to have recourse to tranquillisers! And if those don't do the trick, then we'll have to fight this mythical enemy until we die. Or, as has become popular with the younger generation, 'drop out'. But certainly don't make any ripples!

So we learn to resign ourselves and do and wish for as little as possible. But the whole nature of our being is to LIVE, and withdrawing from it leaves the way wide open for all the different psychosomatic problems to attack us.

It is therefore high time to say: "Enough is enough. Let's do something!"

WHAT IS STRESS?

S tress is a **state created by an aggressive situation.** On a mental level, it's a feeling of tension, of a rush of jumbled ideas. Physically, it's a collection of metabolic and visceral changes. If it is intense or lasting, it leads to various illnesses and/or neurotic complaints.

The parts of the body most susceptible to stress, apart from the nervous system, are the cardio-vascular apparatus (hypertension, vascular sclerosis ...), the digestive tract and its associated glands (sluggishness, dullness, indigestion, pains, gastric ulcers, colic irritation, constipation and disturbed digestion leading to nutritional deficiencies ...) and the neuro-hormonal reproductive system (trouble with menstruation, spermatogenesis, sexual difficulties ...). But we also call 'stress' the aggression itself that brings on these disorders.

And then, finally, stress can be defined as the pair formed by the aggravation AND the reaction to that aggravation.

- There are **two types of stress:**
Certain stress releases a biological – or **emergency – reaction.** This is essentially a discharge of adrenaline, and similar hormones, into the body and the brain. That leads to an increase in the cardiac and respiratory rhythms and a continuum of biological reactions accompanied by a feeling of alertness, of urgency. The entire mind and body is modified as it prepares for an unusual, violent action in order to survive.

These discharges don't last very long, their effect wearing off within an hour or two . . . But they can be repeated at more or less frequent intervals. Some people can experience this type of stress in an almost uninterrupted succession of states of emergency.

Clearly fast repetition of this kind of hormonal and metabolic reaction is not without worrying consequences. Biologically, there comes a moment when the body no longer produces enough of these adrenal hormones, which are needed in appropriate doses in the brain to guarantee to maintain our good humour, dynamism and normal levels of desires and aspirations. And they do this so well that any lack of the correct hormonal mixture leads to depression, introversion and indifference.

But too frequent a repetition of emergency reactions can also lead to an abnormal increase in sensitivity; so much so that for those who are in this situation the least stimulation becomes stress. And so one arrives at a most damaging vicious circle.

The other type of stress releases what is sometimes known as the **adaptation reaction.** Here the discharged hormones are all connected with cortisone. The effect of the changes caused by these cortisonal discharges is to make the body set up reaction systems adapted for long periods – several months or more. It is as if it was preparing itself for a state of siege!

As in the previous case, this type of stress produces both physical and mental energy, but of a less violent kind. The body's exhaustion appears more slowly than before, due to a change in the adrenocortical gland which produces cortisone. This exhaustion leads to very specific illnesses, those that are otherwise called 'illnesses of adaptation'. In comparison with the everyday (yet sometimes serious) problems caused by the state of stress, these are rare.

• Aggravation is only stressful if the person affected considers it as such. As a result, we can say that **stress is in the mind.**

During one of the public transport strikes some years ago, the television showed interviews with passengers reduced to walking to work instead of taking the bus or tube. One of the them was complaining, saying: "It's a real stress!", while others looked on the bright side: "It's a chance to walk a bit and to see places I don't normally get the opportunity to see. It's not so bad!" Nevertheless, looked at objectively, all strikes cause disruption, as irritating for one person as for others. So it is not the strike which is stressful, but what different people make of it! So what can one say of stress that we create from all sorts of situations, without there even being any objective aggravation as a root cause? It can, for example, boil down to the suffering one feels from not being 'properly considered' or again to the anger that stirs inside when one can no longer put up with the mother-in-law living in the same house, despite the fact that from an objective point of view all is working well: her presence has numerous advantages . . .

But it is not only the way of considering an aggression that makes it a stress or not. The way in which we react to it is also very important. In fact, the person who complains of having to make his journey on foot (during the strike) does it with his anger repressed. He breathes too quickly and badly, walks all tensed up and risks twisting an ankle. At the end of his journey he obviously arrives worn out! This reaction is stress. For others, this healthy and pleasant walk provides them with extra energy, the equivalent of a good dose of vitamins!

• **Stress can be good**

This difference in how we each react is clearly the proof that aggravation cannot in itself be either good or bad. If we react negatively, it becomes bad. But if we handle it well, it becomes beneficial.

In fact, all aggravation produces a reaction, an increase and often a momentary change in mental and physical activity. These modifications are made possible by the hormonal secretions released by the aggravating situation. And these hormonal discharges generate the internal release of energy. When this energy is used in an action *with which the person concerned agrees*, the energy build-up and the biological movements accompanying the action provide the body with a boost of youthful vigour. This is 'good stress'.

It is therefore in the brain that the switch occurs between favourable and harmful stress reactions – and causes of illness. And we will see that the management of stress consists not in suppressing it but in drawing from it all the dynamic benefit we can.

Finally stress, the 'bad stress', can be defined as an **aggravation against which we cannot defend ourselves.** We could almost say, more simply: **"To be stressed is to be trapped".** As long as one struggles with some chance of escaping, everything is all right. If there appears to be no way out of the situation, the energy released by the aggravation is spent in vain, in futile efforts. Since the body does not use this energy, it finds itself overlooked and the biological systems seriously upset. This physical suffering is doubled by the fact that one devalues oneself and, as a result, the feeling of insecurity increases. "I'm not capable. . . I'm a failure or an unfortunate victim. . ."

WHAT CAN CAUSE STRESS?

When one realises that each of us can make anything a reason for stress, it's possible to say that everything can cause stress and that there can be nothing in particular about stressful aggravation. In fact, it can be something as objective and material as the loss of a job or it can be totally mental, as some might say, imaginary. That would be the situation, for example, of a person who, coming from a family that was very religious and deeply attached to tradition, declared himself a materialist and joined the Communist Party. Such a person could well suffer from a nagging feeling of guilt: "I have betrayed my own . . . But if I tried to be like them, I would be betraying myself!".

So, causes of stress are many and varied. Nevertheless, an indepth study has come up with a group of categories which are useful for us to get an angle on the whole subject when we decide to manage our own stress.

Interruptions and changes

We have already talked about the thread that runs through most people's lives: a chain of habits in every area of our existence.

162

Each of us gradually creates our habits and, conversely, we are affected by them. This way of existing is a reassuring necessity, faced with the growing chaos that apparently marks societies the world over. These habits provide a framework as much for our professional life (the little idiosyncrasies, the mannerisms, the rituals . . .) as for our personal and family life: kissing our spouse on the cheek, the glance at the children's school exercise books (we don't always have the time to look at them properly, but we make the gesture . . .), etc. All these gestures, these words, repeated every day, overlap like bricks in a wall. Any change, even if chosen voluntarily, starts by toppling everything as if we had removed a brick from the middle of the wall. It's always an aggravation and we can find ourselves sadly de-stabilised by it ('bad stress') or stimulated to find a new equilibrium ('good stress').

The phrase (habitual!) among those who react badly to interruptions – and we have surely all heard it, if not said it ourselves! – is: "It's not like it was any more . . . I can't manage to do it!"

Constraints

Nothing is more unbearable than to be prevented from doing what we want, unless it is to be forced to do something we don't want! This happens so often that no further comment is needed!

Frustrations

The links each of us have with frustration go back to the earliest years of childhood. Education from the most tender of ages is an apprenticeship – more or less skilfully taught by both teachers and parents – in frustration. We have been longing to go to the circus . . . and bang, the day before the great event we have done something stupid we shouldn't have and that's blown our treat!

Over the years, we have had to train ourselves, with more or less good face, to overcome our disappointments and look for the compensations. Nevertheless, as mature adults, we still very often find ourselves affected by frustrating situations. This type of stress hits us in one of a couple of ways:

- There is an apparently unbridgeable gap between our hopes, our expectations and reality.

- We haven't the means to fulfil our ambitions. "I want to, but I can't!"

Conflicts

A conflict results from two opposing forces: one wants to go right, the other left. While the tension between these two opposites lasts, the stress of the conflict continues. But if, finally, one side carries the day and it is not the one we expected, then we are obliged to behave in a way with which we don't agree. Thus stress of conflict becomes stress of constraint. Or we remain bitter at having finally been beaten, and stress of conflict becomes stress of frustration . . .

- The conflict can be 'external' when it places us in opposition to others in a family, professional or social context. Let's be clear that a stressful conflict is not a simple discussion, not even a stormy one. It is a state of fact which makes us live in a permanent situation of conflict.

- The conflict can be 'internal' when we are torn between two tendencies, obliged to live a contradictory situation. The best example is when we are obliged to choose between our desire and our duty. It can also amount to the apparently impossible option between two desires or two duties . . .

Threats

When we fear aggression, we are a lot more stressed than when it appears and we can face it. At least we then know what we have to tackle!

This experience, which we have certainly all felt, is in perfect harmony with the biological mechanisms of stress. It only becomes beneficial when we react effectively and actively against the stressful aggression.

But in order to react, we must still have something to react against! The threat is not a reality; it's only an immaterial evocation of it. Shipwrecked victims may not die from drowning, which would be the sea's aggression, but from fear, which is the threat of drowning . . . And in fact it seems that the stress of a shipwreck releases, even among those who can barely swim, a phenomenal energy which enables them to swim for an incredibly long time. A victim may die from fear when this energy turns against the person and obstructs his heart . . .

The Chinese water-drop torture

Small repetitive aggravations are terribly insidious, too unimportant to react against and therefore too easy to resign ourselves to. So we let ourselves suffer from them . . . But, over a period of time, these irritants can fester and transform themselves into real sores! Something wears away in us and, when we finally take notice of it, it becomes difficult to find a solution.

It's like the small stone in the rambler's shoe. With those thick woollen socks, it's hardly an irritation. But, by the end of the day, the heel is bleeding, the calf muscles are smarting with cramp and the prospects for the next day are painful!

⊠ EXERCISE

Reading all this, you will most certainly have realised that you must at some time have suffered from stress without having identified it as such . . . Or if you have been aware of being stressed, you haven't clearly seen what caused it.

To handle this situation effectively, you must know what the cause is. From now on, practise reflecting on your stresses, both past and current, and class them in one or other of the categories already discussed.

⊠ QUESTIONNAIRE

	never 0	a little 1	often 2	always 3
1. *Do you consider yourself stressed?*				
2. *Do you feel an unexplained mental fatigue, do you have difficulty in concentrating?*				

	never 0	a little 1	often 2	always 3
3. *Are you very quickly bored with what you do? Do you frequently need to change what you're doing? Are you a systematic 'flicker' between TV channels?*				
4. *Have you the feeling of never having the time, of always having to run and of being in a hurry?*				
5. *Do you feel obliged to play a role? Do you force yourself to say (even if you don't think it): "I don't have a problem"?*				
6. *Do you always feel in competition in all situations, even family ones?*				
7. *Do you drink more alcohol than normal?*				
8. *Tobacco?*				
9. *Tea or coffee?*				
10. *Do you take 'comforting medicines' (tranquillisers, laxatives, indigestion tablets)?*				
11. *Do you feel that jobs accumulate and you never get to the end of them?*				
12. *Do you feel that you can never really relax?*				

COMMENTARY

This questionnaire can only provide you with some indications. If you do not recognise yourself in the results, take some time to reflect, quite simply, on your situation as regards stress. A careful and honest look at yourself is an excellent way of making the point to yourself!

0-12:   You are hardly stressed at all. Do you lead a protected life or have you mastered your situation very well?

13-20:   You live 'on the edge', which is normal for a fully active person ... If not, have you some badly handled difficulties?

21-30:   It's stress, in the normal sense of the word. You feel overwrought or a prisoner of your difficulties.

Over 30:   Your difficulties are probably so overwhelming you can no longer face them. Before attempting any personal training, you should perhaps seek the help of a doctor ...

Your handicap

Studying the difficulties of thousands of people, I have noticed that certain conditions predispose us to stress. That is to say they encourage us to live, as stress, incidents that we would otherwise overcome quite readily.

Statistical studies have even enabled us to understand the relative weight of some of these situations, which constitute a basic handicap. We must recognise them in order to place ourselves in the right position against life's many possible aggravations.

- **items +++**
- death of the spouse
- divorce
- marriage break-down
- criminal conviction
- death of a close relative
- accident or serious illness
- recent marriage
- redundancy
- infidelity of spouse
- burglary

- **items ++**
- return to ordinary life after a separation
- taking retirement

- sexual difficulties
- change in professional status
- change in financial situation
- death of a close friend
- change of job
- change in marriage relationship

- **items +**
- bills to pay for hire purchase
- changes in professional responsibility
- departure or marriage of a child
- difficulties with mother-in-law
- change of spouse's job
- difficulties with boss
- change of home
- decision on hire purchase
- holidays
- small illegalities (papers not in order, fines not paid, etc.)
- change of social relations

Don't be surprised that certain items, like 'marriage' or 'holidays' are considered as stress factors. First of all, the statistics have shown it, but also, even if these are happy circumstances, they are times when we have to alter our habits!

So work out your handicap, which is based on the number of +s you have scored depending on what items you have found that concern you. A handicap, even a heavy one, is not a condemnation. It is down to you to be more vigilant. Better than that no-one should have a handicap is that you should train yourself to cope automatically with all those stressful situations.

COPING WITH STRESS

S tress is at the same time the aggravation AND the way in which we react to it. To cope with it, we need to control its cause, but also the person who lives with stress, that is to say ourselves.

The person faced with stress

When we are caught in a stressful situation, we suffer at the same time being a victim of our situation and feeling that we are no longer master of anything, particularly ourselves. This feeling of insecurity, especially if it is repeated, lowers our self-esteem. We cheapen ourselves and no longer know how to be assertive.

In order to cope with stress, even more than controlling ourselves during moments of emotion, we must be the captain of our own ship, self-assured in the face of events in so far as they concern ourselves.

You should therefore begin by practising to increase your self-confidence (we never have too much!), jotting down in your notebook your characteristics in three essential areas:

- Your physical self
- The image others have of you
- Your moral self

PHYSICAL STATEMENT
■■■■■■■■■■■■■■■■■■■■■■■■■■■■■

–   Are you subject to **illnesses** that upset your activities? Do you know your weak areas: heart, respiratory systems, digestion, etc? If the answer is yes, then make a note of your weak points so that you can always take account of them. This consists of finding strategies that dispense with those skills that you lack ... Don't forget that one-legged people go skiing and that the hard of hearing have a sign language which is superior to all national languages because it is universal! So whatever your weaknesses, don't consider these as shortcomings, but only as the need to be more crafty than the others.

If you have never had a real illness, jot down: *good physical health.*

–   Do **you fall asleep** spontaneously as soon as you switch off the light? Or do you need your personal nightly rituals, like watching some television or reading a thriller? Or do you have to take sleeping pills?

If the first, clearly jot down: *good physical health.*

If the second, jot down: *good adaptation* (in effect, you knew how to adapt to get round your difficulty).

169

In the third case, make a note of your weakness. It will be useful to get to the bottom of the reasons for your need of sleeping pills. Start by asking yourself if, when on holiday, you can sleep without your pills. If yes, that shows you have a stressful tension as far as your professional life is concerned (or what surrounds it: journeys, for example . . .). You are going to make it a priority to tackle this problem. Otherwise, make the point with your doctor.

- Your **appetite** and **digestion:** everything all right? Jot down: *good health.*

You are subject to unreasonable pangs of hunger and guzzle just about anything? Before thinking about a psychological cause, ask the opinion of your doctor. Perhaps you have a metabolic imbalance that needs to be corrected. . . You have absolutely no appetite and always have to force yourself to show willing at table? See your doctor.

You nibble sweets between meals? Jot down: *lack of self-control.* And take a grip on yourself.

You take a long time to digest food, which weighs on you and makes you sleepy? Perhaps you have eaten when you were under tension, in a hurry or feeling uncomfortable. Or have you chosen a menu outside your normal diet? Take the time to think about this problem. Look for the best dietary conditions and put these into practice. And jot down: *sensitive digestion.*

- Being **physically active** is very important to you and you grab every possible opportunity? You avoid lifts and you practise some form of gymnastics or sport quite regularly? Jot down: *good physical health.*

On the contrary, you avoid the least effort and you get out of breath quickly. Check with your doctor. If he finds you have a heart or breathing weakness, make a note of this. If, according to him, everything is okay, all you lack is some exercise. Jot down: *in need of physical exercise.*

- Your **sexual activities** pose absolutely no problem. Jot down: *good health.*

You have no – or practically no – sex life and you put up with that. Take some time to ask yourself questions on the subject. Is it tiredness, the lack of desire, the absence of a partner – and the absence of desire to meet someone. . .? Whatever the results of your reflection, you must either find an adapted mode of behaviour or talk with yourself until you reach a satisfactory conclusion, without any reticence! And jot down: *low sex drive.*

At the end of these questions, you can appreciate the importance of your 'good health' and characterise your weaknesses. You should take account of these in your final plan of action.

THE IMAGE GIVEN TO OTHERS

We are constantly interacting with other people, professionally, but even more personally and socially. Even if we believe in relatively cool relationships, there is always an emotional hint in what happens between human beings. They hurt us, they deceive us and most often, without us always being conscious of it, they help us. The question: "What am I to them?" is central, because from the answer stems your feeling of being able – or unable – to count on them.

Ask yourself if, in general, you are 'popular', someone people like, easily, straightaway … Are you tolerant (accept that others have tastes, opinions, customs, different from yours)? Are you touchy? Aggressive? Are you sociable (someone who talks freely to other passengers or people waiting in a queue)? Are you difficult ("I don't like youngsters, red-heads, people who don't speak properly, etc.")?

At the end of this reflection, create a small quick portrait of the way in which others see you – which will clearly not correspond to what you think of yourself. One says that clowns are sad. But we always see them laughing! Perhaps like the clown you feel yourself to be melancholic. But for others, you could well be the life and soul of the party!

You must know how you appear to other people, because they can have an essential anti-stress role to play. But very often you have to ask … And, to know how to ask, and get back what you need, you have to know what others think of you!

THE IDEA OF ONESELF

It is very difficult to know oneself … Even a lifetime isn't long enough!

We propose only a little test using headings as pointers to your character. Below is a list of epithets and you have to underline the one that is most appropriate for you. Think carefully, because you must only choose one! If there are several that seem to apply to you, underline them in pencil but afterwards choose the one that is really your personal `stamp`.

a.	anxious	k.	happy
b.	easy-going	l.	nervous
c.	sad	m.	excessive
d.	obliging	n.	quiet
e.	grumpy	o.	strong
f.	enthusiastic	p.	self-assured
g.	joyful	q.	morbid
h.	reliable	r.	unlucky
i.	aggressive	s.	unsociable
j.	impatient	t.	sociable

These epithets denote five traits or tendencies of your personality. They have been defined after statistical studies carried out on a large number of `guinea-pigs`.

If you have several words belonging to the same group underlined in pencil, that only reinforces the significance of the trait revealed by the questionnaire.

- **1st group: a-i-j-l**

You live in a state of tension that is harmful for your health as well as your morale. You know it and have a tendency to resign yourself to it. That implies a reduction in your control over your own existence: you accept – for want of something better – being cornered by life. It`s time to react!

- **2nd group: c-e-q-r**

You clearly have a depressive tendency. Perhaps you are so used to it that you haven`t been conscious of it. That`s what`s happened, so now you must react!

- **3rd group: d-p-s**

Relations with others are very important for you. If you have underlined the answer `s`, it shows in addition that you are not getting the satisfaction you expect from your relationships (we are never `unsociable`; it`s a defence against deception . . .). But you gain nothing by turning your back. Look to make yourself `popular`.

- **4th group: f-g-m-t**

Your good humour seems well fixed. At least you tell yourself so ... And that surely produces results. But, especially if you have replied 'm' and 't', ask yourself if you haven't gone a little too far? It would perhaps be worth the effort, when you have a moment to think about yourself, to delve more deeply into your reasons for optimism. If they are genuine, your examination can only strengthen them. If not, you will avoid an underlying tension ... and perhaps you will find some real reasons for optimism.

- **5th group: b-h-k-n-o**

You feel in complete accord with yourself, and so very likely with what is around you. Whatever the aggression you have to face up to, you can count on your own solid confidence.

Keeping yourself fit in preparation for coping with stress

The personal attitude required to prevent stress is summed up in three instructions:

- Maintain the body in good condition
- Keep a good image of yourself
- Encourage good relationships with others.

THE BODY IN GOOD CONDITION

To say that one looks after one's body is an outward way of expressing one's thoughts, because the body and the mind are such a closely knit unit that if I think: "The weather's fine this morning", certain hormones are secreted in my brain. And we must all know how much a little physical exercise can improve the spirits.

1. If you suffer anxieties, weaknesses or physical difficulties, don't hesitate to talk to your doctor about them. Ask him for explanations and understand the significance of his advice. For it's you, first and foremost, who looks after yourself with, eventually, the technical advice of the professional.

173

Know the numbers you have to know: arterial pressure, level of urea and sugar in the blood, etc. Don't put up with those 'little troubles' by telling yourself that you haven't the time to spend on them (constipation, toothache, back pains . . .).

2. Practise relaxation. Practise it regularly in periods of tension. Practise abdominal breathing and think about using it during the day, as soon as you feel yourself tensing up.

Go out of your way to practise some physical exercises regularly, the ideal being daily aerobics. Seize every opportunity each day to 'move about': journeys on foot, climbing stairs, short runs . . .

3. Pause-flash and mini-relaxation. In a tense situation, waiting in anticipation of a difficult moment, or in the event of a break during the day, make use of one or other of these techniques.

The pause-flash consists of completely stopping, what you are doing for a few minutes: intense work, difficult meeting . . . You decide on or you ask for a few minutes' break, even if the meeting is in full flow . . . No point in waiting for it to finish, because the tension or fatigue will produce nothing worthwhile. And, as for your colleagues, everybody is probably feeling the same way.

You can make the most of this break to isolate yourself, at least mentally, and empty your mind. Shut your eyes and THINK OF NOTHING. You will easily succeed if you have mastered the habit of relaxation, which provides the practice for this mental trick.

You can profit from a pause-flash to practise a mini-relaxation.

4. Eating well is an art . . . of living! Of course you must educate yourself in the basics of diet (quantities of protein, minerals, vitamins, etc.) and keep an eye on the nutritional balance of what you eat during the day. But, most importantly, you must be in complete agreement with yourself. Don't feel obliged to eat just to 'please' when you're not hungry, or to put yourself on a slimming, anti-cholesterol or whatever else diet without really understanding the principles involved. And, on this subject, watch out for fashion!

The atmosphere of your meal is more important than what you eat. If you are in a hurry or tensed up, you'll spoil the meal for yourself and everyone else, without even having had the pleasure of eating those 'forbidden delights'!

Know how to make your meals, whatever the situation, moments of pleasure. With business lunches, compensate for the professional tension by eating light food. And keep your richer dishes for those happily relaxing occasions with the family or among friends.

Wage war on the 'useless' extras. That starts with the salt and the sugar, which you add without thinking and before even tasting. But also the accumulation of *hors-d'oeuvres*, the desserts, the cheese on top of the main dish which very often constitutes a meal all in itself.

Alcohol, tobacco and the rest ... Why do we consider the aperitif obligatory? To prove that one is a man? That dates us a bit, doesn't it? Do you really hold the view that 'a meal without wine is like a day without sun'? If we really appreciate the taste of a good glass of wine, it would be criminal to deprive ourselves of it ... But let's own up that most of the time we swallow table wine for lots of reasons other than a gourmet's pleasure – and for bad reasons, at that. And the liqueur? How could we dare taste a glass of fine port other than in the comfort of an armchair on a Sunday, with a good cigar, in an atmosphere of complete serenity, which is indispensable for such a refined pleasure? And what about the quick drink at the bar on the way home? That amounts to admitting failure in the face of the difficulties of life. We don't solve anything with cheap drinks. Abusing one's health never improves the situation!

Tobacco should purely and simply be banned. The satisfaction it brings is due to the imagination, which can itself secrete 'pleasure' hormones in the brain ... But it is too dear a price to pay. We should find other reasons for pleasure!

It is useless to go on about this subject, which is well known to everyone. I will simply refer those readers who feel suitable concerned to the paragraphs in Chapter 1 which were dedicated to the techniques of cutting the smoking habit.

5.   Leisure. Learn how to seize and use this time well. It need only be short, but to a rhythm that suits you. The tension that accompanies stress almost always fuels itself in a vicious circle: leisure activities have every chance of breaking this.

It's not as easy as it seems to know how to use leisure time properly. You must be at ease with yourself in order to do it. It amounts not so much to a moment of rest as a period of FREEDOM. You must know how to do what you wish to do. What if the family have different ideas? So be it. That's a problem that must be resolved and the solution has to respond to your desire without making you feel guilty ...

A GOOD IMAGE OF YOURSELF: THE INNER DISCUSSION
■■■

In order to judge yourself in a positive way, which allows you to assert your authority effectively, the study you have just made and noted is certainly useful. But it is not enough. Life flows on and with it runs ceaselessly, like the running river, our own internal monologue. Have you noticed it? Just very occasionally it is noticeable, with someone who is very tired: he talks out loud! Most of the time it's a question of our train of thought. It sometimes involves what we are in the middle of doing: "I'm turning the switch to the left ... the blue light has come on ... now I'm pressing the button marked 'on'..." etc. Most often these thoughts concern ourselves. "Clearly, they haven't taken me seriously ... As for tomorrow, I'm certainly not going to make it ... I'm tired; I must be getting old ... In any case, it's not working ..."

This discussion is far from being harmless. It attacks us insidiously like erosion or termites. This has been proved in experiments. Clearly it would. The inner discourse works by repetition, just below the level of the conscious, like subliminal advertising! But we can prevent it from taking hold by first of all being attentive to ourselves and by being really conscious of what we are saying, as well as making sure we immediately follow any disparaging remark with a positive comment. This too, by repeating itself automatically, will make its way into the deepest levels of our beings and will strengthen our opinion of ourselves. Gradually the critical downbeat themes will disappear from our inner discourse all by themselves.

The most common self-critical phrases and their 'anti-stress'

1. *Things or people upset me.*
Perhaps you don't put it exactly like this, but you think it and you say it in your own way.

- **The anti-stress discourse**

It is essential not to take the passive position, even in speech. Thus these are not things that affect me but ME LETTING MYSELF BE UPSET.

Evidence of failure, you might say? Certainly, but a failure that depends on ME and not other people or other things!

From the moment when it depends on me, I can do something. With the internal monologue, we don't really reflect and the ideas flow all on their own. So it is not the moment to say to ourselves: "I can do something: let's think what!" Instead you should simply let this notion that YOU CAN DO something impress itself on you.

2. *I'm half pleased with my success, but I did fail on . . .*
Of course it's motivational to be demanding with oneself. But be careful about the way in which you formulate this. If you are half pleased, it's because you know you can do better.

- **The anti-stress discourse**

What you must take note of, first of all, is satisfaction (the reward) and the project, with the assurance of success. I AM HAPPY TO HAVE ALREADY SUCCEEDED THIS FAR. THAT'S PROGRESS AND I KNOW IT'S GOING TO CONTINUE.

3. *I am as I am. I can't do anything about it.*
This is the admission of resignation *par excellence!* And it's wrong. We change all the time; the whole world changes! What happens on its own can also be controlled. We can master the change and lead it in the direction we want.

- **The anti-stress discourse**

You must immediately tear yourself from the statement you have just made and note down: I HAVE SUCH-AND-SUCH WEAK POINTS? YES, BUT I ALSO HAVE SUCH-AND-SUCH STRONG POINTS. IT'S UP TO ME TO MAKE USE OF THEM. And continue your monologue: "With what I have – or thanks to what I have – I'm not so bad!".

4. *I have such-and-such a weakness. It's hereditary. My mother (or father) was like me.*
To see that we have such-and-such a weakness is an incentive to struggle against it. But in saying that it's hereditary, we are hiding

behind our fate. We say: "I can't do anything about it!". That's false. Because even hereditary tendencies – and scientifically we don't really know what the notion of a hereditary tendency means – can be altered through education.

A great philosopher once said that education can do everything, since it even makes the bears dance! And education doesn't content itself with what parents or teachers practise. We educate ourselves (or are able to do so) all our lives.

- **The anti-stress discourse**
I AM WHAT I MAKE MYSELF.

Our most frequent gestures mould our muscles and this is particularly true for the face. Optimism, even if it doesn't manifest itself in a permanent smile, has a tendency to contract the muscles that lift the corners of the mouth. People with a good humour have upturned mouths.

5. *I don't understand what's happening to me. It beats me!*
This again is an admission of impotence, which means we don't feel we can foresee the path our own existence is taking. We just accept it as a state of fact. Totally passive resignation is, in itself, already a stress. But, what's more, every admission of impotence is an attack on our self-confidence. It always chips away at it that little bit more.

- **The anti-stress discourse**
MY BRAIN IS EQUIPPED TO CONTROL WHAT HAPPENS AND TO FORESEE IT.

If you have trained yourself to control your emotions, you have learned to live every moment consciously and to automatically programme your existence. If you haven't, you always could!

6. *It's horrible, I won't be able to stand it.*
First of all, mistrust superlatives. Few circumstances really present a horror. A meal slightly burnt may be annoying, but it's not 'horrible'!

Next, you certainly can put up with it. Human beings have clearly proved that they were able to put up with things so abominable that, quite obviously, we as fellow human beings, no more and no less, can face up to what happens to us (probably nothing like the 'horrors' that we regularly watch on our television screens . . .).

- **The anti-stress discourse**

TO START WITH I'M EXAGGERATING. IT'S ONLY
ANNOYING. AND I'VE SEEN OTHER EXAMPLES OF IT.

Think back to previous challenges. In some cases you came
through all right, didn't you? And this time you failed . . . so much
the better, because now you know what you shouldn't do!

7. *Other people don't think much of me. I don't either!*
It's the recurring problem for depressive people . . . without always
being aware of it since so much has become automatic for them. If
we really wait around to be put down, we are resigning ourselves to
being that kind of person! In the days when it was the boys who
invited the girls to dance, those who weren't invited from the start
adopted (the poor things . . .) such a surly attitude that no-one
approached them! And if someone was unfortunate enough to
dare, it was like waltzing with a prison door!

But the idea we have of ourselves is intimately linked with
what we think the opinion of others is of us. If we feel unsociable
(and we give that impression by the way we behave), then others
will find us unsociable.

Our relations with others are essential to the way in which we
live stress. We must therefore be very wary of this way of under-
valuing yourself.

- **The anti-stress discourse**

OTHERS WILL LIKE ME AS MUCH AS I LIKE MYSELF.
THEY WILL THINK OF ME WHAT I THINK OF MYSELF.

This is self-fulfilling, a perfect virtuous circle. Having a good
idea of yourself necessarily leads to others appreciating you. And
this, in its turn, reinforces your self-assurance.

8. *There's nothing to hope for. Things can't be sorted out.*
It's the depth of pessimism? And this kind of internal litany sup-
ports it. We certainly know that you don't always need something
specific to hope for in order to live in the expectation of the
future.

Of course a project, a precise expectation, makes the life force
that we all have more conscious, because HOPING IS A
BIOLOGICAL FORCE. If we are lacking in it, it's because we are
ill (depression) and we must be treated. And the care sometimes
starts with this internal re-education: to be conscious of the discourse we hold and to master it.

- **The anti-stress discourse**

WHILE THERE IS LIFE, THERE IS HOPE, BECAUSE LIFE AND HOPE ARE SYNONYMOUS. THINGS DON'T SORT THEMSELVES OUT ON THEIR OWN. IT'S ME WHO IS GOING TO SORT THEM OUT.

If you do not at this minute feel like sorting things out, remember that nothing is done in a day. Get used to telling yourself: "I HAVE MY WHOLE LIFE IN FRONT OF ME."

GOOD RELATIONSHIPS WITH OTHERS

We can never repeat often enough that we are intimately and biologically linked with other people, whatever type of relation exists between us and them. They are our principal source of re-inforcement (the 'rewards' or 'punishments' of all our education and training). They continually bring us encouragement or criticism, sometimes imperceptibly (a glance in the Underground ...), sometimes in a vital way (the role played in an emergency situation ...). We must feel and know who these other people in our personal world are.

◘ EXERCISE

Make a list of the people around you, from the closest to the most distant. In the middle of a piece of paper, write the word 'ME' in a circle. Then spread all round the word bubbles containing the initials of the people you know, representing the closeness of the relationship by the distance each appears from the centre. This visualisation of your personal world is an important element in your understanding of yourself.

Think of all the people mentioned. To whom can you talk easily? Mark these bubbles in green. Who can you ask for something? Mark the corresponding bubbles in red.

For example, you have a baker who chats away freely. When you feel a little lonely, you know that he will always be happy to discuss last night's film on the television with you ... Another example. You have a friend who is always ready to do you a service. You know you can always ask him for help ...

Having charted your situation, you must examine your behaviour and perhaps think about changing it. Are you yourself obliging? Do you know how to listen? Can people come and talk

with you? Do you know how to make yourself available if someone asks you something? Perhaps you have never thought about
it? Perhaps you feel too timid for open relations with others?

Practise by giving yourself modest goals to begin with. "I will
have a few words with the baker ... I will ask the young recep-
tionist if she had a nice weekend ..." And then, get yourself to ask.
Ask a friend to help you clean your car or to give you a particular
recipe ...

Give yourself the goal of being the person that other people
can ask, and the person who can himself ask.

The stressing situation

Before anything, you must fix indelibly inside yourself the following maxim: **NEVER GIVE UP.**

First there is always something to do.

Next, you mustn't confuse resignation and acceptance. If you
find yourself faced with a really intractible situation, you must
look for a way of removing part of the blockage and find reasons
for adapting yourself to the result. In short, you must keep trying
right up to the moment when you find yourself at one with the
situation.

While resignation is passive, acceptance results from a
real strategy.

The stressful situation is treated in three stages:

- studying the situation
- acting
- defending oneself

STUDYING THE SITUATION

As with resolving problems, you must begin by examining the
cause of your stress.

We have seen that there are six major categories of stress:
- Class your stress in its category.
- Have you already suffered from this kind of stress? How was it
resolved or how has it developed?

Next, examine your role in the stressful situation.

Let's remind ourselves that stress is the link between an

attack and the manner in which the victim considers it. Each of us has our way of seeing people and things, influenced by our beliefs and the image we have of ourselves.

1. Beliefs:

Political, religious, social, moral . . . They give us rules of judgement. We get annoyed by different things according to whether we are 'on the left' or 'on the right'. We don't accept the same things depending on whether our background is Catholic, Protestant, Muslim or Hindu

If you are aware that a particular conviction is playing a role in your situation of stress, you must ask yourself 'questions of confidence': "Am I in total agreement with this conviction? Whatever my suffering from stress, will I refuse to renounce it?". In this case, you will need to find a solution that takes your attitude into account. But you must also watch out for and avoid two stumbling-blocks:

– Rigidity. All conviction, however powerful, can be adapted in a given situation. Religious fundamentalism (all of it) expresses itself through signs of rigidity which make its followers very vulnerable – which in turn often leads to unfortunate compensatory behaviour. All rigidity, the refusal to soften or adapt, is a form of fundamentalism . . .

– Being at variance with those around you. It is difficult to be alone with one's conviction in a hostile world. It's possible – and history provides us with enough cases where this has been taken as far as martyrdom. But very often the disagreement is aggravated by rigidity: the rigidity of the convinced meets the intolerance of the environment.

2. Self-image:

This can have a direct part to play in the make-up of stress, thanks to the stereotypical positions it makes us adopt. In fact, for most of us, the idea we have of ourselves is marked by the ROLE we play – professionally, in the family or even among a group of friends.

For example, Jack is a doctor. Among friends, he automatically stops himself behaving in certain ways which he judges contradictory to his image of 'doctor'. Marion is a mother. Within the family she cannot say or do what her children or husband can, since they would find this shocking coming from her . . . Gerald is the life and soul of his group: he could never admit he was down in the dumps.

It is very useful to be aware of the idea you have of your role so that you can understand better how and why a particular situation stresses you. And through that you can find the way out.

ACTION
■■■■■■■■■

Action is the great anti-stress tactic, the consequence of non-resignation.

The simple fact of taking action – and deciding to act is already an action – is already an anti-stress measure.

THE AIM OF ACTION IS NOT TO SUPPRESS THE STRESS (at least not necessarily) BUT TO TRANSFORM HARMFUL AGGRESSION INTO BENEFICIAL STIMULATION.

1. Can one act against the cause? In asking this question, keep in your mind the key thought: "THERE MUST BE A KNACK TO IT".

Attacking the cause of stress can require changes, sacrifices . . . which in their turn appear stressful! We will see the method for avoiding this type of stress later.

2. Whatever the action envisaged, it must be done in the way appropriate to you, bearing in mind your strong points and your weak ones. If you like solitude and reflection, don't plan a type of action that requires easy, quick contacts . . .

3. In any action, be like a chess-player: foresee the consequences of what you are going to do, the response you will give to these consequences, etc. Don't hesitate, if necessary, to make a 'model', that is to say a plan foreseeing all the possibilities: "If I say this, it will lead to A, B, C. If it is A, I should do 1, 2, 3. If it is B, I should . . . etc."

It's a method you will be familiar with if you have practised resolving problems.

4. Watch out for the pitfalls. The control of stress involves an atmosphere a lot more strained than that of everyday problems and there is a great temptation to:
- **1st pitfall:** give up. You abandon the struggle. You no longer have the courage . . .

– **2nd pitfall:** break everything. It's a childish reaction: the youngster who fails to fit the pieces back in the box angrily throws everything in the air, pieces and box. Anger is an unconscious way of hiding impotence.

5. The 'don'ts': with the help of this small guide, remind yourself that anti-stress is:

I ACTION

II RESPECTING SOME 'DON'T'S:
- Don't demand perfection, either of yourself or in the anti-stress fight.
- Don't pull too hard: that is to say, don't ask for too much or expect too much from a situation or a person.
- Don't ignore your handicaps, physical as well as psychological.
- Don't force your nature: find anti-stress tactics that fit in with your tastes and tendencies.
- Don't aim too high and don't expect results too quickly.
- Don't let yourself be beaten by a failure: on the contrary, remind yourself that the failure is an occasion to learn better and more.
- Don't try to move mountains. There are situations and people as immovable as Everest. You must consider this and look for a solution WITH such constraints as there are.
- Don't let yourself be seduced by harmful drugs. The cigarette doesn't 'relax' you any more than the little glass 'gives you courage'. If you can't do without them, admit it and think about getting a grip on yourself ... but don't justify it!

DEFENDING ONESELF
■■■■■■■■■■■■■■■■■■■■■■■■■■■■■

This amounts to taking action affecting ourselves. We will resort to it when we can do nothing against the cause of stress, but also to accompany our anti-stress action.
   This defence action involves three strategies:

1. Maintaining our equilibrium.

2. Getting rid of the excess energy released by the aggressing situation.

3.   Reducing our vulnerability.

• **Maintaining equilibrium**

A stressful situation is de-stabilising and part of the suffering from stress relates to our need, physical and moral, to find our equilibrium. To do this, several tactics are available:

1.   Another look:

What we notice when looking at an object from one point of view is very different from what we notice when looking at it from elsewhere. And what is true for objects is also true for people or situations.

If I look at a young boy who has just stolen a bicycle from the position of a magistrate, I will not see him in the same light as if I had the point of view of a psychiatrist . . . and it would certainly be different if I was considering my son!

So if a situation stresses you, look at it another way. For example: "My son, with his independent ways, behaves unacceptably. Clearly, if I was not his father, I would be able to accept this autonomy . . ." So there you have it! Forget that you are his father, only think of what this young man is gaining in terms of maturity . . . and you will not longer be irritated. What's more, by moving around the situation to see it from another angle, you can discover a side of him of which you were previously ignorant, which enables you to tackle the problem head on. One is reminded of the sage of Ancient Greece who said: "If you have a jar of oil that you don't know how to carry, walk around it: on the other side you will surely find a handle which will enable you to pick it up." (These jars were as tall as men!)

This way of taking another look can have two advantages. You put yourself in a different position relative to your stress. And perhaps you discover a new aspect to the problem through which you can tackle it.

2.   Minimising problems:

It's impossible to talk about, or even to explain, the intensity of a pain or a state of tension. Think about a raging toothache. One minute you think your head is going to burst and the next minute it's just about bearable.

However, one thing is certain and has been scientifically investigated. When we believe that a pain, a fear or nervous tension is very intense, we suffer a lot more from it than when we think that it's not there! So, faced with a stressful situation, it's not so much a question of auto-suggestion: "I'm not stressed, I'm not stressed!" as of refusing the tendency to exaggerate and of instead reasoning logically ...

– "It could be worse!" All situations could be worse than they actually are.

– "It's not as serious or as annoying as the last time, or as in the case of so-and-so ...". We can always compare the present state with much worse occasions.

3. Putting in brackets:

A hard knock doesn't last forever. It appears at a certain moment and disappears at another! During this time, we know it will be a difficult period, which we should regard as a parenthesis in our life. And we should start to think about the after-stress (like in time of war, people thought about the return to peace ...).

Perhaps your repeated stress is the journey to and from work every day. Looking on the bright side; start by considering it as an 'inexistent' parenthesis of your day. The twenty-four hours of your day cannot all be equally full! Put your journeys 'in brackets' under 'profit and loss'!

4. Rationalising:

A stressful situation is, by definition, a state of lasting emotional tension. This type of excitement makes us lose our grip on reality (everything is enormous, minute, excessive ...). Judgements become incisive: everything is either good or bad, true or false ... There are no longer any shades or tones. Our normal contact with reality is stretched. We must rediscover our reason, face up calmly to disagreeable things, place them alongside those that are agreeable, rank matters in order of importance and urgency. In brief, we need to put a little order back our lives, even if our life is in an exceptional state!

5. Relaxing oneself:

A stressful situation almost always imposes on our thoughts: we can't think about anything else! And we do need to think about it, as we will see in a minute, in order to act and to organise our control strategy. But it needn't occupy us all day ... and all night!

You must be aware that your stress obsesses you. Ask yourself if, at this moment, you are in the process of resolving a problem or organising some particular aspect of it. If the answer is yes, knuckle down to the task, knowing that you cannot afford to spend too much time on it . . .

But most of the time the thought of stress imposes itself over our other occupations – and this cannot be good either for the control of stress or for our other occupations! So ban these parasitic thoughts. You can do it. All you have to say is: "No! I'm concentrating on what I am doing at the moment.". Clearly, this ban doesn't last long. You will have to repeat your instruction as often as is necessary.

Apart from your usual and professional occupations, look for those occasions of distraction (in the sense of amusement or relaxation. . .). A period of stress is like a period of preparation for a sporting challenge (which is equally a stress – but a GOOD one!).

It's a moment when you must 'look after yourself'. Do it yourself and ask those around you to support you. "Mother's got some worries at the moment, so this evening we're going to take her out to enjoy herself!"

• Burning up excess energy

All stress-related aggression releases in us an energy that is disproportionate to the demands of the daily humdrum of life. If the situation is perfectly under control, it's an opportunity for doing something exceptional (for the person concerned, at least) and the effort required will happily use up all this energy.

But while we continue to suffer from stress, the body chokes on not knowing what to do with the surfeit of biological and emotional drive. It has to use it up, which is what we call 'letting off steam'.

Some well-intentioned people, particularly in the United States, invent 'methods' with clever names, whose principle is always the same: to use up energy, if possible in celebration, but also in pseudo anger. They advise you, for example, to attack a cushion, swear at it and punch it with all your might. Others quite simply suggest that you go to a deserted spot and scream your head off . . .

Yes, such ideas may make you smile . . . But they're on the right track. You only have to adapt them to your own national temperament and your personal tastes and abilities.

One of the advantages of regular physical activity is simply to provide yourself, each day, with the occasion for 'releasing the safety-valve'.

In parallel with this essentially physical 'letting off of steam' (let's emphasise the adverb 'essentially' because everything that is physical is also mental), you can offer yourself escape in the IMAGINARY. It can begin with the 'if': "If I was doing that . . . all would be better." The more impossible and mad the 'that' becomes, the better you feel in telling yourself about it.

Next you can do some real 'daydreaming'. It's the little internal cinema, in which you are the director, the producer, the principal actor and the only spectator. You can invent marvellous stories, as far from reality as possible and without any relation to stress.

As an adolescent, you must have already done this. Then, as an adult, you have allowed yourself to be dictated to by thoughts of reality. You no longer have the time to dream and would even be a little afraid of doing so. Nevertheless, it's an excellent exercise in relaxation just before going to sleep. Afterwards it seems that you are sometimes sleeping with a smile on your lips . . .

• Reducing vulnerability

A lot of our wounds result not so much from harshness of objects (or people) around us as from the fragility of our own spirits. The good old gardener grabs the prickly stem of a rose in his bare hand and the thorns break off in his palm! We must train ourselves to be less 'sensitive'.

My values are not recognised by so-and-so? Hard luck! After all, they are MY values and not his!

An American stress specialist has demonstrated that we can learn to develop a 'hard skin' by being attentive to the discourse that we have during our daily wounding, a discourse that is always positive for us. Certainly a fragile skin leaves us a lot more vulnerable to stress than a tough skin! This specialist has suggested a comparative chart of reactions which different people have when faced with a stressful challenge.

Thanks to this chart, we can see that faced with a given stress, a similar type of reaction is produced, but in the destructive sense for some with a 'thin skin' and in the positive and effective sense for someone with a 'thick skin'.

STRESS

THIN SKIN	THICK SKIN
• ruminating over worries and problems in a vacuum	• preoccupation for a brief moment, then establishing plan of action
• fear, humiliation	• annoyance, initial discomfort, then compensating and forgetting
• hate, desire to destroy (without doing it)	• antipathy: taking measures to avoid an unpleasant situation
• feeling of inferiority, incapability, failure	• facing the situation: detecting causes of failure; putting in hand plans to remedy it
• anxiety, panic	• apprehension: increasing vigilance to facilitate reactions
• hostility, aggression	• objective appreciation of others; measures to avoid harming them; internal attitude of ignoring them
• depression	• sadness; urge for reflection; search for support near others
• exhaustion, fatigue, feeling that everything is insurmountable	• conscious of 'trough of the wave'; decision to rest; search for comfort from others

THE TOOL BOX
■■■■■■■■■■■■■■■■■

To end with, here are a certain number of keys to have on you all the time! They are only effective if you have previously practised the training proposed in the preceding pages.

1. To avoid living under continual pressure

- *It all starts in the morning:* get up at least ten minutes before the 'necessary time'. You will begin your day in the euphoria of a kind of gift: "I've got time". And the relaxation will flow through the rest of the day.

- *Logic:* more than 30 per cent of our actions are useless, illogical (like persisting in overtaking a continuous line of traffic!). Before undertaking any action, ask yourself: "Is it logical? Is it necessary?". You will save 30 per cent of your time, which will give you that valuable breathing space.

- *Being realistic:* Most of the time we are in a hurry because we want to do something in an hour that takes an hour-and-a-half. Time cannot stretch: allow for realistic hours. Useless to say: "I must": that doesn't lengthen the hours or the minutes. If 'you must' really, decide to work longer, but not to squeeze more into a given period.

- *Hunting the leaks:* Those little spare moments are like dripping water from a leaky tap: just a little, but at the end of the month the bill shows it's actually a lot! How many journeys (which could have been grouped together), repetitions or uninteresting chats could be erased from your day? Just think how much you could have relaxed with this extra time.

2. Failures

You must:

a. Consider them as normal: we say that an academic's gown is made of lots of shirts!

b. Consider them as the opportunity to go deeply into a situation. In fact they very often result from the fact that we have thrown ourselves in too quickly without having properly studied all the parameters of the question.

c. They are the opportunity for learning what we wouldn't do. And this is precious, because the majority of our training rests in 'what we must do'.

3. Constraints

Faced with a constraint, you must create a checklist on which you will reflect in those lost moments. On a piece of paper:

- note down the cause or subject of the constraint,

- then prepare three columns. On top of the first will be: "Why am I forced to do that (or stopped from doing that)"; on top of the second: "Is there a remedy?" Against each item in the first column, try to find a remedy (even unrealisable: your brain will occupy itself with the question). On top of the third column put: "Is it worth the bother of doing this or that," and WHAT CAN I GET OUT OF IT?

You will be surprised to find that after a few days the stress you feel from constraint will be eased. Either you have got round the obstacle or you have become conscious of the advantages it brings you.

4. Frustrations

The mechanism is as follows:

$$\text{expectation} \rightarrow \text{deception} \rightarrow \text{STRESS}$$

The key consists in preparing your expectations astutely in order to avoid deceptions.

a. You must know yourself well in order to anticipate what you are capable of doing or receiving. If, for example, you learn to play the piano in your sixties, don't expect to become a great international soloist!

b. You must know the people who may participate in what you anticipate. If your great-aunt has always held a grudge because, as a child, you never went to spend your Sundays with her, don't expect too much from her will!

c. You must understand exactly what you have at your disposal to bring about a desire. If you want to make an important purchase, for which you need a loan, you must not only make a plan for the loan but also present a precise programme of repayment to the lender. Don't be frustrated if, after twenty-four hours, you cannot complete the deal: something wasn't prepared correctly!

d. Lastly, keep the final key. If you are facing disappointment, ask yourself if you REALLY want or need the thing whose lack is causing the frustration!

5. Changes

These are often one cause of internal shock. Transform them into useful opportunities.

a. Find a way of introducing a progression into the change. It is often possible when you can foresee and control its existence. At least brief yourself on the future conditions you are expecting. For example, in the case of moving house, have a good look round your future home, several times if possible.

b. Put your curiosity to work, since all change involves discovery. Don't be blasé and don't put on blinkers so that you only see what the previous situation reminds you of. Look on the contrary for everything that is strange and live your reactions as so much adventure.

c. Stay young. The young haven't yet (theoretically) got habits or customs, which is why they easily welcome new things. They even make it their currency, because they repudiate or reject what belongs to the world of the 'old'. Believe that a change is, for you, the chance to rediscover the adaptability of youth.

6. Conflicts

Conflict with others offers you an interesting experience: to test what happens in a DIALOGUE. That starts with real mental gymnastics. You must not only know and understand, but also get inside the point of view of the other person. The more successful you have been at putting yourself in his place, the greater your chance of convincing that person or changing his mind.

This is clearly a personal enrichment. When you live, even for a moment, the life of someone else, you benefit from two lives in place of one!

But also, by analysing the other's point of view, you can discover new arguments to convince him or to help reinforce your own. What is more, all the rules of conflict demand that you 'seduce' your adversary. And this seduction is a game full of pleasure.

7. Threats

Stress from a threat is due to the fact that the aggression isn't real and that you cannot fight against 'windmills'. The key to this comes logically: make the threat real – IN YOUR IMAGINATION!

It boils down to a game of "And if..." Think about and perhaps note down all the "And if..." that the situation inspires in you. "And if someone was entering by the back-door... And if he got in through the loft window... And if he had a gun... etc". And for each "And if...", reply with an "I could..." or "I would do...".

Go as far as you can with all the "I could...", the possibles and even the impossibles. You are going, imperceptibly, to make a game of them! And at the same time the weight of the threat will be reduced.

Calmer, and thanks to all your imagination, you will even be able to think up a possible defence strategy before the threat becomes reality!

CHAPTER SIX

BEING
CREATIVE

W e live in a society remarkably organised through all kinds of techniques, from systems of social support to household gadgets (machines and pre-prepared food!), and instant correspondence across the world (television, fax machines ...) nowadays even in colour.

Nevertheless the engineers, sociologists and other magicians of our mechanical, automatic, electronic world cannot completely predict our needs. Which leaves us with some things we have to cope with ourselves. And, in fact, hardly a week or day goes by without us meeting some difficulty. Something stops, which no machine and no function of the social security can put right ... Then we have to 'have an idea' .. .. There must be some way, if only it could be found ...!

What we tell ourselves

We say to ourselves: "Yes, I should be able to sort that out. It's nothing, just the 'whatsit'!" Yes, but ... This situation doesn't exactly fall into the category of 'problems to solve'. For that, we have our strategy: observe, classify, reason then skim through the possible solutions until we arrive at the best.

When we know how to manipulate our own mental operations, it's easy. But there are cases where reasoning doesn't get us anywhere. It's not a 'solution' that we have to find; it's a 'thing', a device. We have to invent or fabricate something.

For example, the car breaks down in the middle of the countryside. We have to remove some screws to release the cover of a particular part of the engine to clean it. Unfortunately we haven't got a screwdriver or a knife. What are we going to do? We have to find some ingenious way. . . Very often we start by saying to ourselves: "Well, I can't fabricate something like that! I can use what there is, but it's beyond me to build anything new!" Even worse, we sometimes say to ourselves that we must be slightly hair-brained to go looking for unconventional methods: "It's not my style to have ideas like that!". We tell ourselves that an adult must have dignity, which distinguishes him from being childish. (We know only too well that children make just about anything from almost nothing. . .) And new ideas come from the imagination . . . and we have all learned to mistrust that! We don't know where that will lead us. No, reason must always carry the day.

What we don't tell ourselves is that all the great discoveries, from the invention of the wheel to the space probes that travel through light-years, are born from a moment of mad ideas. Of course, for most of these extraordinary inventions, there had to be enormous numbers of calculations, masses of reasoning, a literally gigantic logical workload. But at one moment in the journey, often right at the beginning, there had to be the idea of a genius, the moment of madness by the inventor or the creator.

Very often, it's true, it simply makes you smile or even refuse any further attempt at analysing the idea. It isn't enough to *have* the idea. One has to believe in it and get hooked on it despite everything. Clearly it is all a question of degree. The great thinker can find himself exposed to the purging trials of the Inquisition – and you to the incredulity of your family and your friends . . .

Marconi, one of the inventors of the radio, had at the beginning of the century launched the idea of communication through hertzian waves across the Atlantic. So he wanted to link up England and the United States by radio. All that was needed, he said, was to have a very powerful transmitter on one side and a particularly sensitive receiver on the other. Everyone laughed at him. All the scientists knew that hertzian waves travelled in a straight line and, as the earth was round, the radio waves sent by Marconi's master transmitter would be lost in space. That was the logical reasoning that this 'half-witted' Marconi wanted to ignore. He still wanted to try it! And it worked!

Later it was discovered that hertzian waves were reflected by an upper layer of the atmosphere, as light rays are by a mirror, and that by correctly calculating the angle of reflection, they were naturally sent on to the chosen receiver. (Marconi had reached his receiver by trial and error.)

WHAT IS BEING CREATIVE?

To be creative is at the same time to show an aptitude and to demonstrate it in a way that gives this aptitude the opportunity to prove itself. Not everyone is inventive and even less a creator. On the other hand, we could all be 'creative' if only we did not stop ourselves from being so!

In fact, to create or to invent is to *produce* something new, which perhaps requires a talent that we don't all have. But before producing, we have to start by working on our imagination, which requires us to move away from the known, the habits and even the certainties – and perhaps even logic. And that we can all do.

In Marconi's day, knowledge – and the logical reasoning from such knowledge – held that the radio waves transmitted up into the air went on to be lost in infinite space. Marconi had the *courage* to overstep these limits imposed by the knowledge of the time: "And if one tried all the same?", he argued.

Being creative is daring to question what one knows as much as what one believes. That doesn't destroy anything, but it encourages research for more facts ... which can only reinforce the knowledge and the beliefs, if they are well-founded.

Thus Marconi's discovery destroyed neither the knowledge of the rectilinear movement of hertzian waves nor that of the earth's curvature. On the other hand, it did lead to finding the existence of a certain atmospheric layer possessing particular physical properties that made it possible to reflect radio waves.

Being creative is also being able to withstand the discomfort, conscious or unconscious, which comes with any novelty or change in our habits. We willingly complain about routine, yet in reality we loathe the insecurity that comes from leaving the rails!

Our way of behaving, like the way we see the world, develops gradually through our experiences and our training; and these depend on what we are – and especially the idea we have of ourselves. This enables us at any moment to *know* what we must do, what we can expect, within our own situation, and in the context of what we are. "I believe I'm a joker and I expect others to laugh when they hear what I say ...". The security of knowing that everything in our life links together as predicted allows us to say with satisfaction that 'there is nothing new under the sun'!

This is not the case of the child who still doesn't *know* and whose personality, even if it is accepted that he has one, still doesn't tell him what he must do or think. And the child continually imagines stories and things to do, so much so that we very often ask ourselves with some disquiet what he is likely to invent next!

We have all been children and we have all 'invented' ... If only we could manage to lose our inhibitions and leave the rails as adults, nothing would stop us from inventing all over again. Because to leave the rails is to be creative and *when we are in this state, ideas come all on their own.*

To leave the rails is to dare to see what is around us, what is happening to us, differently. We need to remind ourselves that what is a disaster for a Londoner could be a benefit for a Tunisian – or even a Parisian! It is also to get away from the image we have of ourselves: a woman of forty, a workshop foreman, a father of four, etc. It is true that these little compartments in which we place ourselves provide very practical points of reference. As a 'doctor', I must behave as such and even think as one. The ready made is without problem: we follow instructions and everything turns out as predicted!

But if, for one moment, we were to get rid of all these reference points, everything would be turned upside down and we would feel totally confused.

As was once said, disorder is the condition in which the brain is fertile; because it is from the unknown, the unexpected, that novelties, that is to say ideas for inventions, creations, are born.

But we should note carefully that to be CREATIVE doesn't only consist in letting our imagination run wild. It must also PRODUCE something! It is a *condition* in which we are then going to make the mechanics of reason work. The person whose car has broken down in the countryside must find the *means* of unscrewing and fixing back on the cover of the engine part. This means establishing *the link between imagination and reality.*

To put it another way, being creative means finding a way of being which *allows the ideas to flow forth and carries the drive thanks to which we can move from the idea to its realisation.*

HAVE YOU GOT TENDENCIES TOWARDS CREATIVITY?

In this section there are three little games which, without being tests in the technical sense, will enable you to understand your creative skills before doing the exercises.

Take your notebook and:

1. Jot down:
- all the round objects you can think of
- all the objects that make a noise
- all the things that fly.

Count up the number of words you have in each list...
less than 15: your mind is really very 'clogged up'.
16-25: you acquit yourself quite well.
more than 25: you have a good creative aptitude.

2. Unconventional uses: note down all you can do with:
- a crayon   - a cork
- a tyre   - a shoe
- a newspaper   - a key

Count up everything you have written down ...
less than 30 uses: 'clogged up'.
31-45: average.
more than 45: that's good or very good.

3. Note down everything that each of the four following outlines can represent:

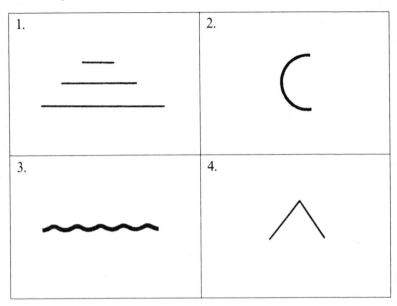

You can reproduce each design on a piece of paper in order to turn them in every direction. Then count up the number of different interpretations you have found ...

less than 12: clogged up.
13-20: average.
more than 20: that's good or very good.

➡ EXERCISES

The aim of the exercises that are going to train you to be creative is to help you rediscover what we sometimes call the 'innocence of youth'. They will aim at making you throw off the shackles and restrictions of your certainties and your adult 'dignity' (however young you are!) to enable you to change your outlook.

It is clearly easier to rediscover and to invent afresh when we see everything as if for the first time. And looking from a new stand-point is enough for it to be a first time. When we have always seen the street from our front window and, one day, we go to our neighbour's on the other side of the road, what we see is another street . . . Equally, if I say to you: "Tree", you know exactly what I mean! The roots are at the bottom, at your feet, the foliage above your head and the trunk in between. But imagine looking at the tree another way: the foliage is above your feet and the roots below your head.

We are used to living with things and notions that 'are what they are'. We are literally imprisoned by this certainty. But why? Dali painted soft watches . . . Why not imagine birds with teeth? The aim of these exercises is to give you the taste for freeing yourself of all your preconceived ideas about what is said, done and known.

HOW TO BE CREATIVE: THE BASIC PRINCIPLES

1. You are creative: we all are. What you don't do (perhaps) is to let your creativity work.

2. The obstacles and blockages to our creativity are always the (false?) obligations and certainties that organise the conscious thread of our life. We must therefore:
   a. release the buried riches in our unconscious.
   b. overcome the obstacles and blockages:
   – by changing and softening the way in which we see the world.
   – by challenging our certainties and distancing ourselves from them.

3. Use others: we are an integral part of a human group. Others stimulate us by their expectations, the support they give us and the ideas they can offer or arouse in us: "Hang on, what you are saying makes me think. . .".

4. Use whatever is available:
   – by living in direct, constant and conscious contact with what is around us. The configuration of, and relation between, objects and their movement around us will give us the idea we are looking for . . .

201

– by seizing on meanings, functions, physical or mental objects ... For example, thinking of the 'external trade balance' can stir up a lot of images ... from our great-grandmother's purse to the one in which we like to hear our coins jingling!

All the exercises that follow are like games. You can do them on your own or in the company of others. AMUSE YOURSELF, while bearing in mind that this part of your training is one of the most serious, the one that must give you the golden key.

Creativity is a freedom which goes much much further than the art of finding how to remove a screw without a screwdriver!

SOME QUESTIONS TO PUT YOU IN THE MOOD

The 'why's' of childhood

Find as many answers as possible to the following questions. Don't be afraid of giving fanciful or even (apparently) absurd replies.

- *Why is the sky blue?*
- *Why are there men and women?*
- *Why do animals have fur, feathers and scales and not us?*
- *Why do we have to wash every day?*
- *Why are there laws?*
- *Why don't we walk on all fours?*

Be sure not to dismiss these questions. Remember that companies pay a lot of money for seminars in which such exercises are a key part ...

How does the cat ...

- *How does the cat see (hear, feel, etc) my family life, my house (or that of any other family if you don't have a cat)?*
- *What does the fly in my kitchen see and think about?*

LEAVING THE RAILS
■■■■■■■■■■■■■■■■■■■■■■■■■

New look

For those of us who 'know' lots of things, all sorts of objects, ideas flow from them.

If, for example, someone asks: "What is a station?", we could say: "It's a large building into which trains arrive and from which they leave. It is where we go to catch a train." That's fine. But what if the person we are talking to doesn't know what a building is – or a train? What if he has no fixed reference points?

So practise looking at things afresh, imagining that you are explaining to an extra-terrestrial who is asking you what the following are:

- a building
- Europe
- social security

- a train
- energy
- rock music

- unemployment
- television
- a microbe

You will not be wasting your time, particularly to start with, jotting down in your notebook all the ideas that spring to mind. Each time ask yourself: "Can he understand?" Assuming of course that he understands English! But it's illogical if he understands English yet doesn't know what a building is? And so?

When you have amused yourself sufficiently with this game, imagine that you are going to the planet that your ET comes from – where there are no buildings, no trains, etc. What are they doing for accommodation, eating, getting about? How do they organise their society? And so on . . .

Upheaval

We think, we *know*, that what surrounds us is 'like it is', with its faults, of course, but we know that since, most of the time, we can do nothing about it. But why not dream? And if the little genie of our childhood were to escape from his lamp . . . and if he gave us the magic word . . . what would you like to change – just once, even the most improbable things . . . or particularly those?

- means of transport
- religious practices
- money and its use
- children (in general – or yours)
- adolescents (the same)
- men (males of the human race)
- women
- beds
- songs, etc.

Good reasons

Our days are made up of a succession of actions that we do because we must, because it pleases us or simply without thinking. In reality, with EVERYTHING that we do, we can of course find a list of reasons, often incongruous, illogical, improbable ... But tough luck or so much the better! The important thing is to find reasons! For example, I wear a hat because I am English ... to avoid the sky falling on my head ...

Now it's your turn to look for reasons – the most improbable will be the best – for:

- buying a newspaper
- wearing a tie
- living in a house (or flat)
- taking photos
- liking wine
- liking jazz
- liking children
- eating fish
- using a wallet
- going to the lavatory, etc.

Faults

I have called this the exercise of 'defectology'. Why? Because it amounts to finding all the defects, even the most hair-brained, in objects, situations and notions – both important and silly.

For example, wine has the fault of not being water. If it was water, it would flow from the taps and we would drink it until we were no longer thirsty without making ourselves ill! What other faults has wine got?

Practise this exercise by finding a list of similar type faults for:

- the car   – a station   – a pen
- the television   – an armchair   – a sailing boat
- the Inland Revenue – friends   – rock music
- love, etc.

In other words

The way in which we express ourselves, relate stories or events or speak to others depends on how we see the world and the idea we have of ourselves. We will always find the way back on to the rails, on which our life runs . . . if we don't constantly react to our surroundings. Equally, our way of talking and saying things influences the type of feelings we have. You must not think that this is auto-suggestion. It is a mechanism, admittedly automatic, that makes sure that we are as far as possible at one with ourselves.

If, for example, we say in the morning: "Brrr, it's cold", we feel a lot colder than if we were to say: "Hang on, it's not very warm! But there again it's still not really winter!". In the same way, if we decide to speak in popular clichés like: " That's cool . . . I'll give it five out of five . . . It's a drag . . ., etc.", our thoughts gradually become restricted to these coded slogans. We start to think like the media, like the rest of the world, in stereotypes. Our own personality grows smaller and smaller . . .

In reality, there are perhaps more than a hundred ways of saying that everything is all right, without being obliged to say: "That's cool". We must get used to manipulating the language so that it is our own, with all its originalities. . . Practise saying the following things in as many different ways as you can find, even inventing words if someone else can understand them! And jot them down in your notebook so that you can appreciate the growing richness of your inventions.

- it's tiring   – I want to . . .
- it's going to rain   – I fully understand
- roll on the holidays – it's time to go

Then stir up your imagination by finding new words for some well-known expressions. Why not have a look through those dictionaries of quotations to find something suitable; it's worth the effort!

- The darkest hour is just before dawn.
- There's none so deaf as those who will not hear.
- You cannot get a quart into a pint pot.
- A trouble shared is a trouble halved.
- A bad workman blames his tools, etc.

Smashing up

This exercise is used a lot by the experts in creativity training. It is based on the principle of attacking the dogma of our contemporary society. Things, objects, institutions, notions, etc... are what they are. Let's accept them in the usual way and life can only be better. NO. If men had continued to accept things as they were without at least dreaming of other things, we would all still be living in caves! We must continue to move ahead and to retain or rediscover enough of the child in us to imagine what things would be if they were otherwise – even to the point of absurdity.

For example, think about a plate. What if it were square? (Not so absurd, that, since square plates do exist!) And if it were convex? And if it were perforated (it would be a sieve)? And if it were cylindrical or spherical like a balloon? And if it were made of blotting-paper? And if we pushed it around in the garden? And so on ...

By dint of going through crazy ideas, you are almost certain suddenly to come out with an interesting one, about which "you would never have thought!". Above all, enjoy yourself and play with your hair-brained ideas. Imagine, for example, that you are serving your Aunt Agatha with custard on a plate made of blotting-paper!

To help you with this creative work, here is a 'smashing-up' plan to put you in an inventive frame of mind.

Prepare a list of things that you are going to 'smash up'. For example:

– a plate	– university	– a slipper
– a pen	– rain	– democracy
– a tap	– a person	– digestion

For each of these things or objects you are going to:

a. Increase it: increase its weight (what will that produce? How will that be? etc.) – increase its volume – its price – its length of use – the people concerned – the frequency of use or meeting – the social or political scope – the qualities – the faults. . . (NB: it may seem difficult to apply all these procedures to all the various things listed, but try just the same!)

b. Reduce it: the opposite of the previous exercise. For example, reducing the size of the slippers you could have one for each toe, then one well padded for the heel and quite a game for the sole of the foot, to wear according to the temperature . . .

c. Combine it: with a similar object (for example, a combination of trousers and slippers like a baby-suit; how would this be made?) – with an opposing object – with a function – with a person – with a political party . . .

d. Invert it: in its form (for example, a convex plate) – in its functions or use. You have to create an 'anti-object'. For example, what would be 'anti-digestion'? And where would that lead you?

e. Modify it: change the moments or places of use, the material, the shape, the name – make it mobile on the ground, in the water, in the air – make it immobile – modify its constituent elements (for example, a democracy without votes?).

f. Sensualise it: make it more exciting to look at, listen to, taste, touch – or less so.

USING WHATEVER IS AVAILABLE
■■■

When we read a biography of one of the many inventors, we notice that not only do they have a 'different view' of the world, but they also make use of what this view brings them.

Take the story of Archimedes in his bath. He wasn't content to feel, like the rest of the world, the agreeable freshness of soaking in water. He had noticed *something else*. When he got into the water, he felt lighter than on his two feet, in the dry. So, he told himself, water doesn't just serve to refresh; it can also push upwards and serve to support us!

We could also quote the discovery of Newton. An apple fell on his head, which was unpleasant . . . But let's go a little further. Why did the apple fall? Nobody pushed it . . . 'something' had to have attracted it towards the ground . . .

We could just as well cite Gutenberg, walking among the grape-pickers and watching them press the fruit . . . "And if I was also using a press to push (print) my inked characters down very hard on my paper?"

We are surrounded by objects and movement of all sorts, which could be used for so many other things than we expect of them – like the transformation of an old railway carriage into a holiday home or even a permanent one! – Particularly if we add a little bit of fantasy. But we have to practise to overcome the blockages and the more or less unconscious barriers.

What we can do with. . .

Jot down in your notebook all that you can do – even if it is at first sight impossible – with:

- matches
- a piano
- a fireman
- a pencil
- a computer
- a clothes-hanger
- a bottle
- a convent
- an architect
- and, why not, a racoon!

To do without

If certain things had just been missing or had never existed, we would have had to scrape by somehow, living perhaps differently from the way we are used to.

So try to imagine how you would manage and what you would have to find in order to live normally in present-day society if there wasn't:

- paper
- shoes
- ways of knowing the time (clocks, watches, sundials, egg-timers . . .)
- money
- taps
- electricity

(NB: you're not allowed to just say that you would invent the missing object!)

APPEALING TO THE UNCONSCIOUS

Both scientific experiments and the observation of behaviour confirm that we all have the ability to be creative. But most of us aren't – or believe we aren't – because all the blockages we have already discussed prevent ideas from bursting forth. However these ideas do exist in abundance inside us, in our unconscious. We have to go and find them . . . Obviously we cannot really rummage around in our own unconscious as we would in a desk drawer. But, through indirect means, we can bring out a stock of ideas, of images – sometimes even pearls! – that we thought we were completely incapable of having. And I'm not referring here to the psychoanalyst! There are simpler ways, like loose associations and analogy . . . In this type of exercise, the psyche forgets the blockages and takes no notice of breaking its own rules!

The more you train yourself, the more easily you will see your unconscious treasures blossom forth, all on their own, into your conscious, each time you look for an idea.

Loose associations
or "That makes me think of . . ."

When you decide to devote a few minutes to loose associations, you should at first take your notebook and jot down everything that comes to you. You will very quickly find this comes easily and you can then amuse yourself by doing the exercise in your head.

Think of a word; it doesn't matter what: window, lover, gratitude, noise, cake, anger, etc. Jot it down and ask yourself immediately: "What does that make me think of?". For example, 'window' makes me think of a curtain, which makes me think of a shower, which makes me think of Hitchcock, then suspense, then suspension, then car, then ...

This is an excellent exercise, but it is also a way of fishing for ideas. By leaving words that link up to flow on their own, you can suddenly say: "Great! I've got the idea!".

'Semi-led' associations

This is really a method of looking for ideas, but you must practise it in order to master the technique for when the moment to use it arrives.

Take a word that is full of significance for you: the subject where you really need a brilliant new idea. It might be 'screwdriver' for the person whose car has broken down, or 'lover' or 'digestion' if yours is too slow ...

Try linking this word with all the others that pass through your mind and think about what that word gives you or evokes. If the ideas don't come, there's no point in continuing to look for them. Move on to another word that comes to you.

For example, screwdriver and rain? Screwdriver to fix my umbrella, but I can't think of anything else. Screwdriver and constitution. Ah! Laws ... The Highway Code should make the carrying of a screwdriver in cars obligatory. I don't need laws! From now on, I will always have a little tool-bag ... Screwdriver and toothbrush! Wait a minute! I've got a nail-file in my pocket comb-case ... That's what I can use for a screwdriver! I would never have thought of that! Etc. ...

Analogies or "That looks like ..."

The vast majority of inventions didn't come out of the blue. They were inspired by comparisons, like Gutenberg and the wine-press. If we train ourselves to use whatever's available, we can have ideas **through analogy** with what we observe.

There is even a scientific discipline known as bionics, which consists of observing natural phenomena – from birds' flight to the underground development of mushroom roots – from which one can draw guiding principles for industrial, aeronautic or other research.

The child (always the one to show us the way!) often makes such comparisons or analogies naturally. When, for example, he sees a plane he cries out: "It's a bird with an engine" or sadly even more often these days when he discovers a bird, after becoming very familiar with planes thanks to television, he tells us: "Look! It's a plane without an engine!".

Practise finding more and more **resemblances**. To begin with you will find one or two... You must get used to this game in order to progress – at the risk of making far-fetched analogies, which are often the most fertile in ideas! So, what do the following resemble?

- waves in the sea: horses, locks of hair, merry-go-rounds ... and what else?
- the exit from the cinema (the audience leaving)
- a large cross-roads
- adolescence
- a policeman, etc.

• Playing with allegories

Numerous works of art, paintings, sculptures – but also poetical images – are allegories, objects which through analogy resemble an abstract idea. For example, representations of Fertility are often statues of well-endowed women with ample naked breasts, sometimes surrounded by chubby little children ...

Imagine you are a painter or a sculptor. Through what will you represent:

- kindness
- freedom
- Latin America
- work
- justice

- the Atlantic Ocean
- life
- love
- the solar system

• The Chinese portrait or "If it was ..."

This is a game you can play with friends, or on your own. It consists of thinking about an object (concrete or abstract), a person or an event, then asking yourself what this object, person or event would be if, for example, it was:

- a stone
- a sport
- a tree
- a colour
- an item of clothing

- a river
- an animal
- a smell
- a food

For example, take the French Revolution. If it was a stone? Depending on your ideas, you could say it was a large standing-stone or a pile of pebbles. Courage . . . If it was an item of clothing? A helmet! And so on . . .

When you play this with others, you must choose your resemblances carefully, because the aim of the game is for the other players to guess the object or person or event about which you are thinking!

• The methodical search for analogies

This is the meeting of two opposites because a method is logical while an analogy is irrational! But we mustn't forget that creativity is not the flight into the illogical. It's an approach to *reality* free from the stereotypes imposed by society and from the prohibitions born of our blind conviction. We can rationally explore the irrational!

When you feel comfortable with the previous little games, this type of exercise can be very rewarding. It amounts to working out resemblances and pouring out ideas.

Take some paper and a pencil and make a list of objects out of the blue. Start with four items. If you enjoy this and get results easily, then add to your list . . .

For example:
1. football
2. plate of noodles
3. sofa
4. flowers

Note down the chosen words across the page and write the characteristics and functions of the first word – football – underneath (see example below).

Football	Plate of noodles	Sofa	Flowers
Round	+		
Amusement (pleasure)		+	
Sport (health)		+	
Children	+		
TV (matches)	+	+	

Under the other words, put a cross if a function or characteristic of 'football' can be applicable, however hair-brained or tenuous the link.

Thus 'plate of noodles': round plate, food for children, advertised on television. And sofa: we sit on it for pleasure, we relax there which is good for our health and we watch television from it.

If you get nothing out of this first table, repeat the exercise but this time list the characteristics and functions of your second word and see what corresponds to the other words:

Plate of noodles	Football	Sofa	Flowers
Dish	+ (contrary)		
Hot			
Soft	+		
Healthy	+ too much food		
Italy	+		
Symbol of stupidity			

For 'football': it's the opposite of a dish (or plate); it may be soft for children; our stomachs blow up like footballs if we eat too many noodles; in Italy they are mad on football, so the analogy between a football and a plate of noodles is Italy! And so on ...

SEARCHING FOR IDEAS
■■■■■■■■■■■■■■■■■■■■■■■■■■■■■■■■

All these exercises that you have done, and will perhaps continue to do to amuse yourself, will give you a mental liveliness (relatively) free from the constraints of all the stereotypes of your everyday life. They will develop lots of routes in your brain, along which your ideas will flood, both spontaneously and at your command.

You will become creative as your mind works in its new climate of freedom, with no criticism of the ideas that pop up, no saying "It's impossible, it's stupid ...". You have trained yourself already in resolving problems, and searching for an idea comes just before solving problems. Having ideas is being creative, and being creative comes just before inventing something – which is what we must do to solve problems. You look for an idea because you are missing an object and because you want to find something that might do the same job – or you want to improve output or facilitate a task. In brief, you are looking for something that might fulfil a *function*.

So you are going to:

1. Formulate, in one word, if possible, the thing about which you are looking for an idea.

2. Make a list of the characteristics and functions of this object.

3. Look for all the objects that have certain of these characteristics and functions.

For example:

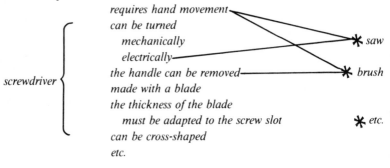

So some analogies appear (sometimes unexpected), from which the ideas spring forth: for example, the analogy between a saw and a screwdriver. Can I saw with a screwdriver or unscrew with a saw? Why not, if I have a saw with an end that is a screwdriver? That could be a very useful tool . . .

EPILOGUE: A LITTLE GAME

You are about a dozen people who find yourselves on a desert island after a shipwreck. Make a list of the survivors: their differences, the sexes, ages, geographical and cultural origins, levels of knowledge, jobs ... all different. Each one sees the situation and what they must make of it in their own way, depending on who they are. Imagine what each thinks ... as well as your own reactions and suggestions.

You will find your ideas coming to mind as if you were reading an adventure story! Why not jot them all down and try to write a story? This will not necessarily make you a writer: being creative does not, alas, mean being a creator! But one thing is sure: you are creative (if you want to be) quite simply because you are a human being.

And another thing is also certain: being creative is being free.

CHAPTER SEVEN

STAYING
YOUNG

S taying young isn't just a preoccupation for senior citizens. In today's society, the world belongs to the young; everything is made for them and by them. And so to stay in the driving seat we must stay young. That doesn't seem easy ... or even logical, since each year the whole world is a year older! But in fact youth has very little to do with your date of birth. It's an attitude and a way of life. And if we feel ourselves ageing, it's not because we are counting the years. It's because everything changes so quickly these days that we feel we are not keeping up with it. When we are not – or no longer – in the group of people who make the changes, we look at them on the crest of their wave and tell ourselves we are getting old.

Professionally, we have to stay young. When we reach our forties we begin to sense the knives coming out. The young wolves are ready to tell us we are out of date – and apparently that's unforgivable!

But we must also stay young for personal reasons. The greying temples of father's best friend give him his charm – perhaps add to it – but they don't underline his youth!

And we must stay young longer and longer. At least the statistics offer us the hope of twenty more years of life compared with those who were born twenty years before us! It's a question of living these years to the full. And we can only really live them if we stay young.

What we tell ourselves

"I'm getting old . . .". Why do we say that? Tiredness perhaps, of a different sort from that we felt in the past (we start to use this phrase 'in the past' more and more often!); weariness even? Another face in the mirror each morning, more wrinkles, a complexion that has lost its colour? The spring lacking in our step?

We tell ourselves: "It's not right at my age." Certainly it may be an age at which it's inadvisable to go hang-gliding (or whatever . . .). But people who say: "It's not right at my age" are thinking neither of hang-gliding nor of having a 'fun time'; they don't even know what that is! They say it, and this is more significant, about a short skirt, a bicycle ride, a rock concert . . .

We tell ourselves: "It's beyond me . . .", "I've no more punch left . . .". The wave of younger people takes over, sometimes brutally it's true, and wants to turn everything in the business upside down. They walk around with their pocket organisers permanently switched on, like the stars of some original science-fiction film with their electronic superman helmets. Thanks to their organisers, everything is decided in a split second, even what they are going to eat in the cafeteria.

So we tell ourselves: "I can't manage any more. It's too different, too complicated, too quick . . ."

Finally – and here is the admission that we have let ourselves be trapped – we tell ourselves: "It's no longer worth the effort." Not worth fighting any more, not worth moving . . . It's not even worth the effort of living . . . "I might as well resign myself to it" . . . and die!

Of course it's always worth the effort, even when you have told yourself it isn't.

WHAT IS 'STAYING YOUNG'?

I t doesn't consist of countering "the irreparable ravages of time" ... The years pass by, we change (ever since birth!) and everything changes around us. But these changes are 'ravages' if we think they are and unnecessarily restrain our desires and activities.

Staying young is basically *changing* in line with the evolution of the world around us.

Of course the world evolves ... It's never the same water passing under the bridge! But everything in us alters just as much. This perpetual movement involves all the cells in our body. Each is a factory that works twenty-four hours a day. And, on the whole, these cells renew themselves – right up to the moments following our death.

Our whole body participates in this constant change, the spiritual either following or preceding the biological. At least, normally. It is possible for our spiritual self to take up a position at a certain moment in time and refuse to change it. This position is necessarily an artificial one since real life is continuous movement: it's the start of old age.

THE LOSS OF YOUTH LIES IN INFLEXIBILITY

Inflexibility of the mind, of course, because plenty of youngsters have inflexible bodies.

SO YOUTH IS VERSATILITY, CONSTANT ADJUSTMENT

And that hasn't necessarily anything to do with our actual age.

It is true that, during the early decades of our life, we are in general naturally adaptable and even look for novelties; we live unknown experiences. And it is equally true that this becomes less natural when we let ourselves be charmed by the 'Sirens' song' – otherwise known as habit. And once habit sets in, it becomes a kind of skeleton for our existence. It's well and truly rigid; and youth turns tail ... But this stiffening is not obligatory. For a good thirty years we shouldn't even think about it. After that, it's enough just to reflect on it – and avoid it – to stay young!

Staying young doesn't consist of maintaining, at the age of sixty, the same tastes as when we were twenty. If we think we have them, then we are stuck with an idea that is only based on ourselves and our life. By refusing to accept reality we are denying ourselves everything that it could bring. We are trying to live a substitute existence and so, whatever we may think, we are just a little old man (or woman).

So does this mean that at sixty I have to resign myself to not having the same desires as when I was twenty? Of course! But it's not a matter of resignation! It's just that my desires when I was twenty, which I no longer have at sixty, seem to me completely out-of-date! After all, we certainly have to give up the feeding bottle – or our mother's breast! That 'weaning' is quite forgotten about, and we don't have any feelings of resignation about it. Certain tastes change *naturally* with age. However, a change is clearly not a loss of something. You no longer have a desire for that nice porridge you were given in your first year and you are probably dreaming about a juicy steak instead. We all change ...

In any case, if you are living in perfect accord with yourself, you would not have the time for nostalgia: whatever your age, so many other desires come to you, year after year, about which you would never have thought ten years earlier!

Staying young is therefore about keeping in contact with ourselves as much as with the world, seeing our tastes, our needs, our activities evolve in unison with the changes in that indissoluble unity that is the person (rightly) in his or her own world.

And it is as important to keep young as it is to control stress:

WE ARE YOUNG AS LONG AS WE DON'T RESIGN OURSELVES TO NO LONGER BEING SO

And this goes for people of all ages, particularly those who have just turned forty ... They especially must know how not to resign themselves to being cast out by the young wolves. In any event, business, like society, needs not just young wolves but also more mature ones ... And even old wolves have their uses! Everybody's skills are different and those that we acquire with age – even after the eighth decade – are precious.

Just as the word 'youth' doesn't simply refer to a particular age group but belongs to the vocabulary of value judgements, we must equally remember that we stay young for just so long as we respond to our changing environment.

CHECKING OUT YOUR 'MENTAL' AGE

A nswer, in *all honesty*, the following statements and questions, marking + for yes and 0 for no:

- *I feel I have changed.*
- *When travelling, I still need the little comforts I'm used to.*
- *I no longer understand the young.*
- *My memory's gone; I have to write everything down.*
- *What good are projects? They achieve nothing.*
- *I cannot stand changing my hours.*
- *At my age, one doesn't make new friends.*
- *No good will come of all these changes.*
- *I no longer have the desire to go out in the evening.*
- *I think about my diet before good living.*
- *At my age, one doesn't need to please any more.*
- *My favourite entertainment is the television.*
- *I have absolutely no desire to taste all these exotic dishes.*
- *It's very tiring entertaining friends.*
- *I think the world's going mad.*

COMMENTARY
Count up the number of +'s you have marked. If you have:

- **0-5:** you are not too 'deadened'.
- **6-10:** it's old age.
- **11-15:** well past old age!

If you really have scored more than two or three +'s, you should first of all take a good-humoured look at your situation. Then decide seriously to take yourself in hand because, whatever your 'actual age', YOU MUST NEVER HAVE MORE THAN TWO OR THREE +'s!

FIVE KEYS FOR STAYING YOUNG – OR REDISCOVERING YOUR YOUTH

- **The body:**
  Look after it, of course. But what counts particularly is the spirit in which you do this.

- **The image of yourself:**
  Particularly the emotional attitude you have as regards yourself.

- **The mind** (the intelligence machine) **and action**

- **Other people:**
  It's the mature image: "I need them and they need me".

- **Keeping in touch:**
  Staying IN the flow – and running with it.

THE BODY
■■■■■■■■■■■■■

During the whole of that first period of our life, it goes without saying that whatever happens our body 'follows', does what we want and pays the price when we perhaps go that little too far. That hangover, for example, after a night of excess . . . But, when you are only twenty, the suffering only lasts until the following morning. And if the night really has been that good, afterwards there's NOTHING!

Then the moment arrives when the little warning lights start flashing. We puff a bit when climbing the stairs and no longer take them two at a time. We take that bit longer to digest a good meal.

And the effects of that night of celebration leave their mark for several days afterwards!

We find it harder to sleep. We see the outline of our body changing. When playing with the youngsters, we discover we don't have the same agility . . .

The moment when we finally have to admit that things are changing can be painful.

But we must clearly make the difference between what could be **DETERIORATION** and what is simply **EVOLUTION.**

It's undeniable that a life led 'in top gear', without any attention to health, with all the abuses known to civilisation (tobacco, alcohol, rich food, etc.) can result in signs of *deterioration* by the mid-forties. This deterioration occurs when the biological, physiological and physical performances are below normal. You must see your doctor and medical or general health measures will have to be taken. Every effort should be made to get back into shape.

It's normal that at the age of twenty we are not thinking about retirement. But after we reach forty, we can start to foresee it, albeit in the long term. The sooner we begin staying young, the more youth we will accumulate for our old age.

The *evolution* of the body is directed towards strength and the assertion of a physique. If you have never thought about this, look at the reproductions of the great Greek sculptures of the classical period. Compare the almost fragile grace of an ephebe (a young man) with that, for example, of the famous disc-thrower (young maturity) and then with that of a statue of Zeus, the king of the gods. He has the striking elegance of a man sure of himself, in the autumn of his life. The shape has admittedly lost its finesse, but the harmoniously solid body is that of an oak tree.

We could say a lot more about the evolution of the female form: the slenderness of the young girl keeps – and even acquires – an elegance, a catching charm, in the mature forms of statues representing motherhood or the goddesses of fertility.

But it is true that as we mature there can be a very big difference between strength and reassurance on the one hand and excessive size on the other. This difference is not a question of centimetres. It emanates from the inside of the person.

Keeping our body in shape, suitably to our time of life, doesn't consist of keeping 'model-like' measurements, but of taking steps to model ourselves on what we are. If you are active, busy, and constantly on the lookout for something to do, to see or to discover, there is a very good chance that you will develop towards a nervous slimness, your face will more readily get wrinkles. If you have a happy-go-lucky temperament and are open and convivial with others, your natural generosity will express itself in your body. But of course the body's tendencies can be controlled, just like all manifestations of our existence.

In youth, we don't take much notice of ourselves, because we have so much to discover about others and the world around us. But when those little signals (breathlessness, etc.) attract our attention, that is the *moment to discover ourselves,* to learn to love ourselves and to take *pleasure in looking after ourselves.* We don't look after ourselves to 'stay young' but to live better. And in doing this we also stay young; that happens all on its own.

The only major change of the 'coming of age' is that we must look after ourselves. In other words, we can no longer do everything all the time. And this is a new pleasure to be discovered!

Imagine you have a garden with a fine lawn, a marvellous array of flowers and a neat herb patch. Then gradually the weeds, stinging nettles and brambles take over. So you take a big decision. You work hard, reseeding the lawn, clearing the beds and generally tidying up. Then, year after year, you have the fun of choosing new plants and flowers – and keeping an eye on those weeds! Before, you had an area of land that looked after itself. Now you have discovered the pleasure of MAKING a garden.

Finally, don't forget that the moment when the idea comes to you that you 'must stay young' is the turning point when, for your body, 'nothing happens on its own any more'. And this is the age of **PREVENTION.** You must start learning the indicators of your health: blood pressure, pulse rate, sugar levels and so on. To do this, consult with your doctor as to how and when to keep an eye on everything.

- **For your health:**
- Aerobics are the great secret (see the techniques in Chapter 1). Practise them until they become your greatest PLEASURE of the day, just at the moment when you NEED them.
- Everything is allowed ... with common-sense, that is to say within the limits of your current state of health.
- But, *after all excess,* give yourself the time to get over it. Don't try to re-impose your normal rhythm with a body that has just suffered. After the age of forty, it recovers more slowly than when

it was twenty. So, according to the type of excess: rest and follow a strict diet for several days . . . If it's a question of sporting excess: several sessions of massage and hydrotherapy.

An excess is like a little quarrel with your body (even if you have thoroughly enjoyed it!). Someone once said: "Never go to bed on a quarrel: you must reconcile yourself before sleeping." And it's the same with your body. Rediscover the harmony before continuing to live . . .

– You can practise sport well after you eightieth birthday! But it must be ADAPTED to your EVOLUTION. You should increasingly choose those sporting activities involving endurance and strategy that bring physical satisfaction rather than the sudden dash and quick effect.

Even if you are full of admiration for the youngsters and their skill in skiing on water or on snow, would you REALLY want to be doing the same thing? You can wonder at the audacity of the flying trapeze artist without needing to see yourself under the 'big top'!

THE IMAGE OF YOURSELF
■■■■■■■■■■■■■■■■■■■■■■■■■■■■■■■■■■

The essential for retaining the drive that characterises being young (let's repeat, at whatever age) is to have a good understanding of yourself and to appreciate yourself in a VERY positive way.

In general, having passed the crisis of adolescence when romanticism inspires the young to a gracious melancholy (the saddest songs are also the most beautiful . . .), youth has no doubt of its total power and freely takes the lead. If there is a failure youth blames others people or circumstances. . . But we mustn't mock this attitude because, thanks to it, all forms of progress are made. Then a moment arrives when the critical – and particularly the self-critical – mind takes on more and more importance . . . And very quickly a new wave of young people comes on to the scene. In the professional world as elsewhere, they push both others and themselves to make a place and to be recognised. Clearly their first weapon is criticising those older than them, so that the preceding generation has a double reason for being undervalued: self-criticism and that of the young!

Thus we no longer have as naturally good an idea of ourselves as before! And if we let ourselves be ensnared by self-criticism, then it is true that we will cross over to the other side of the ferocious divide that separates the young from the others.

It must be said that this is also the moment when, as we look at ourselves in the mirror each morning, we notice the first signs of change ... There have been plenty before, but we haven't been aware of them!

Thus the terrible temptation comes of proving to ourselves that we are still young. And, as we approach our fifties, we set ourselves up to try to do and like the same things as when we were twenty. What's more, as fashions change, we secretly watch the oldest of the children to pretend that we are 'in step' with them. In fact, we risk creating artificial desires that are totally out of harmony with our own potential.

In short, the period of change is that when building up your own image not only doesn't happen on its own but even sometimes demands a real effort against opposing influences.

Reinforcements

Normally we need signs that will reinforce our feeling of self-appreciation. These 'reinforcers' come from all directions.

Our professional life offers us occasions for success, our judgements bear material fruit. Very often the career structure in a business enables us to get favourable evaluations from our superiors and to improve our own image in relation to colleagues and people junior to us.

Our salary provides material satisfaction, of course, but this is doubled in value through a very satisfying pride: "It's me who earned it!" ... Our emotional, family and love lives, as well as that of friendship, multiply these reinforcements – or at least can do so.

As we get older we become a less good audience to these appreciative occasions and more sensitive to the blows we receive (negative reinforcers), which become more and more numerous with age because the pressure from young people pushing us out becomes greater and greater. It isn't always easy to see the clumsiness of these attacks before being wounded by them ... But we *have to convince ourselves* that it's in the nature of things, just as it's in the order of things not to let ourselves be 'walked over'. We must be vigilant *not to accept criticism* – even if it seems justified (we may take mental note, but we never admit it!).

It's imperative that we put people and things back in their place and at least make ourselves respected.

A moment will come when our income is going to diminish ... and with it plenty of reinforcing signs! This is the time to reflect on our needs. Perhaps the children have gone to live elsewhere? We no longer need such a large house ... With the reduction in our income, perhaps we should 'abandon' certain things? But if we have got used to a certain style of living within the last thirty years or so, shouldn't we think it's a good time to change – to stay young?

Certainly the young encourage us to simplify our lives. All sorts of little comforts (often costly) appear to them useless, if not ridiculous ... Perhaps they are right? The duvets make those fine wardrobes full of bed-linen inherited from a great-grandmother rather obsolete ... And aren't paper serviettes a lot more practical? And so we discover that, by simplifying things, we arrive more easily at what is essential. Friends who turn up by surprise, for whom we casually bring out extra plates, feel so much more comfortable than if we had made a big fuss about not being able to feed them. And if they are the sort of people we can't receive like this? Then they're not really friends; so why have them round? For professional reasons? Then find a solution – a restaurant!

It's not a question of working out *all* the measures necessary to enable us to live as well – if not better – but cheaper. What is essential is not to look for 'how to cut back' but how to find the best quality of life in a genuine way, that is to say in satisfying our TRUE values.

A lot of positive reinforcements are provided by those close to us. And there is also a period when certain positions change. Children sometimes distance themselves geographically, but even more so emotionally. They have their life and get-togethers with parents no longer contain the intimacy that allows for an exchange of reinforcements ... Professional changes can distance us from our friends, as well.

Whether such distancing is relative or absolute, we must rediscover ourselves' and learn to live without things and people we were used to, by living differently and by finding other sources of reinforcement.

◗ EXERCISE

Nothing is gained by ignoring the changes that happen in or

around you. If you ignore them, you will see your sources of re-inforcement diminish or even disappear. And you must know what these are in order to be better motivated to change and find new ones.

Take the time to visualise your loss of reinforcers by writing them down in lists, groups, charts . . . Then, for each item, look to see whether you have an idea for a 'replacement'.

For example:
My sons have left home now. I used to like going down to the sports ground with them and advising the team. They thought of me as a kind of trainer. That made me feel of some value . . .

So why not go back there, chat with the captain and the club organisers and offer your services as an assistant trainer?

Whatever the results of this exercise, you must train yourself to feel you are of value. Self-satisfaction is the best reinforcer. This training involves three areas:

- Inner discussion
- Taking yourself seriously
- Pleasing yourself

• Inner discussion
You are perhaps already familiar with the 'anti-stress' inner dis-cussion? The principle is still the same: from time to time you must listen to what you are telling yourself, non-stop and above all in moments when you feel low . . . You are perhaps saying to your-self: "Ridiculous! I'm too old for that . . . I'll never manage that . . . My God, I'm so tired . . . etc". Even if we don't really listen to this litany, the words going through our head make their mark on the way in which we are feeling. Sometimes we aren't really tired, but it's enough to tell ourselves: "How tired I am!" in order to feel an enormous fatigue.

This self-deprecating inner discussion happens of its own accord at that moment in life when we become conscious of the fact that we are no longer as young as we were. And it's a trap into which we mustn't fall, because it's the best way of forcing our-selves effectively towards an age . . . the next one!

◼ EXERCISE
....
Watch yourself for a few days and make a note of those self-

lowering phrases that appear most often. A little later, look for what could be the self-appreciative answer to counter them.

For example, "I can't find the word I want ... it's obvious I'm seriously starting to lose my memory ... It must be my age!". Pause a moment with this sentence. When you look for a word, a name or whatever and it doesn't come immediately to mind, are you REALLY searching for it? Are you making associations in order to find it? Moreover, do you ever play those little memory games like the ones described in Chapter 2? Your answer to these questions has to be 'no', because if it were 'yes' you wouldn't be putting yourself down so much! So, when you catch yourself saying: "I have lost my memory, etc...", reply: "Wait a minute! I've temporarily let my mind wander a bit. I'm going to concentrate. I know it's not going to take much to get back into form."

• Taking yourself seriously

Don't be the first to be self-critical when you do something that isn't perfect. It's human error! Take your own opinions, like your desires and your projects, seriously. Don't let yourself be influenced by a youngster who has just told you that you are 'past it', that you no longer have what it takes or you're not in a position to judge.

If what you want doesn't please others, don't give up too easily. Defend your aspirations, argue them and behave as you always have done. There is no age at which you must say: "Never mind". What you want is as imperative and important now as when you were twenty or thirty.

Defend your projects, even and particularly if someone makes you think that they are going to interfere with those of others younger than you. It's not a question of declaring war against young people, but of remaining vigilant so as not to be pushed on to the sidelines.

• Pleasing yourself

Very often, at the end of a career or because the children have grown up, we have more time on our hands than previously. For such a long time we never had a minute to ourselves; so when we do get this leisure time, we don't dare use it for doing whatever we like. When we have for such a long time only read the business press, we don't dare suddenly to spend time reading the review of a novel or an article on tourism. We don't dare, in the middle of the afternoon, to settle down in a comfortable armchair and listen to some music ... Isn't this a sign that we don't trust ourselves? So reject this attitude. Offer yourself all the satisfaction you can obtain. You deserve it. Enjoy yourself just as you would try to give pleasure to a loved one. Even if you are alone at table, lay out a pretty tablecloth and prepare your food attractively ... 'for the pleasure'.

All this mustn't make you forget the reinforcements that come with the interest of others in you. Here again, perhaps you have attracted this all your life without doing anything to win it. And now you discover that it doesn't happen as automatically as before? Your first reaction could have been: "It's normal. It's my age.". Perhaps in fact age does make you less attractive ... but not directly! It's because YOU no longer like yourself that others distance themselves from you.

There is, in effect, a complete parallel between the appreciation we have of ourselves and the attraction we hold for others. First we have to like ourselves and appreciate ourselves in order to maintain or rediscover this game of attraction.

Attraction isn't necessarily linked with sex. Moreover, whatever the satisfaction we gain from a sexual encounter, it is never as powerful a reinforcer as the displays of INTEREST that someone can express towards us. We often feel that if somebody 'only wants to go to bed', they aren't really attracted by us. This doesn't mean that the attraction must be devoid of sexuality. But sex isn't just about the 'act'; it's a way of being that necessarily has an influence on people of the opposite sex, even in the most platonic relationships!

Too often we invest so much of our sexual identity in the physical side of our relationships that when we become less sexually active we lose the more or less conscious feeling we have of being 'a man' or 'a woman'. We've become 'neuter'!

But we are not 'a person'; we are a man or a woman. To deny this is like amputation, the disappearance of a part of our life. Seduction, even that which involves being a good salesman, a mother, a teacher or a priest ... implies sexed personality. We attract and from that we receive reinforcements through all that we are, including this aspect of our personality. And this AT ANY AGE. What could be more charming than the femininity of an old lady with an immaculate hair-do and delicately made-up? Well before we confess to being a senior citizen, femininity gains a gentleness which expresses itself in a very appealing tenderness that is clearly not always the case with every young woman. As for men, we don't have to explain the charm of gentle strength and the feeling of reassurance that maturity brings. As age progresses, there is a HUMAN LEVEL that we don't find among those who 'rap' the night away in discos, which is powerfully seductive. We must recognise this when we reach that time of life and not look to please with pretences, giving a false impression of 'youth'. It's enough quite simply to use this jewel that the years, one after the other, have given to all of us.

Good humour

It is quite normal, when we feel we are losing our youth, for our humour to deteriorate further and further. It is normal for us to have less and less desire to have fun and feel it a waste of time to plan projects. And, in fact, it is classic that with increasing age we become pessimistic, 'kill-joys'. We settle into having a bad temper, sometimes chronic. In contrast, good humour gives us a real desire for life and a urge to keep our youth.

- **What is humour?**

Humour is an internal glass that makes us see life as either rosy or black. This glass can vary in shade. When it is vivid it instils strong desires in us. This can be to act, if it has the colour of optimism, or to fold up inside ourselves and refuse all that is pleasant in life, if it has the colour of pessimism.

If the shade of a dark humour is black enough, it can push us to self-destruction, bit by bit or more brutally by suicide. So humour is at the same time both a source of inner dynamism and the colour of our mental life.

This extraordinary mechanism, on which depends our joy of living and our desires, works through the intermediary of hormonal secretions in the brain and all over the body. We can affect it medically when its excesses reach the level of illness, but we can also influence it spiritually because it constantly adapts to what we are experiencing. A good humour makes us want to do things, to project ourselves towards the future. But also, when we are in a gloomy humour but manage to give ourselves that desire for action through self-control techniques, we can transform our own humour and feel much better.

➡ A LITTLE TEST OF YOUR HUMOUR

- *Do you have a taste for the past (yours)? Was everything better before than now?* **YES/NO**
- *Are you using the word 'before' all the time?* **YES/NO**
- *Are you wary of novelties? Do you think they lower the quality of life?* **YES/NO**
- *Do you refuse to think about the future? Your future? That of your children? That of society?* **YES/NO**
- *Do you think the destruction of the planet is near?* **YES/NO**

Circle YES or NO for each question and see how many of each there are. This will give you an idea as to how balanced your humour is, between optimism (NO answers) and pessimism (YES answers). If pessimism comes out on top, danger – be careful. You are on the road to diminishing desire and reduction in the possibilities of encountering positive reinforcements – in short, on the road to ageing!

YOU MUST TAKE YOURSELF IN HAND
to maintain a good humour!

1. Pay attention to your conversation: internal or with others... Don't continually refer to the past. Anecdotes and interesting memories should be recounted only from time to time, if the situation lends itself (if you are a lively and interesting story-teller, you will be asked for them!).

But pay ATTENTION not to wound younger people with comments like: "It was better . . ." or comparisons that run down 'today'. You can make allusions to the past, because it was different, but find in these differences some reasons for appreciating the present. Young people cannot make comparisons; they 'don't know their good fortune'. Talking about the past in a certain way can help them become conscious of it.

And you can rejoice in knowing both!

2. Explore the present: discover all that technology offers you. Before saying something doesn't suit you, try it! Imagine, when the wheel was invented, the old grumblers saying that they preferred to carry everything on their back. Ridiculous, no? You should not be like them, with totally fixed ideas that prevent you from enjoying the benefits of life like buying something frozen, when you've no time to cook, or going on holiday via a 'package tour' when you couldn't afford to travel independently!

3. Look forward to tomorrow with interest, even impatience: adopt the slogan 'tomorrow is another day', in the sense that "I am very curious to know what it will bring!". Launch yourself into tomorrow and the future, that is to say ask yourself how you will be, what you will be doing ...There are for each of us SO MANY possibilities!

And make up some projects, create some strategies for your future, and that of those close to you.

Finally, to keep your humour in a good state:

- Live your past with tact and elegance.
- Live the present to the full and with curiosity.
- Live the future with confidence, desire and craftiness.

THE MIND
■■■■■■■■■■■■

The mind and its intellectual faculties evolve with the years in two contradictory directions: one for gain and the other for reduction – if you let them ...

- **The gain:**

This concerns the daily increase of our store of experience. Even if we have never done any special exercises, simply by accumulating those known things, that is to say knowledge (you shouldn't reserve this word just for what you learn at school!), the brain automatically groups our experiences internally.

We don't need to remember our school lessons to know that a cat belongs to the class of animals, like an ant or a duck-billed platypus! We can forget how a duck-billed platypus looks, having seen it just the once on television, but we will never forget that it is an animal and not a vegetable! Our ability to classify things gets better as the years go by. And since all reasoning rests in the use of classified information and associations, it follows that we are able to reason better, more quickly and more reliably as we get older. We reason more quickly, even though sometimes we have the impression of being slower than before, because we go more directly to the essential. We don't lose time in mental groping, as we did when we were younger.

• **The reduction:**

The reduction involves perception. We perceive less, because we 'know'. The slightest clue is enough for us to know what something is about. The tip of the tail of my cat tells me: "That's my cat". I don't need to look at the rest of it! That can mean a gain in speed, certainly ... but with two consequences – which in turn lead to a slowing down!

Firstly, since we 'know', we no longer bother to look. We lose the motivation to search for new perceptions (which existed automatically before). We become blasé. And when we are blasé, all our energy fades.

Secondly, memorising happens on its own, particularly when we have perceived something better, more thoroughly. With the reduction in perception, we lose the capacity for automatically memorising new things. And little by little, even when we make a conscious effort, this memorising become more difficult.

The brain is like the muscles. When it is no longer exercised, it gets rusty!

What we must do

It's ABSOLUTELY essential to remain vigilant. We must appreciate the growing strength of our reasoning but also watch out for the bad habit of no longer paying attention, of 'knowing before having read or heard!'.

Value your reasoning and look for any opportunity to play games of deduction and strategy. Young people use computers to play often very cunning strategy games. Why not play with your children?

Above all, fight against your loss of attention. Cultivate DIVINE CURIOSITY. And cultivate it in every area. You are reading a book or looking at a film set in the period of Elizabeth I? Can you imagine life in those times? Difficult! Look for the information in history or reference books and throw yourself for a moment into that time in history. Your new knowledge will fascinate your audience and you will live a double existence – in the 16th century and in the year 2000!

During conversations, don't hesitate to inform yourself. Someone tells you: "My son's got measles.". Ask them what that involves and how they manage with the other children, etc. Of course, you mustn't be nosy! But there is a way of questioning which stems from genuine interest for the person and which is felt therefore not as an intrusion but as friendship.

◪ EXERCISE

For this exercise, settle down to your personal and family archives. Rediscover them, group them. Arrange them into a presentation file that will enable you to look at the whole story time and again and to show others, particularly your children. It's a very nice present to give them!

ACTION
■ ■ ■ ■ ■ ■ ■ ■ ■ ■

Action is as necessary as being able to drink water or to breathe. This starts at the most tender of ages with the need to move about ... which is not as simple as it seems. It's a push towards the discovery of one's body and the training in what one can do with it.

The baby very quickly expresses his need to act. He wants to feed himself, hold his rattle and say: "It's me ... it's me". And then this **BIOLOGICAL** need for action starts to take shape. He must *work on something or someone*. It's not simply a question of playing, but of obtaining results.

The human being needs to DO something. But gymnastics don't produce anything, you say? If they are properly performed, that is to say not in a simply mechanical way, they produce the feeling of having achieved one's aim, which is as satisfying a result as getting someone else to do it. Sport is often regarded as more attractive, because competition, even at a friendly level, provides a point to the action.

With life in today's society we learn to respond first of all to the demands and appeals that it makes on us. We don't chose what we do and we don't act through a need that comes from within us. We react! Even with pleasures and distractions – which should be the area where our spontaneous action expresses itself – we are remotely controlled (very often ...) by publicity, television and so on.

In periods full of activity – professional advance, demanding family life thanks to the children – we are so busy reacting that we don't take into account that we're not acting any more.

Sometimes, a little signal can sound the alarm, when for example we suddenly find ourselves with an hour or two or maybe a day 'to ourselves' and we don't know what to do. Or perhaps, the holidays (we hardly dare say it!) seem long and we're not that upset about going back to work!

Then, when our professional life stops for retirement or, worse still, early retirement, when family demands drop away and the children are grown up, it's a CRISIS. The sudden realisation of old age is serious. Although most of us have always been looking forward to this moment of freedom – of release! – when it comes, we don't know how to cope with it. We don't know what to make of it . . .

It's because we have forgotten the basic instinct for action. We are like a bird for too long shut up in its cage who can no longer remember how to fly!

We have to rediscover our drive to enable us to express ourselves. Because letting ourselves be trapped by (imaginary) laziness, those purposeless gloomy reflections, is to turn our back on life. Not only is this physical and moral ageing, but it is also the certaintity of an early decline. We will make ourselves die before our time.

BECAUSE ACTION IS LIFE AND LIFE IS YOUTH

So how do we rediscover the genuine need to act? There are several ways of doing this and you should practise all of them.

1. Curiosity

It's impossible to over-emphasise all the benefits to be gained from curiosity. It encourages action in several ways. ·

First of all, it creates or leads to a 'state of awakeness' in us, in other words, it gently increases our mental tension and muscular tone. And it maintains us in a state of expectancy, ready to grab at anything . . .

Next, it pushes us to know more about things, in whatever area, whatever subject. For that, very often we must do something, such as undertake research or go to meetings. And, very often, by looking to satisfy our curiosity, we discover something that stirs up our desire. This can be a desire to do something or acquire something, which requires us to take action, sometimes involving a strategy, in order to achieve it.

2. Desires

Like the caged bird that no longer knows how to fly, we can get to the point where we don't even know what the desire to act is any more. When we do become aware of this, we are ready to resign ourselves: "It's my age!". It's true that if we accept the lessening of our own desires, especially those for action, it is because we are already damaged. But nothing is forcing us to accept this. On the contrary, out of self-respect, we must stay young and, to do that, we must practise rediscovering our desires.

You have a very good way of practising: it's the **daydream.** Prepare your little cinema session in which you do something – mad, impossible, whatever you like – that pleases you. Think about it once more and then, the next day, invent a situation where you do something else that this time *is* possible, even if only when certain conditions are met. Now examine these conditions as a problem to be solved, looking thoroughly at your project from every possible angle ... and you will find you will quite quickly want to implement this with action!

3. Pleasure

The essential for an active life consists in responding to the demands of any situation – which happily often brings pleasure, although this comes as an extra. First, we do what we must do because we have to. Then we find pleasure from it. We no longer know how to act FIRST for our own pleasure.

So we must reverse the priorities: to do something first for the pleasure – and so much the better if at the same time it is useful or helps something or someone. For example, I decide to prepare a lemon meringue pie, because it will give me pleasure to succeed in making it. This evening my family and friends will benefit from it. So much the better for them, because I will have made it anyway!

Perhaps you no longer know how to please yourself? That brings us back to the problem of desires. Give yourself the desire to please yourself, to re-educate yourself. Read the travel brochures cover to cover, find out what shows are on in your town (or further afield ...), read some magazines, make a note of the lists of activities: riding, dress-making, amateur dramatics... Think about them. Imagine yourself participating in these activities. Are you thinking about finding some pleasure?

When you have decided to give yourself some pleasure, don't start by saying to yourself: "It's impossible. I'm too old. I couldn't do it ..." If you really imagine yourself doing it, if that brings you a feeling of anticipated pleasure, if you are being sincere with yourself ..., you can give yourself that confidence. You are not too old.

And as for any financial or material conditions, that's a problem to be resolved. Launch into a strategy for resolving it and start work on the measures you have decided necessary.

4. To dare

Very often we give ourselves as an alibi the well-known formula: "I'm no longer the right age", because quite simply we don't dare do certain things. Children, young people do it . . . or professional adults . . .

For example, psychologists sometimes use drawings in their initial analysis, be it diagnostic or therapeutic. When they ask children: "Draw me a house" they generally have no difficulty in doing so. But the grown-ups! They reply: "I don't know how to . . . I can't . . ."

Who is really INCAPABLE of drawing a house? In reality, the adult is afraid of doing a 'childish' drawing that makes him (or her) look stupid. And it's the same with music. "I'm not going to learn to play the flute (piano, etc) at my age." And why not? Because it is a little late to envisage a career as a great soloist? That's hardly necessary in order to gain some pleasure from a musical instrument!

You don't have to imagine painting a picture that will be hung in the Tate Gallery. But you can nevertheless dare yourself to get pleasure from a paint-box . . . or by writing some poems . . .

5. Authentic action

There's a trap, knowingly sprung by advertisements and the media: it's the action that doesn't exist . . .

When we no longer have any desires, when we no longer know how to please ourselves, we risk doing something for the sake of doing something, instead of looking for a real incentive in our action. Through boredom, we go in for any old activity, a group that takes us on a holiday we don't care about. Is there anything sadder?

Whatever you do, never be tempted into something of this kind. It's better to stay at home and do the crossword puzzle!

If you let yourself sink to the bottom of the swimming pool, when you give a slight kick you rise back to the surface. It's better to do nothing until you really have had enough – and then feel the DESIRE to do something!

To practise, apply yourself to practical activities – useful and even necessary, like some DIY. There must surely be some repair or renovation work to do at home for which it is difficult or costly to find a professional . . . Make something (clothes, small pieces of furniture . . .) for your family or even for yourself . . .

Naturally there are activities that you cannot manage if you have never learned them. So go and find some books on the subject and learn how to do it!

The art of discovering the world

Travelling is certainly a choice activity for staying young . . . on the condition that we do it properly. Very often a fully active life and family necessities prevent us from making those great journeys of which everyone dreams. This is the moment to think about them.

1. Clearly you must REALLY desire it.

2. You must prepare the material conditions. There are, in practically every country in the world, places to stay: with one of the inhabitants, in shelters, youth hostels (or the equivalent) that are open to people of any age and accessible to every pocket. Clearly this won't offer the same comfort as a hotel and you must take your sleeping-bag. But, unless your doctor forbids it, the discovery of a new country is well worth the effort.

3. Naturally you must prepare for your journey: reading up brochures and books and seeking the necessary information.

4. During the journey, you must collect and keep as much as you can: photos, sketches, tape-recordings, notes . . .

5. On your return, you must arrange all your documentation and think about getting together with your family and friends to show, tell and eventually discuss all that you have experienced.

THAT'S ALL PART OF LIFE . . . AND THE MORE YOU LIVE IT THE LESS YOU WEAR YOURSELF OUT

OTHER PEOPLE
■■■■■■■■■■■■■■■■■■■■

Have you noticed the 'Mafia' among the young? When they arrive somewhere that's new for them, they immediately establish contact with others of their own age and chat together as though they had always known each other. They are mates, even if they don't speak the same language! And it seems they are all dressed the same way, boys and girls, the world over (at least in the large towns): scruffy jeans and T-shirt . . .

Observers note that this state of affairs, which didn't exist to any real extent thirty years ago, could well serve us as a model. It confirms, they say, the universality of the young . . . it confirms their youth, THE youth.

– It's the pleasure of discovering the ways of other human beings – without being weighed down with all our impedimenta (having to 'be presented', having friends in common, knowing who is who, etc.) – by sweeping aside the apparent differences (another language, another colour).

– It's the search for new friendships: the more people we know, the better the chance we have of making ourselves appreciated (multiplying the reinforcements . . .).

– It's the occasion to make ourselves known, to explain who we are, how we live . . . and, through that, to know ourselves better! And to appreciate ourselves more.

Of course, the young don't tell themselves all that. They go towards others spontaneously because they want to. But the deep roots of this desire show us the way.

Those of us approaching our fifties, on the other hand, have a tendency to remain bombastic about our reserve. It's embarrassing to approach others or to appear too familiar when replying to them . . . "What might they think?" And so we remain alone, an old couple (old before our time!).

We must refuse the temptation of solitude, refuse the good reasons we give ourselves for avoiding contact. We must refuse to condemn ourselves to solitude. The young have made up their own class of youth. What's stopping us from feeling that we BELONG to the class of humans?

• **So what should we do?**
It happens on its own. Look at others around you. You will surely

find some people who seem to you interesting, to whom you would like to speak.

• **PRACTISE** when you're waiting in a queue or on a journey. Be attractive to others quite simply by demonstrating that you are ALIVE, that you are ready to show an interest in everything. Know how to seduce by interesting others, of course, but also by listening to them. Make yourself available, ready to help. Hold open the door for people, help someone cross the road, pick up something that has fallen ...

It's a deeply-rooted attitude that expresses itself in small gestures but can also show itself as a more important solidarity. And this makes us someone that others like immediately. We all know these people that 'everybody likes'. Have you noticed their youthfulness?

• We say and we believe that we make friends during our youth, at school and when we're students and then afterwards it's finished. It's true that in a period of great activity, between professional commitments and family demands, we are hardly able to create new friendships. But when that is passed, it's the moment to rediscover the 'student life'. We can start to learn all sorts of things again, perhaps a new way of living. We also need to discover new people and make new friendships: we are ready for that!

• **Love as well**

'It has no age' is not a vague expression floating in the air. Love does become more difficult as we get older, it's true. We do take a fancy to someone less rapidly than when we were twenty. We are more willingly wrapped up in our little egoisms (even before our fifties!). And we think about all the consequences and sometimes the complications before thinking quite simply of the fun ...

To live demands a certain courage ... to be young at heart! But let's say in passing that this repays a hundred-fold.
– It can be the love of a couple starting to relive their lives. Yes, that does happen! You must, with the heart's intelligence, do all that's necessary to ensure this new venture succeeds. Sometimes this could mean changing habits or attitudes or the style of life generally ... starting from scratch and discovering afresh, seducing afresh ... What youthful delight!

– It can be an encounter . . . You must forget your age, theirs, let go of the ropes and set off in your bubble like any other lovers of any age, of any time . . . You must *have the inner generosity not to have false fears.*

KEEPING IN TOUCH
■■■■■■■■■■■■■■■■■■■■■■■■■

It is interesting and important to keep in touch with everything that happens. We buzz with events. And when we buzz, we live . . . and stay young!

We must know what is happening in the world generally, but also in the world of the arts – by following the development of paintings, sculpture, music and so on. Novelties in art have always been badly received. And it's true that we must make an effort to adapt to what is new in those areas that directly touch our most sensitively held views. Unfortunately we have a tendency to refuse to make that effort, once we have become a 'grown-up person'! In order to accept a new form of art, we must see and see again the new works as we stroll round the galleries. We must force ourselves to listen several times to music we don't like. Sometimes that remains disagreeable. Never mind . . . it's a pity! From time to time that marvellous moment comes when the veil is removed and suddenly we feel an emotion of pleasure. Each new creation we like is an additional pleasure and one pleasure more is always worth the effort of obtaining it. Equally, this effort is an exercise in adaptation, which makes the brain more flexible. So much won for LIFE!

We should know what is happening in our town, in our district. Perhaps it's a period in our life when we start to be afraid of time? Why not join in the local activities? Why not think about taking on some local responsibility or joining an association? It's not a question of 'doing good deeds to keep ourselves busy', but of actively participating in the social life around us, of entering like an actor the stage of our society or hobby. This is certainly useful for others, but even more so for us.

We must know what is happening to our family, to our friends. Perhaps we need to help them or encourage them? In any case living with them (in our thoughts!) enriches our life with theirs.

Being in touch requires us to act, to look for information and sometimes to adapt ourselves. It also requires us to open up in front of the world, in front of others. That trains us to live with others, like living with the victims of a disaster when we receive the information and pictures of the tragedy. Perhaps that will motivate us to live – at least a little – for others ...

In short, being in touch is being **IN LIFE'S CURRENT**, staying on the crest of the wave and advancing with it. It's the proof of our youth and, in return, it's one of its sources.

A WORD ON DIET

There's no 'diet' that will suit everyone: each person, in each period in life, in relation to their state of health at the time, as concerns their own biological needs, will have different dietary requirements. We need to inform ourselves about this with the help of our doctor and, if necessary, that of a specialist. And we must respond to these needs, notably and above all through our food and the way in which we eat it.

Here, however, are a few general indications that are worth keeping in mind and using as guidelines – except in the case of illness.

1. Breakfast

It's a meal and a moment that is essential for each day. You must take it quietly, with the feeling of having the time, in order to get an advance taste of the day that's beginning. Your breakfast should contain:

- Liquids: at least half a litre – weak tea or coffee with half-cream milk and no sugar or sweeteners.
- Cereals: replaced perhaps once or twice a week by bread and butter or jam or honey.
- An egg or slice of ham or gruyere cheese (alternating).
- A yoghurt.
- A fruit or freshly squeezed citrus juice.

2. For the two other meals

If you lead a sedentary life, you must have:

- Meat (white or red), fish, liver or kidneys once a day (alternating).

- An egg when you haven't had one for breakfast.
- Salad or fruit with each meal.
- Cooked vegetables once or twice a day. Vegetable soup is excellent.
- Pasta, rice or potatoes (starch) once a day (alternating).
- Cheese at the meal when you don't eat meat, fish, etc.
- Sweet dessert two or three times a week, at a meal when you don't eat meat, fish, etc.
- Bread: 300-400g each day.

3. Drinks

Remember that **WATER is the best drink.** You must take about two litres of liquid every twenty-four hours. Wine, beer . . . yes if you **REALLY** want to. And *to taste*.

Don't forget the formula:

YOU MUST EAT TO LIVE AND NOT LIVE TO EAT

And, if you don't abuse them, those 'special' little meals aren't necessarily off the list!

IN CONCLUSION

You have come to the end of the book ... Do you think it's asking too much of you? But what is too much if you haven't yet reached it? Another reason for you to tackle it with vigour.

Perhaps it seems a bit heavy when you read it. But once you have got into the action, you will very quickly find satisfaction and it will become quite easy!

We are the most extraordinary instruments – of music for ourselves and harmony for others. We must all the same do as much as possible to ensure we play as well as possible?

This book is a tool – or, better still, a box of tools. Use it to oil the wheels, top up the battery and tighten the bolts ... But to do that, you need to know the instrument well and practise using it.

It's a question of running-in, that's certain. But isn't it exciting to feel the machine loosening up little by little?

And above all you must do it with pleasure, FOR THE PLEASURE.

YOUR NOTES, OBSERVATIONS AND EXERCISES

YOUR NOTES, OBSERVATIONS AND EXERCISES

YOUR NOTES, OBSERVATIONS AND EXERCISES

YOUR NOTES, OBSERVATIONS AND EXERCISES

YOUR NOTES, OBSERVATIONS AND EXERCISES